MW00607520

KEEPING YOUR BOAT LEGAL

THE BOATING LEGAL GUIDE

Curt Epperson, JD, LLM
Attorney at Law

FINE EDGE
Nautical & Recreational Publishing

IMPORTANT LEGAL DISCLAIMER

Both the publisher, Fine Edge, and the author have made every effort to ensure that all the information in this book is accurate. However, errors may exist, due to transposition/typographical errors, and misprints.

Neither Fine Edge nor the author warrants this information to be exact and disclaim any liability for errors or omissions or for any loss or damage incurred from using the information in this book.

Publisher: Mark J. Bunzel
Book design by Melanie Haage
Copyedited by Polly Lane and Leslie Bunzel

All photos and illustrations are provided courtesy of the author or the U.S. Coast Guard, unless noted otherwise.

Cover boat photo by Mark J. Bunzel

Copyright © 2006 FineEdge.com, LLC. All rights strictly reserved under the International and Pan-American Copyright Conventions. This books contains unique proprietary information including, but not limited to, detailed diagrams. No part of this book may be reproduced or transmitted in any form or by any means, electronic or mechanical, including photocopying, recording, or by an information and storage retrieval system except as may be expressly permitted by the 1976 Copyright Act, or in writing from the publisher.

Address requests for permission to:
Fine Edge
14004 Biz Point Lane
Anacortes, WA 98221
www.FineEdge.com

LIBRARY OF CONGRESS CATALOGING-IN-PUBLICATION DATA

Epperson, Curtis N., 1953–
    Keeping your boat legal : the boating legal guide / Curt Epperson.
      p. cm. -- (Fine Edge nautical knowledge series)
    Includes index.
    ISBN-13: 978-1-932310-12-2 (pbk. : alk. paper)
    ISBN-10: 1-932310-12-6 (pbk. : alk. paper)
    1. Boats and boating--Law and legislation--United States--Popular works.
I. Title. II. Series.
KF2558.P5E67 2005
343.7309'6--dc22   2005033699

DEDICATION

Dedicated to my parents, Dan and Connie, who paid for the education I needed to earn the money for a beautiful sailboat and especially to my wife, Mary, who patiently tolerates spending so much money on that boat.

About the Author

Curt Epperson is a practicing maritime lawyer and also an avid sailor. His passion for the sea is evident in both his professional and personal life. Curt saw a need to help boaters stay organized and informed about the many legal aspects of their boats. Hence he developed the *Keeping Your Boat Legal* book and accompanying binder. Although the legal profession can be intimidating, Curt wrote the *Keeping Your Boat Legal* book in a simple to read question and answer format to easily disseminate important information.

CONTENTS

Introduction

Detailed knowledge of government rules and regulations is essential, regardless of how much experience you have as an owner or operator of a boat. Your boat must be properly equipped and in compliance with a myriad of state and federal regulations. If you have not been boarded and inspected by the U.S. Coast Guard, it is likely that you will have the experience sooner, rather than later. Knowing and understanding all the various equipment, documents, safety regulations, and keeping your boat properly outfitted, will ensure your first inspection by federal or state authorities goes smoothly and quickly. Your first inspection by the U.S. Coast Guard may be time consuming and unpleasant if you do not know the requirements or if your boat is not in compliance.

Our first boarding and inspection occurred in our twentieth year of cruising. My wife and I thought we knew all the relevant requirements. We were fortunate in that we did not receive any notice of deficiency. However, we were alerted to some potential problems. Additionally, we realized that our record-keeping system could be better.

Information about boat insurance, chartering, legal requirements, equipment requirements, and operational rules for recreational vessels is widespread and voluminous. Most of us do not have the time or expertise to sift though all the sources, web sites, publications, and the data to really know the basics.

Boating accidents often occur at ports far from home. Your insurance may help pay the financial losses, but maximizing the recovery and expediting an insurance claim is heavily dependent upon good record keeping. Well-organized records and documents aboard your boat and at home, along with an adequate understanding of your insurance policy, will allow you to quickly resolve an insurance claim and get back on the water.

In the quest to cover everything, most resource guides do not communicate the most important concepts and regulations in a clear, concise, and coherent manner.

Each section in this book addresses specific legal topics and requirements for owning and operating your boat. The book uses a simple question-and-answer format of legal requirements ranging from safety equipment to immigration and customs. We have even included resources you may use to get more detailed information if you desire. A corresponding section in the Appendix contains additional explanations and examples of forms that you may use to record and store important information. The question-and-answer format is based on analysis of the most important legal issues surrounding boat ownership and operation. The questions are indicative of those the author has frequently encountered during his twenty-five-year legal practice.

The *Keeping Your Boat Legal* binder, offered as a companion to this book, is a convenient way to store necessary documents and information in one place. It is designed to organize and store the documents for your boat, as well as the information described in the following chapters. The loose-leaf binder can be kept aboard your boat and easily brought home for safekeeping. Alternatively, you can use two binders and maintain copies of your records aboard and at home. You may purchase the *Keeping Your Boat Legal* binder from your local nautical bookstore or directly from Fine Edge (www.FineEdge.com), or you can build your own records manual by using the forms included in the Appendix and a standard three-ring binder.

Whenever you use your boat, you must have all the documents and equipment required by federal and state laws. Additionally, if you charter your boat, the operators must have easy access to the documents and information. Organizing and maintaining good records can be tedious, but the *Keeping Your Boat Legal* binder simplifies the task with a uniform approach.

Law enforcement on the water is increasing dramatically due to the threat of terrorism and new requirements issued by the Department of Homeland Security, increased environmental regulations, new equipment requirements, and the simple fact that there are many more boats now than in the past. If you carry the necessary documents, have the required equipment aboard, and follow the correct procedures, your encounters with law enforcement officials will not be a problem. You will be happily on your way in no time at all.

A recreational boat or yacht is a significant personal investment. The information and recommendations in this book will help you protect that investment and save future heartaches. Most important of all, you can focus your attention on relaxing and having fun on the water.

Name and home port is no longer sufficient information. Always carry complete information about your boat and yourself.

Important Basic Vessel Information

Keep certain information about you and your boat permanently aboard. Know the basic specifications of your vessel to make it easier to contact and question the manufacturer or dealer, boat yards, and repair shops, as well as answer questions from government agencies and officials. If you or anyone else is asked to provide the name and address of the vessel owner, the documentation number or registration number, or information about the dinghy or tender, he or she will be able to easily do so. Have the aforementioned information on a form in one easily accessible place. You can make multiple copies of the form with the information filled in and have copies available for immigration, customs, and enforcement officials, or even for boatyards. The information for your dinghy or tender is especially important and will be invaluable if it is lost or stolen. A full-page form is included in the Appendix. Additionally, the *Keeping Your Boat Legal Binder* includes printed forms and a CD with forms in Microsoft® Word format so you can fill in the information on your computer.

The following information about your boat is the minimum that you should carry aboard at all times.

Vessel Information

Name: _____

Date of Purchase: _____

Vessel Home Port: _____

Documentation #: _____

State registration #: _____

Vessel Manufacture Information

Make: _____

Model: _____

Engine(s) make/model: _____

Hull #: _____ Year Built: _____

LOA: _____ Displacement: _____

Engine: _____

Owner Information

Name: _____

Mailing Address: _____

Street or P.O Box: _____

City: _____

State: _____ Zip: _____

Phone: _____

Tender/Dinghy Information

Make: _____

Model: _____

Serial #: _____

Horsepower: _____

State registration #: _____

Vessel Ownership, Income Taxes, U.S. Coast Guard Documentation, and State Registration

The following section addresses in what form you hold ownership of your vessel, some income tax considerations, and how you choose to register your vessel with the government. The questions and answers that follow are important to consider while you are in the process of buying a boat and before you close the transaction. It is easier to take these matters into consideration before you own a boat, thereby avoiding additional paperwork and transaction costs trying to correct mistakes or oversights.

A. Vessel Ownership
Personal, Corporate, or Limited Liability Company (LLC)?

Most boat owners never address the idea of having a corporation or some other legal entity own their vessel and for most boat owners the issue is not very relevant. However, it can be important if the vessel will be used frequently with guests aboard or if the vessel will be used for business purposes. Liability and tax considerations are directly relevant to using a corporation or an LLC to own your boat.

Are there choices for how I own my boat?

There are some different ways that you can own your boat. Instead of simply owning it in your own name you can set up a separate legal entity to be the owner. It is possible, and often prudent, to have a corporation or LLC own your boat.

- **Personal ownership.** It is the simplest, easiest, and most common way to own anything and means you own the boat and hold title in your name just like a home, a car or truck, a snowmobile or motorcycle, or any other item of personal property. A couple can hold title as husband and wife, or as joint tenants with right of survivorship, or as tenants in common, or the title can be in one person's name only.

- **Corporation.** A corporation is a separate legal entity that must be formed in compliance with state law and registered in the state or states in which it does business. A simple, closely held corporation can be formed with minimal cost in most states using forms that are available from the Secretary of State's office.

- **Limited Liability Company.** An LLC is a separate legal entity that is formed in accord with state law and can also be formed with minimal cost using standard documents.

Why should I have a separate legal entity own my vessel?

Most people rarely consider the liability consequences of owning a boat. We often assume that if an accident occurs our insurance will cover the damages. However, that is not always true. We live in a very litigious society and lawsuits alleging extraordinary damages are commonplace, particularly against wealthy persons. Damages or injuries may occur that are not covered by your insurance or that exceed your policy limits. You can help protect your personal assets and net worth from excessive liability if you have a separate legal entity in place as the owner of your vessel. You might lose your investment in the boat, but other assets (like your home equity, stock market investments, rental properties, etc.) can be protected. Taking simple steps before you purchase your boat will help protect your assets.

If you just have a small to medium recreational pleasure craft (power or sail) that you intend to use yourself then it makes the most sense to simply own it in your name, just like your home, your RV, or your personal truck or car. There probably is not a big advantage to using a separate legal entity in such a situation. However, if you use your vessel for business purposes, (commercial fishing or touring, whale-watching, client entertainment, etc.), have it in charter, loan it out to other persons, or

4

frequently take guests aboard then it makes some sense to use a private, closely held corporation or an LLC to hold title. Every boat owner should question his or her liability exposure and consider whatever legal means are available to protect themselves.

What is a closely held corporation?

A corporation is a business entity that constitutes a distinct legal person, with rights and liabilities separate from its owners (the shareholders). A closely held corporation is not publicly traded and is usually owned by just a few people. Many small, private corporations have just one shareholder, who also is the only officer and director. Initial registration and annual license fees, renewal fees, and reporting requirements vary from state to state and deserve some attention. If you live in one state but your boat is located in another, it may be worthwhile to see which state has the lower costs to form and run a corporation.

Under federal tax law, a closely held entity can qualify as an S Corporation. This means that it does not pay taxes on income. Its income and expenses are passed through directly to the shareholder(s). An S Corporation is a good entity to own a boat that will be put in business use or for charter. However, in many situations, an LLC may be an even better choice.

What is an LLC?

An LLC is a Limited Liability Company. It creates the liability protections of a corporation but can be managed and taxed like a partnership. Like an S Corporation, an LLC does not pay taxes on its income. Its income and expenses are passed through directly to the LLC members. Furthermore, if your LLC has just one member then it can be a *disregarded* entity for federal tax purposes and it does not have to separately file any federal tax forms. A single person LLC is an excellent method for owning

---

How Bad Can It Get?

It is not difficult to envision circumstances where liability for damages caused by an accident are not covered by your insurance. For example, some yacht policy provisions provide for a reduction in coverage if one or more of the named insured persons (owners) are not aboard the boat when it is being operated. Imagine that prior to leaving the dock for a weekend of cruising you ask your friend and crewmate to motor over to the fuel dock and fill the gas tank on your 32-foot powerboat while you make a quick trip to the convenience store. While you are at the store your friend ties up to the fuel dock and begins fueling the boat. He forces the fuel cap inside the handle of the fuel nozzle so as not to have to sit and hold it to keep the gas flowing. Your friend is a little cavalier with the dock lines, especially when he is eager to get on the water and start enjoying the trip. In fact, he is so eager that he goes below to check a chart. A gust of wind comes up, the stern line comes loose, and as the boat slowly blows away from the dock, the fuel hose and nozzle pull out of the deck-fitting and spills gas onto the deck. Some of the gas quickly leaks into the engine compartment below the deck sole. As your boat moves farther from the dock, the hose falls in the water and happily pumps gallons of gasoline into the harbor before your friend comes back up. He panics and yells

for assistance to the young employee who is busy talking on his cell phone to his girlfriend. Of course, he forgets where the emergency shut-off is located. While struggling to control the boat your friend decides to start the engine. Kaboom! The boat and dock are on fire. Your boat is a total loss, as is the beautifully restored 1966 Chris Craft tied to the other side of the dock. Luckily, no one is killed. You see the fire and smoke from where you stand, but by the time you arrive on the scene, it's a total disaster.

Total damage to your boat is the full amount of the Agreed Value of $85,000. Other damages are estimated to be in excess of $500,000. Unfortunately, the Chris Craft was waiting for its insurance survey and uninsured at the time, so the owner demands full payment from you. However, because you were not on your boat at the time of the accident, your Agreed Value coverage is only 50 percent of the policy amount and your liability limit for protection and indemnity is only $25,000. Because you are a well-established businessman with annual income of over $350,000, everyone expects that you will simply pay for the damages from your personal savings. Your friend has no available assets or cash to help with the payments and declares bankruptcy. You are left to pay everything on your own.

a boat that is frequently or occasionally used in ways that could cause significant liability. Like a corporation, the LLC costs and requirements vary from one state to another.

Setting Up a Corporation Does Not Have To Be Expensive

In most cases you should get some professional advice when you are thinking about setting up a corporation or LLC. But do not believe you need to spend an arm and leg to set one up. It's just like buying equipment or gear for your boat. You can spend a lot if you want to but often times it's possible to buy things at substantial savings.

Not long ago, the son of one of my clients called me to inquire about setting up an LLC for his new business. He did not intend to have any employees or partners; hence a single-person LLC was a perfect fit. He asked how much it would cost to set up. At the time, the costs were about $175.00 for the filing fee and another $25.00 for the various registration fees. I offered to meet with him to explain the operation of an LLC and how to keep the books, file the form and provide him a simple member agreement. The total cost would be around $500.00, give or take. He was shocked and told me he had two other quotes for nearly $2,000. Then I told him he could do it himself using the Secretary of State forms from its web site. He said he needed to get it done in one week and would rather I just "take care of it". I said there would be an extra fee for expedited service by the Secretary of State and he asked how much. "That's an extra $25.00 for them to hurry up the filing," I replied. Again, shocked silence for a few seconds. "One of the other lawyers told me that the expedited fee would be $500.00," he said.

The bottom line is you do not need to spend big bucks to set up a simple, single-person LLC or for a simple, one-person shareholder corporation. In some states the application is a one-page form that can be printed directly from the Internet and mailed to the Secretary of State. Furthermore, good bookstores have various "How To" books, some with perforated edges that you can pull out and send in ready-made forms. An excellent source for do-it-yourself information is NOLO Press (www.nolo.com). Examples of corporate and LLC application forms for one state are in the Appendix.

Other than liability protection, are there reasons to have a separate legal entity own my vessel?

If you are going to use your boat for business purposes or put it in charter, you may be able to deduct expenses associated with the boat and depreciation (subject to the rules and regulations in the tax code). Sometimes it is easier to keep business income and expense records delineated and separate if you have a distinct legal entity with separate bookkeeping and bank accounts. If you use your boat in business and deduct depreciation and expenses, you must comply with the complicated statutes and regulations governing such deductions. Being properly organized and structured can help with the compliance issues and help convince the Internal Revenue Service (IRS) that you are running a real business, not just someone trying to take a deduction of personal expenses.

How do I decide if a corporation or LLC is right for me?

The information above is only intended to convey some basic principles. If you think you should use a corporation or LLC as an entity to own your vessel, you should first get professional advice from an attorney and a Certified Public Accountant (CPA). You need to understand the full implications for your particular situation and get proper advice to ensure you are not just creating unnecessary complication. Some of the benefits to using your vessel for business or charter are the tax deductions, but the laws and regulations are complicated and must be followed correctly. You can file the forms yourself to set up an LLC or a corporation, but if you do not do it correctly and follow all the necessary procedures, it can backfire on you. It is best to get professional advice and assistance in the beginning, at least for some background information.

The *Keeping Your Boat Legal* binder has space to keep copies of your corporation or LLC business license and records. Your binder should contain the following:

- Articles of Incorporation for a corporation or Articles of Formation for an LLC.
- Certificate of Incorporation or Certificate of Formation for an LLC.
- Federal Employer Identification Number.
- List of officers and directors for a corporation.
- List of members for an LLC.
- Copy of annual state registration or license renewal.

B. Income Taxes and Boat Ownership

It is possible but relatively complex to take tax deductions for boat expenses, such as: maintenance, moorage, insurance, etc. The tax code and IRS rules are very specific. The reason is simple. For most people, ownership of a boat is personal and the expenses are not deductible unless the boat is used for a legitimate business purpose. However, many boats qualify as second homes under the tax code, allowing you to deduct interest payments on your boat loan. If you want to deduct boat expenses from your income you should talk to a tax professional with knowledge and experience regarding boat ownership. A competent boat broker or charter company should be able to refer you to an appropriate adviser. However, exercise caution when receiving tax advice. For example, the guy at the boat show who is trying to sell you a new $400,000 boat is not a good source of independent information and counsel. Some boat brokers and most charter companies may recite an interpretation of the tax code that is biased toward their best interests, not yours. With that in mind, please note also that the following discussion is a general guide and is intended to provide just enough information for you to decide whether or not to go further with the concept.

Can you deduct the loan interest on a personal recreational vessel?

You may deduct loan interest on a recreational boat if the vessel meets certain criteria of a second home. Obviously, most boats are not second homes in the same sense as a house located somewhere on the land. Nevertheless, the income tax code allows deduction of loan interest for a boat if the vessel contains specific elements. Those include an on-board toilet, equipment for cooking, and space for sleeping. If your boat has those elements it will qualify as a second home for tax purposes, and you will be able to deduct your interest payments if you borrowed money to purchase your boat.

What if you own a business that occasionally uses your boat?

If you own a business that occasionally uses your boat for legitimate business purposes that are related to the business, the expenses incurred by the business during the actual use of the vessel are deductible against the income from the business. However, the key is that the use of the vessel is directly related to, or associated with, the conduct of your business. If the use of the vessel is for customer, client, or employee entertainment then the expenses incurred must be reasonable and not extravagant or lavish. If you intend to use your boat for purposes associated with your business, talk to your tax adviser. Make sure you understand all the laws and regulations, and make sure you follow them closely.

If your business owns a boat and uses it for business purposes can you still use it for personal recreation?

A business itself may own a vessel, use it for legitimate business purposes, and deduct the costs of ownership. For example, a fishing company may own a boat used for fishing, and a transport company may own a boat used to carry passengers or cargo. However, if the business owner also has personal use of the boat, it must be clearly recorded. The owner will either have to pay the company a fair price for the use of the vessel or declare personal income of the fair value for use of the business asset. It is usually not a good idea to have your company own a boat if you intend to use it for personal recreation. In most cases it is not advantageous for a small, closely held business to own a boat that will have infrequent business use or more than occasional personal use.

When may an individual owner deduct depreciation and expenses such as insurance, moorage, maintenance, and repairs?

This is one of the most complex tax questions associated with owning a boat. For an individual owner, the key to taking tax deductions for expenses is to place the boat into a trade or business, and this question most often arises for recreational vessels in the context of buying a boat and placing it in charter for use by others. For decades, the IRS has scrutinized boat chartering to see whether or not it is a business with an expectation of profit. If the business is not operated to make a profit and is mainly a hobby, sport, or recreation, you may not use losses from the activity to offset income from other endeavors. However, the IRS has recently also taken the position (supported by at least one tax court decision) that use of a vessel in a charter business is a rental activity and must satisfy the regulations associated with passive activities. In general, unless an owner is engaged in chartering the vessel himself without the assistance and participation of a charter company, the chartering activity is passive, and passive activity losses may only be deducted from passive activity income. In other words, if you buy a boat and turn it over to a charter company, you may very likely be prohibited from deducting expenses (including depreciation) that exceed your charter income.

What is the most common business use for a recreational vessel?

Many privately owned recreational vessels are placed in charter, either with an established charter management company or privately by the boat owner. A charter company will act on behalf of the owner as a manager or as a lessee of the boat and take a percentage of the charter fees in exchange for its participation. Another example of business use for a recreational vessel is as a small tour boat or for whale-watching. In either case, the use of the vessel will be fairly frequent (depending upon the geographic area and the nature and size of the boat) and the wear and tear will be moderate to severe. However, income from the business activities will alleviate some of the costs of ownership.

What is an expectation of profit?

The following discussion assumes that you are using your boat in a trade or business that is not a passive business and is not a passive rental activity as defined in the tax code. If your boat is used in an active business then ordinary and necessary business expenses are fully tax deductible. However, full tax deductions are not allowed for hobby losses. A hobby loss is one that is incurred from an activity that might look somewhat like a business but really is not because there is no reasonable way that the activity can generate a profit over time. In most business situations, expectation of profit is not an issue because the business generates actual profits or fails. However, our tax laws recognize that some business ventures may be totally in good faith, with real effort and ingenuity, but still not create an annual profit after depreciation and expenses.

What facts and circumstances count to establish an expectation of profit?

If you want to convince the IRS that your boat business (charter, ecology tours, whale-watching, sailing school, etc.) is an active business and not just a hobby, you need to act accordingly. Basically, an owner must show a real endeavor to make a profit with appropriate business effort and adequate records. The owner should be prepared to show examples of other similar situations where owners make a profit and prove that it is reasonable to expect his

With thousands of boats in hundreds of marinas, will you make a profit in the charter business?

operation to be profitable. The IRS looks at a variety of factors, including the following:

- Whether the operation is business-like.
- The amount of time and effort put into the activity.
- Attempts to change the operation to generate more income or reduce expenses.
- Past successful experiences in similar activities.
- The possibility of profit from sale of assets.

In general, you need to show that your activity is not just a hobby or a ruse. You need to show that you are genuinely conducting the activity in a way that leads to a reasonable expectation for a profit.

What if the boat business is not a passive activity and cannot generate a profit?

If you use your boat for business and generate income (without any expectation of profit) you can still take some deductions for your expenses, but there are clear limitations. You will only be able to deduct expenses up to the amount of the actual gross income earned from the boat. If there is no expectation of profit, deductions are allowed in the following order:

1. Deductions you can take for personal as well as for business activities are allowed in full (such as interest, taxes, and casualty losses).
2. Deductions that do not reduce the basis of property are allowed, but only to the extent that the gross income from the activity is more than the deductions taken under the first category.

3. Deductions that decrease the basis of the property are allowed (such as depreciation and amortization), but only to the extent that the gross income is more than the deductions taken under categories one and two.

If you have a boat in charter, may you still use it personally?

We discussed above how a boat qualifies as a second home for purposes of an interest deduction. If you have your boat in a charter business, and if you fully deduct expenses, your personal use of the vessel is limited by the vacation-home rules. You may only use the boat for personal enjoyment for 14 days each year or 10 percent of the time it is used in charter, whichever is greater. You can also spend some time aboard for reasonable maintenance and repair. If you exceed those limitations then you will be deemed to be using it as a home, and you will not be able to fully deduct your expenses. If you personally use the boat, you must keep accurate records of everything you do (maintenance, repair, upgrades, etc.). Include notes on where you go, who is on the boat with you, and any conceivable business rationale for the use of the boat. If in doubt, write it down. Good records and bookkeeping will never harm you. Bad records and bookkeeping may come back to haunt you.

What is a passive activity?

The discussion above focused on activities where you actively participate. Now we will talk about passive business activities. The tax code limits the deductions you may take when you engage in a passive activity. In general, you may deduct passive losses only from passive income and you may carry excess losses forward to following years. *If the business use of your boat is a passive activity, you are not legally entitled to take deductions that exceed the amount of your passive income.* If you are counting on tax deductions to help pay for a boat that you might not otherwise be able to buy, proceed with extreme caution. The passive activity regulations are complex and not for the faint of heart. The following discussion summarizes the basic principles but is not an exhaustive explanation. ***Consult your tax attorney or CPA for guidance on handling income and expense from passive activities.***

The two kinds of passive activities are:

1. Trade or business activities in which you do not materially participate during the year.
2. Rental activities, even if you do materially participate in them, unless you are a real estate professional.

What is a passive trade or business?

If you have a business involving your boat (usually a charter business), it may be a passive business if you simply turn the boat over to someone else and sit back and wait for your checks and tax deductions. There is a certain amount of common sense involved in understanding this situation. If you have a boat that you use for whale-watching, and have the necessary training, skills, and licenses, advertise the business, personally take people for excursions, you should not have any trouble establishing that you are not engaged in a passive activity. However, if you live in Vail, Colorado, buy a boat in Florida, have a charter company manage all aspects of the business, it will be difficult to avoid definition as a passive business.

Are there specific tests for a passive business?

A non-rental business is not passive if you materially participate. There are multiple tests for material participation, and if you satisfy one or more of the criteria you may be able to fully deduct expenses from the business. The IRS regulations state that you materially participate if:

- You participate in the activity for more than 500 hours during the tax year.

- Your participation is substantially all the participation in the activity of all individuals during the tax year.

- You participate for more than 100 hours during the tax year and at least as much as anyone else.

- Your activity is a significant participation activity and you participate for more than 500 hours. A significant participation activity is one in which you spend more than 100 hours during the year, and in which you did not participate under any of the other material participation tests.

- You materially participated for any five years of the preceding 10 years.

- The activity is a personal service activity in which you materially participate.

- Based on all the facts and circumstances, you participate on a regular, continuous, and substantial basis during the year (and not less than 100 hours). Additionally, no one else may have received management compensation or spent more hours than you did.

What is a passive rental activity?

If you own a charter boat and you deduct expenses and depreciation in excess of the income, the primary assertion in the past has been that it is a legitimate business. For decades, expectation of profit was the focal issue for owners of charter boats. However, many charter company contracts require the vessel owner to turn over all management, operation, and control of the boat to the charter company — usually for a period of one year with automatic annual renewal. Some of these contracts even refer to the arrangement as a lease. This is a good system for the owners and the charter companies because it creates certainty and efficiency for both parties and the opportunity for repeat business from satisfied customers. However, this arrangement creates the argument (recently pursued and won by the IRS in court) that the owner is engaged in a *passive rental activity*, not a trade or business. The tax code states that:

> A rental activity is a passive activity, even if you materially participated in that activity, unless you materially participated as a real estate professional. An activity is a rental activity if tangible property (real or personal) is used by customers or held for use by customers, and the gross income (or expected gross income) from the activity represents amounts paid (or to be paid) mainly for the use of the property. It does not matter whether the use is under a lease, a service contract, or some other arrangement.

When is an activity not a rental activity?

The tax code specifies something is not a rental activity if:

- The average period of customer use of the property is seven days or less. If you directly charter your boat to multiple users during the course of a year and the average period is less than seven days, you are not engaged in a passive activity. However, if you lease your boat to a charter company for a full year, you do not qualify for this exception.

- The average period of use is 30 days or less and you provide significant personal services with the rentals.

- You provide extraordinary personal services in making the rental property available for customer use. Customer use of the property must be incidental to the receipt of the services.

- The rental is incidental to a non-rental activity.

- You customarily make the rental property available during defined business hours for nonexclusive use by various customers.

- You provide the property for use in a non-rental activity in your capacity as an owner of an interest in a partnership, S Corporation, or joint venture conducting that activity.

How do I learn more about the tax code and the regulations?

The tax code and the regulations can be fairly difficult to understand. However, there are IRS Publications that directly address the issues and answer the questions about business use of a vessel. The relevant publications are: Pub 463, Pub 527, Pub 535, and Pub 925. Some of the applicable regulations referred to above are reprinted in the Appendix, and IRS publications are available free on the Internet. Before you buy a boat for use (partly or fully) in your business, or for use as a charter, it is imperative that you study and understand the tax code and applicable regulations. Start by reading the IRS publications and then get expert advice from a tax professional.

C. Vessel Documentation and Registration

What is U.S. Coast Guard documentation?

Documentation is how your vessel is registered with the U.S. Coast Guard and, specifically, proof of your vessel's nationality. Documentation is not required for recreational boats, but vessels used in fisheries in U.S. waters or used in U.S. coastwise trade must be documented (unless an exemption applies). Recreational vessels over five net tons may be documented and many are. Five net tons is the vessel's volume, not its weight. Many vessels over 30 feet in length are more than five net tons. Recreational vessels receive a Certificate of Documentation endorsed for recreation.

Where do I keep the Certificate of Documentation?

The Certificate of Documentation must be kept aboard the documented vessel. It is valid for one year and must be renewed annually (no fee). Failure to renew may result in the vessel being removed from documentation. You will receive a reminder notice from the U.S. Coast Guard and a form to fill out and return to them. Call the National Vessel Documentation Center (800-799-8362) if you do not receive a notice of renewal or if you have any documentation questions. If you do not renew the certificate prior to expiration, you may still do so for 30 days past the expiration date by paying a small late fee.

How and when do I document my boat?

The best time to document your vessel with the U.S. Coast Guard is at the time of purchase. You must fill out the necessary forms and send them to the National Vessel Documentation Service.

Good Record Keeping Pays Off

In the early 1980s (before the passive activity rules), we bought our second boat and placed it in charter to help pay the costs of ownership. We set up a corporation as a separate business (this was also before the days of LLCs). After completion of commissioning we went for a 10-day shakedown cruise from Seattle's Lake Union to the San Juan Islands. We left in the evening on a Friday and passed through the Hiram M. Chittenden Locks, tying up a short distance away at Shilshole Bay Marina.

Being a new and cautious owner I checked the bilge about every 30 minutes. Unfortunately, I also had to pump it out each time. "Hmmm," I thought. "This is odd." A bit of investigation revealed a very loose packing box on the prop shaft and a substantial stream of water. I fixed it, went to bed, and made a detailed note in the log book the next morning.

We took a short cruise to the San Juan Islands and returned with a decent list of things for the dealer to fix and a few other items that needed to be added to make the boat suitable and comfortable for charters. Each item was carefully noted and explained in the log book.

I wrote up a short contract between the corporation and myself for maintenance and repair duties, specifying when and how we could use the boat. We could only go out when it did not interfere with charter opportunities. We also had a detailed manual for operation of all the systems aboard, a good checklist for each cruise, and a complete list of all items aboard, right down to the silverware. I made up a nice notebook for easy reference. I even did a business plan with estimated income and expenses. It included plans for maximizing the number of charters, running a few ads on our own, and our investigation of the charter company to be sure it was the best. I sent a copy to our accountant.

During the year we inspected and cleaned the boat ourselves whenever possible (even though we were using a charter company), and we sailed or motored a few times for short cruises. I did most of the minimal repair work. We made careful notations of our use of the boat and clearly delineated our personal use versus times spent on maintenance, repair, etc.

Before April 15 of the next year, our accountant did our taxes and we took full advantage of the allowable depreciation and something in effect at the time called the investment tax credit. We saved a bunch on taxes.

I kept excellent corporate records with regular meetings and minutes for every meeting. The next year we received a notice of a corporate audit from the IRS. Not just a normal audit, but something called a TCMP (taxpayer compliance measurement program) audit. I called my accountant, who said, "Oh."

I gathered all our records, documents, letters, receipts, etc., and the IRS auditor showed up at my office. The auditor spent hours reviewing all our records then left. He called a few days later and requested copies of a few more items. After a couple more weeks he called to tell me, "I have decided to disallow all your deductions for the boat. Your personal use in the first year, taking into account the shakedown cruise, adds up to nearly double the allowable time."

I was shocked, stunned, and silent. Then I began to argue. I pointed out the necessity of the shakedown cruise and the repair that saved the boat from sinking. I pointed out all the items we specified for repair and upgrade and the notations in the log book. I pointed out the business plan, the contract for maintenance, our advertising, and our meticulous records. I talked without stopping, detailing how hard we worked at the charter business and how we could easily make thousands of dollars each year. Then he simply said, "OK, upon reconsideration, we will allow the deductions." I said, "Thank you," and we hung up shortly thereafter.

The moral of the story: Keep Good Records and Do Not Give Up.

Should I hire someone to do this for me?

Whether you purchase your boat new or used you can use a Vessel Documentation Service to assist with the closing of the sale. You can do the job yourself, but you will not save a great deal of money and it will be time consuming. The documentation service performs a function similar to an escrow agent in a real estate transaction. It will complete the necessary forms, check the ownership of the vessel, investigate and identify any loans or liens against the vessel, arrange to payoff loans or clear liens, get all the necessary signatures (with notarization where required), and file the forms with the U.S. Coast Guard. Just as when you buy a home or other real estate, your boat transaction will work best if you let someone with experience and expertise handle the necessary paperwork.

A documentation office can facilitate buying and selling a boat.

What if I am buying a boat that will not be documented?

If you are buying a vessel that does not qualify for documentation or one that you do not want to document with the U.S. Coast Guard, the process of transferring title is much simpler and sometimes is as easy as buying a new or used car. In that case you may not need any assistance from a documentation service. However, if you are not familiar with the process or if you do not know how to properly transfer the title to an undocumented vessel, it may still be worth your time and money to have some expert assistance.

What is required for documentation?

To receive a Certificate of Documentation, you must demonstrate the following:

- Ownership of the vessel, U.S. citizenship, and eligibility for the endorsement sought. If a vessel is new and has never been documented, show either the Builder's Certification naming the applicant as the person for whom the vessel was built, a transfer of the Manufacturer's Certificate of Origin, or a copy of the State Registration or Title.
- If the vessel is already documented, show the signed Bill of Sale naming the seller and buyer.
- If a corporation or LLC owns a vessel, the entity must be registered in a U.S. state, and the Chief Executive Officer (CEO) and board chairman, as well as the quorum of the Directors, must hold U.S. citizenship.

- A foreign-built vessel may be documented for recreation, but only U.S.-built vessels may be documented for U.S. fisheries or coastwise trade.

If your vessel is documented, you must place its name and hailing port on some clearly visible exterior part of the hull. The name may not be more than 33 letters and numerals. Additionally, the name may not be the same as a word used to ask for assistance at sea and may not be obscene, indecent, or profane. Since some vessels may have the same name, the hailing port name is important (city and state). The name and port must be in letters at least four inches tall. Additionally, the documentation number must be marked in three-inch numbers on a clearly visible, interior structural part of the hull. If you want to change the name of a documented vessel you must file an application to the U.S. Coast Guard on form CG-1258.

Documentation regulations are contained in the Code of Federal Regulations, Title 46, Part 67, and selected regulations from Title 46 are reprinted in the Appendix.

What are the advantages of documentation?

- There is a permanent record of the vessel on file with the U.S. Coast Guard, its manufacture, its origin, and its chain of ownership.
- There are official forms to use for transfer of the vessel, the satisfaction of a mortgage, release of a lien, change of the vessel name, and other circumstances.

- Many lenders require a Certificate of Documentation for vessels that qualify. It provides some additional protection for the lender.

Forms are available free from the National Vessel Documentation Center (800-799-8362). The most commonly used forms are the Bill of Sale (CG-1340), the Application for Initial Issue, Exchange or Replacement (CG-1258), the Renewal of Certificate of Documentation (CG-1280), and the Satisfaction/Release of Mortgage or Claim of Lien. These forms are available on the Internet from the U.S. Coast Guard web site by looking under the Services tab for the Vessel Documentation Center tab under the Marine Safety and Environmental Protection header.

D. State Registration

Is state registration required for a documented boat?

Documentation means your vessel is registered with the U.S. Coast Guard. However, some states also require state registration and payment of a fee, while other states do not require registration if a vessel is documented. If a vessel is not documented then U.S. Coast Guard regulations require state registration for motor-powered vessels. In those cases, the vessel must be registered in the state of its principle operation. If a vessel is not documented with the U.S. Coast Guard, the state will issue a number for the vessel that must be displayed on the boat. The state certificate of number, title, registration, and other state documents must be carried aboard at all times.

Documenting Your Boat Is Worth the Wait

A good friend of mine owns a vessel documentation service and handles hundreds of transactions every year. I spoke to him about some of the reasons to get documentation for your vessel if it qualifies.

It turns out there are a few important reasons why you might want to jump through the hoops. Even though the delay for documentation is running about five months, it may still be worth the effort. You can use your boat while waiting for the Certificate of Documentation to arrive from the U.S. Coast Guard.

First, once your boat is documented, it is indisputably a United States vessel. The Certificate of Documentation is proof positive and recognized worldwide. Even a low level bureaucrat in a backwater foreign port will recognize the certificate and not question your vessel's nationality. (The United States flag flying from your documented vessel really means something.) That same bureaucrat may be far less familiar with a state title, state registration, state Certificate of Registration, or state Certificate of Number. In fact, some state titles look just like a title for a car. This is a bit of potential confusion that it is best to avoid.

Second, when you go to sell your boat it may be much easier for a prospective buyer to get a marine loan. This is particularly true when the lending environment is tighter than normal (i.e. interest rates are higher). This is less important during times of easy money, but many of us remember the days when interest rates for boat loans exceeded 12 percent and lenders were very particular. When it comes time to sell your boat, the documentation will lend appeal to experienced marine lenders.

Third, your U.S. documented vessel is only subject to seizure in the United States by a U.S. Marshal pursuant to specific rules of procedure in U.S. Federal Court. Actually, the correct terminology is that the vessel is *arrested* or *attached*, depending on the circumstances. This may be a valuable protection in certain situations. For example, some harbor towns on the U.S. eastern seaboard think they have stumbled upon a neat way to increase revenue by charging visiting boats a fee to anchor nearby. When a local police patrol boat pulls alongside and informs the cruising skipper of the charge (the fine, the possibility of personal arrest, and vessel seizure for non-compliance), most skippers choose to just pay the tax rather than argue the issue or leave the area. However, the arrest of a documented vessel is subject to the exclusive jurisdiction of the U.S. federal courts sitting in Admiralty. An attempt to take possession of it outside the federal required procedures is improper and in violation of federal law. The federal courts have the authority to levy an award for costs and damages incurred from wrongful arrest of a documented vessel.

Does a documented boat have to comply with state laws?

All U.S. vessels must comply with federal laws and also comply with applicable state laws such as noise, lights, marine sanitation, operator age restrictions and safety requirements. In accordance with federal requirements, all states and territories have vessel registration procedures. However, a documented boat cannot be required to display state registration numbers on the hull. Some states require documented vessels to obtain a state title, although this is not in accordance with federal law.

What is state registration?

The process for state registration varies from state to state. You must provide the appropriate state office with information about your boat and pay a fee, usually annually. The registration and title processes create detailed record systems for identification and ownership of all boats. In some states even very small boats (dinghies and tenders) must be registered, particularly if they are used to catch fish, crab, or other aquatic wildlife. Twenty-eight states require registration for non-powered vessels, 24 states require numbering for non-powered vessels, and 16 states require titles for non-powered vessels. Technically, documented vessels cannot be required to also have a state title, but some states require the state title nevertheless.

Most states treat documented vessels correctly and the process of registering a documented vessel is different than the process for a non-documented vessel. If a vessel is not documented, state registration usually includes a title that states the owner's name and address, the lender's name and address (if applicable), and basic information about the vessel. Thirty-six states and territories require titling of motor-powered vessels. The title certificate you receive is similar to that provided for an automobile

How do I find out the requirements for my state?

If you are buying a new boat, the broker, dealer or manufacturer will provide you with the necessary information for transfer of ownership and registration. If you are buying a used boat, the seller should have the registration information and documents. In most states, the registration process is simple and straightforward. The Appendix at the end of this book has a list of state boating law administrators and Web addresses for various states. Most states have small (free) pamphlets available that summarize state requirements.

E. Vessel Documents

The *Keeping Your Boat Legal* binder has space designated for your Certificate of Documentation, State Title, and Registration information. Keep these required documents available for quick and easy access if the U.S. Coast Guard or local authorities inspect you. *Be sure that you always have aboard your State Registration and/or State Title or U.S. Coast Guard Certificate of Documentation.*

Keep the Records on Your Boat

State and federal laws require that you keep your U.S. Coast Guard Certificate of Documentation, or State Title, or State Certificate of Numbers (or other relevant state registration) aboard your boat. This is very important. The registration or documentation is one of the first things that U.S. Coast Guard personnel will request. According to a sample survey of 100,650 Vessel Safety Checks by the National Department of Vessel Safety Checks, approximately 25 percent of vessels failed the check. Lack of registration and/or documentation papers contributed to approximately 5 percent of the failures. It is a simple matter to comply with this requirement and it should not be overlooked. Although it is rare that any fine or other punishment will occur, the absence of the required documents will assuredly lead to greater scrutiny regarding other matters and less tolerance for other violations.

Furthermore, when you cross an international border your registration/documentation papers are absolutely essential. I have personally observed local immigration and customs officials waive requirements for birth certificates or passports for a passenger or for children, go easy with alcohol restrictions, and even allow a boater to eat some fruit rather than dispose of it in the bucket, but there is virtually no chance you will be able to cross a border without the required registration/documentation papers.

Do not ask for unnecessary problems; keep your state registration papers or your U.S. Coast Guard documentation aboard your vessel at all times.

F. Vessel Log Book

What is a log book?

Keeping a log book is a notion that dates back to the early sailing ships and the explorers who sailed them. The details in their log books were necessary for navigation and to document their discoveries, claims, and all the other details of the voyage. The log book on a modern recreational vessel is not quite so essential, but it still has an important role to play when cruising. Essentially, the log book is a history of the use of your boat, a record of your trips and cruises, and a record of events aboard your boat, with the level of detail determined by you.

Is a log book required?

There is no legal requirement that a non-commercial recreational boat keep a log book or other detailed records

of each trip. However, there are some very good reasons to do so:

- When you are traveling to another country, you should have a list of your crew members. The log book is a good place to make the notations.
- When you are navigating a new area it is an excellent idea to make notations in the log book for times and places you have been. Not only will you enjoy remembering your trip later on, you can record details that might otherwise be forgotten. For example, you may experience currents or weather conditions that are worthy of note (to be avoided in the future), or you may visit a port, bay or cove that has a peculiarity (rock, reef, wind, etc.) you would like to remember.
- If you experience any difficulties or have an accident of any kind, the log book is the place to write it down. The details will escape your memory later on, possibly to your disadvantage.

Save Time and Money on Insurance Claims

Several years ago, we visited a favorite harbor in the San Juan Islands and tied up in one of the slips. I left the boat to visit some friends on another boat while my wife, Mary, took a nap.

About two hours later, Mary came aboard to tell me that a medium-sized trawler came into the adjacent slip but, while doing so, got pushed by a cross wind into our boat. Neither boat had fenders on those sides and our boat got crushed a bit by their stern. Mary said she heard some crunching sounds but did not see any obvious damage. Needless to say, I took a walk back to our slip.

I also did not see any apparent damage; nevertheless, I took out our logbook and made some notations. I wrote down the name of the harbor, our slip number, the name of the other boat, the approximate time of the accident, and a brief description of what happened. I also got the other boat owner's name and the name of the marina attendant who witnessed the mishap. Then I went back to visit our friends.

The next spring I hired a guy to do some cleaning and polishing of our boat. That afternoon he gave me a call. "Did you know about the cracks in your gel coat on the starboard side?" he asked.

"No, I didn't notice anything, but I will come over and take a look," I said.

My inspection confirmed his observation. We had two spider webs of cracks in the gel coat right at the spot where the trawler crunched us the previous summer. Yikes.

I called our insurance agent and got a call from an adjuster the next day. He was not very enthusiastic about a claim for damages from eight months ago, until I read him the information from the log book. He perked right up. I faxed him a copy of the relevant page (which also showed other details of our trip before and after the accident) and got a call back about a week later.

Our insurance company paid for complete repair of the damage and collected from the other owner's company. We received an expert gel coat repair with no visible evidence of any damage. It was nice to find out the damage was superficial, but the repairs still were not inexpensive.

The adjuster made it clear to me that the information in the log book made things very easy. The other owner's insurance company did not complain a bit because we had names, times, etc. At the very least, those few minutes spent writing down a few details saved us the amount of the deductible on our policy and quite possibly saved us the amount of the full repair bill. Additionally, even though an accident occurred, we clearly established our total innocence and preserved our excellent safety record.

- When you cross a border write down the time and place and when and how you clear customs and immigration. If you are given a clearance number or an entry number, write it in the log book. Sometimes customs and immigration questions arise months after your trip and a contemporaneous written record can be invaluable.

- We always make daily entries, starting in the morning. I write down the time we leave, the engine hours, the weather conditions, any notes about the previous night, our destination, and how we expect to get there.

- During your trip, make entries for notable events, navigation information (speed, distance, course, etc.), and miscellaneous observations.

- When you arrive at your destination, record the place, time, conditions, etc. I write down observations such as how crowded it is, where we anchored or moored, and how we anchored or moored (stern tie, short scope, long scope, buoy, dock, etc.). If I do not write my observations during the day, I do so after we arrive at our destination while the day's details are fresh in my mind.

There are numerous log books for sale in marine stores with bound pages that are organized for your immediate use. One advantage of the pre-printed log books is that the pages and your entries are permanent. However, many people simply make up their own pages, make multiple copies, and put them in a three ring binder. Either method is fine. Many boaters have a separate log book to record all maintenance and repairs. Printed maintenance and repair log books may also be purchased at marine stores or on the Internet.

What kind of information in the log book will help me with the IRS?

If you have your boat in charter or some other business use and you are taking tax deductions for expenses and depreciation, your log book is very important. In fact, under those circumstances it may be best to invest in a bound and printed log book for permanent records. Then it is easily apparent that the records are contemporaneously entered and they are chronological. For tax purposes, you should record every use of the boat and all activities on the boat.

- If you make a repair or spend time on maintenance, put it in the log book.

- If you go for a short cruise record all the details in the log book. Encourage your charter parties to make regular entries as well (even though most will not do so.) At the very least, you must have a record of all names, dates, and payments for charters.

- If the IRS audits you and wants to investigate the use of your boat, the log book can be your best friend and the financial equivalent of an expensive life jacket. The log book does not have to be fancy or expensive, although there may be some advantage to having a log book with bound pages (as it is obvious that pages have not been inserted or deleted after the fact).

Weems & Plath publishes a simple and useful cruising log book.

Recreational Boat Insurance

A. The Basics of Boat Insurance

The joy of owning a boat is tempered by a few onerous details and vessel insurance is one such detail. Buying insurance is something done by nearly every boat owner. Nevertheless, the process can be complex and time consuming. The following discussion provides some basic information regarding insurance for recreational vessels. However, this discussion does not cover or explain all aspects of insurance for your boat, and commercial maritime and cargo insurance is not addressed. Here are a few things you should know.

Is insurance a legal requirement?

Federal law does not currently require marine insurance. However, some states are urging passage of a federal requirement that boat owners carry marine liability insurance or for the authority to impose such a requirement under state law. Legalities aside, there are many excellent reasons for insuring your vessel.

- Protection of your investment. Boats are expensive, and accidents may mean significant dollar losses. Insurance is not cheap, but it's well worth the cost.
- Lender requirements. If you want to get a loan to buy a boat, the lender will require insurance, just like with a house or a car.
- Marina requirements. Most marinas require proof that you have insurance before they allow permanent moorage. The marina management or owner does not want to get stuck with the bill if your boat explodes, burns, sinks, or otherwise causes harm to the facility or other customers.
- Liability protection for harm to someone else. An accident or mishap involving your boat can cause damage or harm to other property or persons.

Liability insurance on your boat is every bit as important as liability insurance on your home or car.

Will insurance cover all losses?

The complete answer to this question is complex, but the basic answer is no, you are not covered for everything. When you buy any kind of insurance, you enter into a contract with an insurance company that says it will pay for certain losses and liabilities you may incur or reimburse you for payments you make for expenses or repairs. However, in most situations, you will have to pay the amount of the deductible on your policy. Furthermore, the specific incident, expense, or repair must be something that is covered by the contract, and the amount of the loss must be within the policy limits. If the total loss exceeds the policy limits, you may end up paying a substantial amount of money from your own pocket for repairs or replacement of your vessel. It's important to buy sufficient coverage.

How could the total loss be more than my coverage?

There are many accidents that can result in damages in excess of your coverage. If your boat explodes, burns to the water line, or sinks, your policy will probably pay for the loss, up to the market value or agreed value. However, if you negligently run into another boat and both boats explode and sink, your liability may exceed the liability coverage under your policy, particularly if someone is injured or killed. Huge damages could occur if your boat catches fire in a marina and the fire spreads to other vessels. Most policies do not cover intentional wrongdoing, such as intentionally discharging oil or fuel overboard. These examples help illustrate why you must be sure a reputable company issued your policy, why the policy limits must be sufficiently high, and why you should operate and maintain your vessel legally and properly. Insurance companies expect you to comply with the requirements in your contract and will hold you to those requirements before paying for a claim.

This marina fire caused damage to only a few boats, but that's not always the case.

What are the most important aspects of boat insurance?

The common law regarding vessel insurance has evolved over hundreds of years of court decisions and is based upon principles of Admiralty law and Insurance law. Although it can be quite complicated, there are some basic concepts you should understand.

- **Good Faith.** Marine insurance is based upon a duty of absolute good faith. The failure to disclose a material fact (such as existing damage or defects) can be grounds to terminate the policy or refuse payment for a loss. Answer all the questions on your insurance application carefully and honestly. You must not conceal any material facts about your vessel.

- **Policy Requirements.** *Read the policy.* Yes, it is boring, but it is very important to know where you can go on your boat, what equipment is required, and how and when to contact the company. Many policies have geographic limits and do not provide coverage if you travel outside designated areas. If you do not understand something, do not be embarrassed to contact the insurance agent and ask questions.

- **Proper Maintenance.** Always keep your vessel in a seaworthy condition. Policies do not cover losses caused by wear and tear, gradual deterioration, rot, mold, corrosion weathering, blistering, delamination, etc. If you have a survey performed for any reason, repair any deficiencies or problems noted by the surveyor.

- **Common Sense.** Insurance policies require specific action in the event of an accident or damage. Claims can be refused if you fail to follow specified procedures in the event of an accident. You must take all necessary steps to protect the vessel and its equipment from further damage or loss and immediately notify the insurance company. Usually, the steps you have to take are simple common sense, based upon reasonable expectations. Always act reasonably and responsibly if a loss occurs.

What types of insurance are available?

Insurance on recreational watercraft is divided into three basic groups: personal watercraft (jet skis, wave runners, etc), boat insurance (generally vessels between 16 to 26 feet), and yacht insurance (26 feet or longer).

- **Boat Insurance.** This type of insurance covers physical damage to your boat and liability coverage for damage to someone else's property or personal injury to someone else.

- **Yacht Insurance.** This is similar to boat insurance, except it is called hull coverage and protection and indemnity coverage. Hull coverage covers the yacht and its equipment (and dinghies and tenders for additional premium cost). Indemnity pays for damage or injury you may cause to someone else. Both boat and yacht insurance can include protection against persons who are uninsured, payments for limited medical expenses, towing, fuel spill containment and clean up, and salvage.

- **All Risk Coverage.** Most yacht policies are all risk, and they cover all external causes of loss except those that are specifically excluded. For example, damage from named storms may be excluded or limited.

- **Named Perils Coverage.** Named perils coverage is different than all risk coverage. It only covers losses from incidents that are named in the policy. If it is not on the list, it is not covered. Obviously, the all risk coverage is better.

What types of policies are available?

There are two policy types for the calculation of the amount paid in the event of total vessel loss. Payment will either be an agreed value or an actual cash value. Boat insurance will usually cover actual cash value, and yacht insurance (depending upon vessel age) will usually be for agreed value. The figure set for agreed value should be the actual value of your vessel. The higher the value, the more the insurance will cost.

What is a declarations page?

The coverage provided by your policy will be stated on the Policy Declarations Page. Review your declarations page very carefully. Items that are covered will be listed in a column with a corresponding coverage limit for each item. The declarations will also state deductible amounts and cruising limits. Cruising limits are the geographic areas that are included. (Basic yacht policies will exclude blue water cruising, for example.) Policies that limit coverage to selected areas (such as Chesapeake Bay or Puget Sound) are less expensive. An example of a declarations page is included in the Appendix. The declarations page will usually list the following information:

- Insurance amount and agreed value for the vessel and equipment.
- Coverage for investigative services.
- Liability coverage.
- Medical coverage for each person injured.
- Uninsured boaters coverage.
- Coverage for personal effects, the boat trailer, and dinghy or tender.
- Deductible amounts for the various coverages.

How much coverage should I buy?

Most people are familiar with automobile insurance and the minimum requirements. However, insurance for boats is not the same. Every owner has to decide how little or how great the insurance should be, based on individual circumstances. You should consider the type of boat you own, the value of your boat, where it will be used, when it will be used, how experienced and careful you are, and how much money you might lose if you caused serious injury to someone else. Lawsuits can be extremely expensive and judgments can be very high. It is not necessary to over-insure but be careful not to under-insure. If you are concerned about liability and protecting your net worth, consider buying a liability insurance rider for a higher amount.

How can I save some money on my insurance?

Most boat and yacht owners desire to save money whenever possible. Various factors determine the cost of insurance, such as the type of vessel, size, age, location, and owner experience. You should talk to your insurance agent and discuss in detail the type of coverage you need and all the various aspects of the policy. You may learn something specific you can do to reduce the price for your insurance. Here are a few common ways to keep your costs down.

- **Education.** Take an approved boating safety course such as a U.S. Coast Guard Auxiliary course or a U.S. Power Squadron course. These courses are required in some states.
- **Protective Devices.** Installing reasonable protective devices (such as depth sounder, VHF radio, extra fire extinguishers, smoke detector and carbon monoxide detector), may make you eligible for a discount. Ask the insurance agent ahead of time if certain equipment qualifies you for a discount.
- **Appropriate Deductibles.** Set your deductibles as high as you can reasonably afford. If you are a careful, experienced owner, with no history of an accident or loss and if you have enough money in the bank to cover some reasonable costs, you can save on insurance costs.
- **Adequate Insurance.** Do not buy more insurance than you need. If you never go outside inland waters, don't buy insurance to go offshore. If you decide to go outside your geographic limits, see if you can buy temporary coverage for the single trip.
- **Clean Record.** Keep a clean automobile driving record. Insurance companies believe that a cautious and safe car driver will also be a safe boat or yacht owner. If you have a citation for intoxicated automobile driving, it will seriously affect your boat insurance.
- **Safe Area.** If your boat is kept in a safe area away from hurricanes or other severe weather conditions, tell the insurance company. Premiums are higher in areas subject to extraordinary weather. Ask if there are things you can do (like dry storage ashore) to get a discount.
- **Prices.** Shop around. But keep in mind that the least expensive policy will not necessarily be the best. If possible, join an organization or group that offers marine insurance as a membership perk. Always check the policy and the company that offers the policy. If you have never heard of the company, it may be best to continue shopping.

- **Honest Claims.** Never make unnecessary or exaggerated claims. If you have an accident do everything reasonably possible to limit the damage. Remember, your company may promptly pay your claim in full but then decide you are not a good risk and refuse to renew your policy. That can make it difficult and expensive to get new insurance.

Where should I keep my policy?

Once you have paid for your insurance and received your declarations page and your policy, make a copy and keep in on your vessel. No one can be expected to memorize and remember the policy conditions and requirements, especially in the stress and anxiety of an accident or injury. Also keep on your vessel the name, phone number, fax number, email address of your agent and the company claims department. Immediate advice, assistance, and some peace of mind, is as close as a cellular phone or marine operator call away. But if you do not know the contact's name and number, your stress level will elevate accordingly.

What are some common damages and losses?

Fortunately, most boating accidents involve harm to one or two vessels and relatively small amounts of damage. It is rare for a vessel to be totally destroyed, but it does happen. Many insurance claims arise while the vessel is not being operated. Bad things can happen while your boat is simply sitting alone (for example, most boats that sink do so right at the dock).

Many insurance claims are related to maintenance and equipment problems that are preventable. Even if there is not a specific law that requires you to maintain your boat and its systems and even if you have adequate insurance you should never neglect routine precautions and maintenance. If an accident occurs you will end up paying for repairs at least up to the amount of the deductible on your policy and it is possible that damages may exceed your policy limits if an accident from your boat causes substantial loss to other boats, the marina, or physical harm to other persons. The purpose of this discussion is not to address every possible disaster or accident but there are some common and avoidable problems.

Save Money by Shopping Around

Insurance for your boat is not cheap, but it does not have to empty your bank account. In most situations, you should be able to get a good insurance policy at a reasonable price. However, if your boat is in charter or some other form of commercial, business, or shared use, you should expect to pay considerably more.

When we bought our sailboat, we looked around a bit for a good insurance agent (not very avidly, though) and bought a policy as part of the closing of the transaction. It seemed a bit expensive (almost $1,000 per year), but in the excitement of acquiring our boat we did not give it much thought.

We are careful and experienced owners, so we had no accidents or claims in the first two years of our policy. Nevertheless, when we got our renewal notice, we noticed we had a premium increase of more than 20 percent. I asked my wife to do some shopping and look for a better deal.

We began the process by looking in our phone book and by checking the Internet. Then, based on our experience with medical insurance and our membership with the American Automotive Association (AAA), we got the idea to look for some kind of group or organization that might offer better insurance rates. As a result, we joined BoatU.S., a large national organization.

Our insurance premiums plummeted more than 50 percent. Although, we had to join the organization, there are other benefits that make up for the annual dues. The insurance savings alone are well worth the cost of membership.

BoatU.S. is not the only organization for boat owners, and other groups offer various discounts and incentives. Some common incentives are: discounts at marine stores, free towing for short distance problems, boat loan specials for members, and lots of free information. Most groups have a newsletter or magazine with lots of good information and Internet links. The Appendix in this book has a list of organizations for your consideration. If you want to save a few dollars on marine insurance, it is a good place to start. However, you must still carefully review the policy to be sure that the record of claims payment is not tainted. If you have doubts about an insurance company, one place to get information is your State Insurance Commissioner. If there are major problems with a company, your State Insurance Commissioner's office is a good source of information.

High winds destroyed this genoa while the boat sat safely at the dock. The roller furling partly unfurled and the wind twisted the sail making it impossible to roll up.

- **Electrical and wiring.** Poor or faulty wiring can easily cause a fire that will destroy a boat. Electrical fires account for about 55 percent of all boat fires, and DC systems are responsible for most of those. Fires caused by AC systems are typically more severe and costly. Loose wires or corroded connections generate heat, depending upon the load. Often, substantial AC power is brought aboard your boat by a relatively small shore power cord. You must be sure that the cord is securely attached to the dock outlet and that it is sufficient to handle the load. All those conveniences aboard your boat (TV, computer, microwave oven, air conditioner, refrigerator, icemaker, etc.) can result in a substantial power draw. A damaged shore power cord can be a significant hazard.
- **Hoses and clamps, through-hulls and valves.** Modern yachts may have five, ten, or more holes in the hull in the form of through-hulls. A valve usually tops off these fittings with a hose attached to the valve and is held in place by a clamp that goes around the hose and holds it to the valve. These clamps are simple, inexpensive pieces of equipment, but if one

fails, your boat may sink. Clamps used in marine applications must be made completely of stainless steel and properly installed. Hose clamp inspections and maintenance are often overlooked or neglected, with disastrous results. Additionally, the stems that go through the hull and the valves attached to them can corrode over time or suffer deterioration from electrolysis. These should be inspected frequently, especially when the boat is out of the water.

- **Fuel leaks and fumes.** Explosive fuels are present on most every vessel with an engine or cabin. Gasoline engines rely on highly volatile and explosive fuel. A small leak from a damaged fitting or fuel line can lead to a catastrophic explosion. Additionally, many yachts have propane appliances and propane tanks. There are specific requirements for installation of propane equipment and tanks, propane fuel lines, and maintenance and inspection of tanks. All fuel lines and tanks should be routinely inspected for age, cracks, corrosion, loose fittings, and loose attachments. Lines that are otherwise in good condition can quickly fail if they become loose or detached and are allowed to flex or chafe.

Never Ignore Water Inside Your Boat

One year after we acquired our sailboat, I noticed small amounts of water under the engine. I finally isolated the source as a small, slow drip from the raw water uptake hose attached to a valve. I tried tightening the clamps and the drip stopped for a while. When it started dripping again I gave the problem some additional attention.

I started by closing the valve for the raw water. The valve was stubborn and difficult, but I was able to get it closed. I removed the hose and examined the hose barb attached to the valve. Close observation revealed that the white nylon hose barb was clearly on its last legs. It was seriously cracked and ready to totally fail. The hose barb vibrated moderately whenever the engine ran and would have eventually broken off completely. If the valve broke, water would flow freely into the boat.

This is just one example of a small problem that can quickly spell disaster. Most boat sinkings (about 80 percent) take place while the vessel is tied to a dock and unattended. Those little valves, stems, hoses, and clamps are always a potential source of problems.

What should I do if I have an accident?

Your policy will have a specific section (probably one of the first paragraphs) that tells you exactly what to do if an accident occurs. That's why it's so important to have a copy of the policy on your vessel. The requirements are part of the contract with the company and if you fail to comply your coverage could be jeopardized. Some of the requirements are common sense. Here are some of the first things you must do.

- Immediately see to the welfare of any injured person.
- Take all necessary steps to protect the boat and its equipment from further loss or damage.
- Notify the appropriate officials immediately.
- Do not discuss fault or cause of the accident. Do not make any statements that admit you were at fault, assume obligation, or admit liability. Do not try and be overly friendly because you feel bad about the accident.
- Notify the insurance company.

An example of language from a yacht policy regarding the reporting of accidents is included in the Appendix.

How do I understand all those terms in my policy?

Insurance policies are complicated contracts with decades of court decisions to further confuse everyone. However, the government regulates insurance companies in the United States and reputable companies make an effort to provide policies that are understandable. Nevertheless, you will never be able to understand the terms and conditions of your policy if you do not read it and ask questions. Every insurance policy has a section dedicated to definitions of various words and terms used in the policy. It is important to read those definitions carefully or to refer to those definitions while you are reviewing the policy itself. Sometimes, the definitions can cleverly limit the amount of coverage you will have in specific situations.

What are among the most important things to look for in my policy?

Most people never get around to reading their insurance policy, even though they should. It is actually very important to read the policy because it determines how, when, and how much will be paid on a claim. The following are some items that need special attention.

- The definitions section is very important. Words or phrases that are specifically defined are crucial to understanding the policy. Some definitions may be more restrictive than the common understanding of a word or phrase.
- The actions to take if a loss or accident occurs are crucial. The policy spells out your specific obligations, and you must follow the requirements to assure your claim will be paid.
- The policy will have an exclusions section; you must know what is excluded. Those items (such as wear and tear, corrosion, weathering, etc.) are your responsibility and will not be covered by the policy.
- A policy for private pleasure use has no coverage during periods of chartering, leasing, or commercial use. If you have your boat in charter, you must obtain coverage for that activity. Additionally, many policies do not offer coverage for powerboats while engaged in any speed race or test, but they do cover predicted log races and sailboat racing.
- The policy will specifically cover fuel and other spill liability. There will also be an exclusions paragraph in that section. Be sure you know what is not covered. For example, most policies will not cover liability for intentional or willful misconduct or criminal or civil violations of law. That means if you find oil in your bilge and pump it out on purpose, you will not have coverage for damages or fines.
- Check for exclusions related to specific geographic areas (usually specified on the declarations page) and look for exclusions for special areas that might be considered hazardous by the insurer. For example, in the Pacific Northwest policies often specify coverage for Puget Sound and British Columbia waters only, but not west of Nigei Island (the north tip of Vancouver Island) or west of Cape Flattery (at the mouth of the Strait of Juan de Fuca). This means that cruisers going to Alaska, around Vancouver Island, or down the Pacific coast must obtain special coverage for the trip.
- Check for operator or crew requirements. Policies with coverage for offshore trips often require additional crew members (beyond just a husband and wife couple for example) or a specific level of experience by someone aboard, such as a captain.

Insurance Terms and Definitions

Here are definitions for some general insurance terms.
Your marine policy will have additional definitions that
apply to the policy itself.

AGENT: Someone licensed and authorized to sell insurance on behalf of an insurance company.

BROKER: A licensed person or organization paid by you to look for insurance on your behalf.

CANCELLATION: The termination of insurance coverage during the policy period. Flat cancellation is the cancellation of a policy as of its effective date, without any premium charge.

CLAIM: Notice to an insurer that under the terms of a policy, a loss may be covered.

CLAIMANT: A person who asserts right of recovery.

DEDUCTIBLE: The amount of the loss which the insured is responsible to pay before benefits from the insurance company are payable. You may choose a higher deductible to lower your premium.

DEPRECIATION: A decrease in value due to age, wear and tear, etc.

ENDORSEMENT: Amendment to the policy used to add or delete coverage. Also referred to as a rider.

EXCLUSION: Certain causes and conditions, listed in the policy, which are not covered.

EXPIRATION DATE: The date on which the policy ends.

INSURED: The policyholder - the person(s) protected in case of a loss or claim.

INSURER: The insurance company.

LIMIT: Maximum amount a policy will pay either overall or under a particular coverage.

MATERIAL MISREPRESENTATION: The policyholder / applicant makes a false statement of any material (important) fact on his/her application. For instance, the policyholder provides false information regarding the location where the vessel is kept.

PERIL: The cause of a possible loss. For example: fire or theft.

POLICY: The written contract of insurance.

POLICY LIMIT: The maximum amount a policy will pay, either overall or under a particular coverage.

PREMIUM: The amount of money an insurance company charges for insurance coverage.

REPLACEMENT COST: The cost to repair or replace an insured item. Some insurance only pays the actual cash or market value of the item at the time of the loss, not what it would cost to fix or replace it.

REPLACEMENT VALUE: The full cost to repair or replace the damaged property with no deduction for depreciation, subject to policy limits and contract provisions.

REINSTATEMENT: The restoring of a lapsed policy to full force and effect. The reinstatement may be effective after the cancellation date, creating a lapse of coverage. Some companies require evidence of insurability and payment of past due premiums plus interest.

RIDER: Usually known as an endorsement, a rider is an amendment to the policy used to add or delete coverage.

Why Boats Sink In Open Water

Reason	Percentage
Taking Water Over the Gunwales	30%
Leaks at Through-hulls	18%
Leaks at Raw water Cooling System/Exhaust	12%
Drain Plug Missing	12%
Navigation Error (Grounding)	10%
Boat Construction (Hull Split Open)	6%
Leaks at Outdrive Boots	4%
Struck Floating Debris	4%
Other	4%

Source: BoatU.S.

How important are those supplements and updates that I receive?

You will occasionally receive something called an *endorsement* from your insurance company. These are essentially amendments to the policy that explain some aspect of the coverage or that change some aspect of the policy. The endorsement is a standard looking form with what might appear to be inconsequential information about your policy. However, the endorsement may change the coverage in a specific situation or it may change or add a definition for a specific term or clause. It is very important that you read the endorsements and understand what is being changed.

B. Insurance Agency and Company Information

It is very important that you keep insurance information aboard your boat at all times. It is impossible to predict when and where an accident may occur but it is necessary to immediately contact your insurance agent and insurance company. This can only be done if you have the names and phone numbers with you. The Appendix has an example of a simple form you can use to keep important insurance information readily available.

The *Keeping Your Boat Legal* binder has space for you to keep important insurance information and space to insert a copy of your insurance policy and the declarations page.

It Is Not Junk Mail

We carry insurance through BoatU.S. on our boat. The coverage is relatively affordable and the policy is simple to read and understand. The policy is offered by The Continental Casualty Company. Every year we receive some endorsements and I always try to take some time to read each one carefully, then I put a copy in my *Keeping Your Boat Legal* binder and in my insurance file in my office.

One endorsement I received illustrates how important it is to read everything carefully. The endorsement in question, read as follows: "The Yacht Policy, Coverage B, Boating Liability, is amended to provide that unless the Boat insured is operated with one or all of the below listed persons aboard, the Coverage B, Boating Liability, limit is reduced to $25,000 and Coverage A, Boat and Boating Equipment, is automatically reduced to 50 percent of Agreed Hull Value of the boat, and is subject to the deductible as shown on the declarations page. The warranted operators include: Curtis Epperson & Mary Epperson."

This endorsement means that either I or Mary must be on our boat whenever it is operated if we want full coverage under our policy. Prior to this endorsement our constant presence was not required. From now on our boat will never leave the dock without one of us aboard.

Personal Information To Keep on Your Boat

What personal information should I keep on my boat?

Whenever you travel by boat, even as a guest, it is important to carry certain personal identification information. This is especially important if you are in the vicinity of a national border. Any boat in the vicinity of a national border is subject to being stopped, boarded, and searched. This is especially true now that governments are engaged in more serious scrutiny and tracking of all persons crossing national borders. Additionally, the U.S. Coast Guard is on the front lines of the effort to stop the flow of illegal drugs. Vessel inspections, searches, and scrutiny of everyone aboard are increasing. You can avoid problems and make the job easier for government authorities by being prepared. The following personal information items should be with you on your boat.

Beyond People Information

One aspect of cruising enjoyed by many people is the practice of bringing along a pet. However, in addition to the other special considerations (doggy life jackets, trips ashore for walks, dog and cat hair aboard, and uninvited guests like fleas) your pet's presence requires additional documents.

Make sure your pet is correctly licensed in your state or city and that you have the correct tags. Additionally, if you are planning to cross an international border, be sure that your pet has all the required immunizations.

Back in the early days, our friends constantly harangued us to buy a spinnaker. Finances were tight but I eventually came up with a solution. A client bred her dog and offered to sell me a very cute Llasa Apso puppy. I named him Spinnaker and proudly told my friends that we had a spinnaker for the boat.

He and I went cruising for the first time when he was about 12 weeks old. When I checked in at Customs after crossing the border into Canada the officer asked, "Do you have any pets aboard." I replied, "Yes, a little dog." She asked to see his license and proof of rabies vaccination.

I stood silently and then asked, "Is the rabies vaccination required?"

"Yes, unless he's just a puppy. Then he still has immunity from his mother."

"How old can he be?" I asked.

"Twelve weeks," came the answer. "Is he older than twelve weeks?"

"I'm not sure. I think he's about that old, maybe a little more. He's just a little guy."

She eyed me calmly. "Has he had his shots?" She asked.

Well, at this point I was rapidly sinking into a hole. So I punted and said, "Yes, he had all his shots but I don't have any documents with me. But he is not very old and he's very small. He certainly doesn't look like he is more than twelve weeks. He's just a little fluff ball." I smiled hopefully and prayed for a break.

"Well, if he is real little and he had his puppy shots I suppose he will be OK," she replied with a smile. "Just be sure to have his records next time".

I left the office quickly after getting my clearance number. Spinnaker and I enjoyed many cruises together and I always had his records with me.

- **Photo ID.** You should carry your automobile driver's license or some other acceptable photo identification.

- **Passport or birth certificate.** If you will be crossing a national border or cruising in the vicinity of a border you should definitely carry a passport and/or a copy of your birth certificate. You should have proof of your citizenship and that of everyone else aboard. Your driver's license nor even your voter's registration are considered proof of citizenship.

- **Health insurance.** Keep your health insurance information aboard. If you have an accident or illness you will need it.

- **Prescription medicine.** If you use prescription medication you should have information regarding the use of that medication, its side effects and hazards, and proof of the prescription.

- **Copies of credit cards and other valuable documents.** Some travelers store separate information regarding their credit cards (card holders name, card issuer name, and card issuer's phone number) so they can call the issuer in case the card is stolen or lost. A handy thing to do is to make copies of valuable personal documents and credit cards and keep them in some safe location.

When you complete your trip or cruise and you are returning home, take the personal information home with you. ***Do not leave your personal information on your vessel when it is not in use or when it's in use by someone else, such as a charterer.*** You should keep some basic information about yourself and everyone aboard your boat when you take trips or cruises. A sample form for personal information is included in the Appendix.

Vessel Survey and Repair Information

A. Vessel Survey

What is a Marine Survey?

A marine survey is a detailed examination of your vessel. The surveyor makes an inspection and prepares a written report. A good survey will contain valuable information about your boat and include things that you may not readily recall. For example, the survey should include the name of the builder, the place built, the year built, the vessel identification number, the hull number, the length over-all, the beam, equipment aboard, engine information, and other important specifications. Many of

The owner of this boat will need a damage inspection survey. The next owner will definitely want a pre-purchase survey to be sure all the damage has been properly repaired.
Credit: Photo from BoatU.S.

these questions will come up when applying for insurance or moorage and the survey is a handy and easy resource.

It's important that your survey be in accord with standards set by the American Boat and Yacht Council (ABYC), the National Fire Protection Association (NFPA), and the U.S. Coast Guard.

There are different types of surveys used for different purposes. It is appropriate to ask a surveyor for a sample of the type of survey as well as for a resume and references. Surveys are performed for a variety of reasons:

- **Pre-purchase survey.** This is the most comprehensive type of inspection and is strongly advised when purchasing a new or used vessel. It is sometimes referred to as a full condition and value (C&V) survey. The condition and the overall operation of the vessel should be examined. This includes such items as structural integrity, out of the water inspection, sea trial, electrical systems, propulsion system, fuel system, machinery, and navigation, in addition to miscellaneous on-board systems, cosmetic appearance, electronics, and overall maintenance.

- **Insurance survey.** This inspection is performed so that the insurance company can determine whether or not the vessel is an acceptable risk. In some cases, however, a survey that is called an insurance survey will not include enough information for an insurance company to make a decision. Be sure that the insurance survey will be adequate for the intended purpose before you spend your money. Most insurance companies are interested in the structural integrity and safety of the vessel for its intended use, and many companies require a more complete survey, particularly on older boats. They also will want to know the vessel's fair market value.

- **Valuation survey.** This survey is performed to gather enough information to justify or determine the fair market value of the vessel. This is normally needed for financing, estate settlements, donations, and legal cases.

- **Damage inspection survey.** This is performed to assess the extent of damage, recommend repairs, estimate repair cost, and, if requested, the probable cause of the damage.

Do I need a survey?

Most insurance companies and banks will require that a vessel, particularly an older one, be surveyed prior to approving a loan or issuing an insurance policy on a vessel. They will need to know the condition and fair market value to finance and/or underwrite the vessel.

What will the survey report include?

A good marine survey will give the prospective buyer or seller information on the vessel's condition and fair market value. However, the survey will include very little information (if any) about the boat's engine. If you want specific information about the engine, you should hire a marine mechanic to do an evaluation. Ask the surveyor for some recommendations and choose a mechanic with experience that is relevant to the boat and engine that you are considering. Always ask the surveyor and the mechanic how much it will cost. Prices can vary significantly from geographic region to region, from builder to builder, and model to model for seemingly similar boats.

- **Defects.** The marine survey can help identify latent manufacturing defects, shoddy workmanship, and substandard construction techniques and equipment and determine if any U.S. Coast Guard defect notices have been issued on a particular make or model.

- **Repairs.** Most surveys will itemize various items that need repair or replacement. If there is a defect, or if there is damage that requires immediate repair, it will be highlighted by the surveyor. The best practice is to immediately investigate any items listed by the surveyor and take remedial action. In many cases, an insurance company will require that you undertake repairs or replacements suggested by the surveyor. It is important that you keep records of all the repairs and the invoices. Even if a repair is not immediately required by an insurance company or lender, the matter may arise later. If you already paid for the repair, you will want to be able to prove it.

How do I find and choose a surveyor?

The quality of the survey will depend upon the competence and experience of the person you hire. A top quality survey by an experienced and knowledgeable individual will not be significantly more expensive than a quick and cheap report, but it will be worth the extra money. It is worth your time and money to shop around for a reputable surveyor. Here are a few tips for finding a competent surveyor.

Three Years Later The Surveyor Remembered Our Boat

Three years after we bought our sailboat, I decided it was time to replace some of the valves (sea cocks) and through-hull stems. Our inspection showed some corrosion and wear and tear that inspired less than full confidence. However, some of the stems were in good shape. All of them were glassed flush to the outside of the hull so replacement was a significant job. I wondered if we could just add new valves on some of the stems and what type of valves to use. The existing valves appeared to be stainless steel attached to bronze stems. We wondered why the builder would use dissimilar metals and pondered whether we should buy stainless steel valves, Marelon® valves, or bronze valves.

I retrieved a copy of our three-and-a-half-year-old survey and sent an email inquiry across the country to the surveyor. The next day I received a polite and informative reply. He remembered our boat and was familiar with the builder and model. He did a little checking and let me know that the stems were bronze and the valves were also bronze with chrome on the outside. Therefore, the metals were not dissimilar. He recommended removal of any stems that showed signs of corrosion and leaving in place the stems and valves that were in good shape. He also offered his opinion on Marelon® versus bronze valves.

His advice was very helpful and probably saved us some money on the repairs. It was very handy that I still had my copy of the survey and his email address.

- When you are buying a boat, ask the broker for some suggestions or referrals, ask your insurance agent for some referrals, or ask a documentation service for some referrals.

- Call each surveyor and find out how much it will cost, what will be done, how long it will take, what professional certifications he or she has, and what will be covered in the report.

- Inquire about the surveyor's experience and professional background.

- If you are more comfortable dealing with someone who has a professional designation, the National Association of Marine Surveyors (NAMS) and the Society of Accredited Marine Surveyors (SAMS) provide such designations.

- More information about such organizations is in the Appendix. An outline of information contained in a typical survey is also included.

You should keep a record of every survey and the surveyor's name, address and phone number. Keep the information aboard your vessel. If you have a question about your vessel (perhaps in conjunction with a repair or improvement), the surveyor can be a good source of information. You may find it useful to contact the surveyor at some point for information or advice.

B. Repair Information to Keep on Your Boat

It is a good idea to keep track of your maintenance or repair information and history. First, you will want to know simple things, such as when you had your last haul out and inspection and when routine repairs were last performed. Record the boat yard name, address and phone number, and a summary of the work done on your boat. It's often useful to be able to easily contact boatyards, mechanics, and other repairmen who have performed repairs of services on your boat. A particular question or issue that may be confusing and puzzling to you might be quickly answered by the person who installed equipment on your boat or serviced it. Second, detailed record keeping will make it easier to answer questions that come up in conjunction with insurance applications and the resale of your vessel. A sample form for your survey and repair information is included in the Appendix.

This Weems & Plath Maintenance Log book is an excellent example of a printed book for recording maintenance and repair information.

Vessel Navigation Rules and Requirements

A. The Rules Of The Road

What are the navigation Rules of the Road?

The U.S. Coast Guard enforces navigation rules and regulations. These navigation rules are also referred to as the Rules of the Road. The rules that apply to all watercraft are divided into inland rules and international rules.

Do I have to obey the Rules of the Road?

Yes, absolutely. For safe and legal operation of your vessel it is essential that you understand and obey the rules. You will not be stopped by the U.S. Coast Guard and required to quote all the rules but you must know the basics. For example, the rules establish actions that vessels must take to avoid collisions. If you do not understand these basics, the risk of an accident involving your boat increases considerably. So does the risk that it will be your fault. Ignorance is never a defense or adequate excuse. If you violate the navigation rules and cause an accident, you will be legally responsible and may incur a fine or other enforcement action. You also may be held negligent in a court of law and incur liability for damages or injuries.

NAVIGATION RULES

U.S. Department Of Homeland Security
United States Coast Guard

NAVIGATION RULES
INTERNATIONAL—INLAND

COMDTINST M16672.2D

The Navigation Rules are available directly from the U.S. Coast Guard or from the Internet.

How do I obtain a copy of the rules?

You may obtain a written copy of the Navigation Rules (NSN 7642-01-436-9514) from the Government Printing Office or download a full free copy from the U.S. Coast Guard Office of Boating Safety web site. The Internet address is in the Appendix. Purchase printed copies from various marine publishers or at most marine stores. Vessels over 39.4 feet must have a copy of the Inland Navigation Rules aboard.

What do the rules cover?

The rules cover a wide variety of navigation situations.

- **Visibility situations.** They include the conduct of vessels in various visibility conditions and conduct of vessels in sight of each other.
- **Lights, shapes, sounds and signals.** They include specifications for lights and shapes (including towing and pushing, lights for different vessel types, anchor lights, etc.) and sound and light signals for maneuvering, warning, and distress signals.
- **Assistance at sea.** The rules require that necessary assistance be rendered whenever a vessel is involved in a marine accident, and that assistance be rendered to someone found at sea in danger of being lost. The duties to render assistance are only required to the extent that it can be done without serious danger to the assisting vessel or individuals aboard.
- **Negligent or intoxicated operation.** The rules also prohibit negligent operation that endangers the life, limb, or property of any person. The rules prohibit operation of a vessel while under the influence of alcohol or a dangerous drug.

What are the right of way rules?

The following discussion is a simple summary of the navigation rules for the right of way in various situations. There is a hierarchy for vessel rights of way, stated as follows:

- **Disabled vessel.** A broken down vessel, or one not under command, has primary right of way.

- **Supply vessel.** A vessel transferring supplies to another, or a working vessel whose work restricts it to a particular area, or a vessel (such as a dredge or tow) that has limited maneuverability is next.

- **Fishing vessel.** A fishing vessel with gear that restricts its maneuverability (not a sport fisher) is third.

Port, Starboard, Red, Green... Which Way Do I Go?

Do not rely on old charts. The common rule of thumb — red, right, returning — sounds simple, but it is not always as easy as it might seem. In most cases, it is fairly straightforward to discern when you are entering a harbor or proceeding up a channel. But in some situations you will find yourself keeping red buoys and markers on your port side. In other words, it is not always clear when you are proceeding up a channel. Additionally, some waterways (natural or man-made) connect two larger bodies of water; for a portion of the way, you are headed into a harbor, and for part of the way you are headed out. It is important to interpret these situations correctly.

The only sure way to know the correct side to pass a buoy or marker is to check your nautical chart and identify the navigation aid before you arrive. This is another reason why it is important to have current and updated charts. Your chart will show the correct location of a navigation aid and show you on which side you can safely pass. If your chart is old, it may not show new buoys or markers. Additionally, if a shoal or sand bar has moved (as they inevitably do over time), the old chart may not show the correct location of a buoy or marker.

We recently experienced a good example of this problem. We carry many different charts and guides on our boat. On a recent cruise in waters near Seattle, we used a new set of charts and several recent cruising guides. However, we also had one older NOAA chart that included a large scale harbor chart for a particular narrow and shallow pass. It was 20 years old and significantly out of date. While the old chart had accurate data for depths, rocks, obstructions and currents, one of our cruising guides had detailed discussion of some proposed changes for buoys and markers for this particular pass. We studied the chart and the depths and distances and the notes in our cruising guide and studied the locations of various shoals and bars. We compared the information on the old chart to our new ones and saw some important differences.

Although it intuitively seemed like we were leaving a large harbor (and should thereby keep the green buoys on our right), the charts clearly indicated that we were entering a new harbor and that the green buoys must be kept left and the red ones on the right. As we entered the passage we noted the existence of two markers (one buoy and one day marker on a pole) that were not shown on the old chart. We could see by looking at the new chart and reading the cruising guide that the markers identified shallow areas and some rocks.

It helped that the shallow areas were clearly visible due to the low tide. But at high tide, with only the old chart as a reference, it would have been easy to make a mistake and pass on the wrong side of the first two green buoys since they marked a (barely covered at low tide) shoal that extended about three-quarters of a mile from shore. In fact, when we arrived at our destination that afternoon, the marina had a photo posted of a sailboat lying on its side on the shoal, having made the mistake that we avoided.

There are other situations when you must pay close attention to the buoys and your charts. In areas that have connecting waterways, such as portions of the Intracoastal Waterway, the buoy placements may reverse as you navigate along the channel. In some channels that connect bays or ports, red buoys belong to starboard for part of the way, but at certain points they reverse and must be kept to port. Of course, the exact opposite is true for vessels coming from the opposite direction.

This U.S. Coast Guard illustration shows how to follow a channel marked by various buoys, red on the right, green on the left.

- **Sailboats.** A sailboat under sail alone, a rowboat, or paddleboat, is fourth. A sailboat under engine power must obey the rules as if it were a powerboat. For example: a powerboat must yield to a sailboat (not under engine power), and a sailboat must yield to a commercial fishing boat that is actually fishing. Each of those would need to yield to a working vessel with restricted maneuverability, and all must yield to a disabled vessel.

- **Overtaking.** For overtaking situations, the passing vessel must yield to the vessel being passed. This also applies if a sailboat is overtaking a powerboat. When two vessels are approaching each other from opposite directions, the general rule is to indicate your intent early and pass port-to-port.

- **Channels.** In narrow channels or restricted spaces, do not impede a vessel that must stay in the deep water or within the channel markers. Do not impede a large vessel that has difficulty maneuvering in a narrow channel or confined space. If you are crossing a channel or shipping lane, do so at a right angle and as quickly as possible. If you are in an area of large commercial vessels, pay attention, stay out of the way, keep your VHF radio on and tuned to the proper channel, and watch your navigation charts.

Stay Visible While Anchored

Sometimes, it seems that following some of the rules is not necessary under certain conditions. For example, we have all probably anchored in secluded harbors, full of boats, in out of the way places, and noticed how few boats use their anchor lights at night. After all, who needs an anchor light to protect against a collision in a quiet bay with no nighttime traffic? The story that follows illustrates the folly of neglecting this rule. We once stayed at a state park that had eight mooring buoys in a line next to a small undeveloped island. We took the buoy on the south end of the line and settled in for a peaceful weekend.

Later in the afternoon, we noticed an increasing number of small boats (including personal watercraft) passing by the line of mooring buoys at speeds of 30 or 40 mph or more. They were using the bay to pass around the inside of a small island to our north. I recognized the state park was in a traffic lane for lots of small power boats proceeding to vacation homes for the weekend. It occurred to me that the traffic might go on after dark. It also occurred to me that some of the drivers might be getting a good start on the weekend and under somewhat diminished capacity.

Sure enough, dusk fell, and boats continued to go by until late into the evening. Some of the passing boats did not use running lights. Our boat and the others tied to the mooring buoys all had our anchor lights shining. In fact, I also sat out in the cockpit of our sailboat until the traffic stopped, reading a good book under the light of a lantern. The last thing we needed was an errant power boat plowing into our stern for failing to see us in the dark.

Your anchor light is good insurance against an accident that you might not be able to otherwise avoid. Further, if you do not use it and another vessel (fast or slow) runs into you, even if the driver is otherwise acting irresponsibly, you will be held at least partly responsible.

Remember, also, that an anchor light at the top of your sailboat mast may be difficult to see. Many such lights are tiny little things that draw very little electrical current but are also not very bright. Since they are high in the air a passing speedboat may not see the light at all. Sometimes it is a good idea to put a brighter light lower in the triangle in front of the mast. It must be high enough to be seen from a distance, but low enough to be easily visible from up close. You can also do what I did — sit in the cockpit and keep a good light on your book.

This clearly marked channel makes navigation into the harbor easy.

The Index for the Rules of the Road is reprinted in the Appendix. The Appendix also has reprints of Rules 9 and 10 dealing with narrow channels and traffic separation schemes and a reprint of the Penalty Provisions.

B. Aids to Navigation

What are Aids to Navigation?

The buoys and markers maintained by the U.S. Coast Guard (and state officials in some areas) are essential elements of safe navigation and are referred to as aids to navigation. Basic knowledge of the system is required for all boaters. The following summary is an introduction to the system. More detailed study and understanding is necessary and further information is readily available in numerous books and on the Internet.

What are buoys and markers?

The basic system consists of buoys and markers to show channels (natural and man-made), traffic management systems, shallow areas, and submerged or otherwise dangerous hazards.

- Official navigation charts, most chart books, and cruising guides, have an appendix that includes pictures or diagrams of markers and an explanation of each. The diagrams illustrate the various types, sizes, and colors of buoys and markers and their meaning. When you are planning your course each day, look carefully for markers shown on your chart or in your cruising guide. If you do not know what each marker means, check the diagrams. It's very helpful to note the location of these markers on your chart

and then watch carefully for each one while you are under way.

- When you are navigating into a harbor or waterway, you will likely encounter markers that show the channel. The simple rule is *red, right, returning*. When you are moving into a channel or harbor from open water, keep the red buoys and markers on your right. If there are also green markers keep them on your left. When you are moving out of a channel or harbor toward open water the reds go on your left and the greens on your right.

- There are many other types of markers. Some mark reefs, rocks, and other shallow areas, while others mark no-wake zones or areas where speed is restricted. Some markers are very easy to understand. For example, when you see a white diamond-shaped sign on a steel post that reads "Danger, Rock," it is a good idea to check your chart and swing well clear of the sign. Not all markers are so easily understood, but it is still your responsibility to know what the markers mean and to obey the directions they offer.

C. Lights and Signals

What lights and signals are required?

There are detailed regulations regarding lights for different types and sizes of vessels and different situations. These are contained in the Navigation Rules, Part C, Rules 20-31. All vessels are required to display navigation lights between sunset and sunrise and during periods of reduced visibility. Recreational boats are governed by fairly simple rules and situations. Some of the most common situations are as follows:

- Power driven vessels (including sailboats under power) less than 65.5 feet show bow lights (red and green on left and right), a white stern light and a white mast light.

- Power vessels less than 39.4 feet show red and green bow lights and white mast light.

- Sailing vessels less than 65.5 feet show red and green lights and a white stern light (or all three on the masthead).

- Vessels at anchor show a white masthead light.

D. Navigation Charts

Do the rules require nautical charts?

Accurate navigation charts should be carried aboard any boat and may be required in some areas and countries, such as Canada. Although the navigation rules do not specifically require charts on recreational vessels within U.S. waters, it is not a good idea to go cruising without up-to-date and accurate charts. Additionally, even though electronic charts that run on a computer or on an electronic chart plotter (GPS) are available, it is not a good practice to rely on electronic charts exclusively. If a device breaks or the software or power fails, you can find yourself in a dangerous situation with no guidance to avoid hazards. Always carry official paper charts appropriate for the areas you visit. It is not sufficient to merely use electronic charts or cruising guides.

What do charts show?

Your navigation charts will show the location of land masses, harbors and bays, obstructions such as reefs and rocks, water depths and tidal areas, traffic separation areas, buoys and markers, etc. When approaching a buoy, marker, or an obstruction, the skipper or navigator should first note its location on the chart, then find it visually and plan the correct course.

What are Local Notices to Mariners?

It is a good idea to keep your navigation charts up-to-date by purchasing new charts, periodically. Even the latest published versions of official charts may be several years (or decades) old. Newly purchased charts may not show all the latest changes to navigation aids, vessel traffic lanes, and special situations and areas. The U.S. Coast Guard publishes changes in its *Local Notices to Mariners*. The U.S. Coast Guard began publishing all such notices on the Internet as of April 1, 2004. Check the Appendix for the Internet address. Additionally, local cruising guidebooks and marine magazines often reprint important local notices.

E. Vessel Traffic Service (VTS)

What are VTS areas?

The U.S. Coast Guard describes its VTS as follows:

> *The purpose of a Vessel Traffic Service (VTS) is to provide active monitoring and navigational advice for vessels in particularly confined and busy waterways. There are two main types of VTS — surveilled and non-surveilled. Surveilled systems consist of one or more land-based sensors (i.e. radar, Automatic Identification System (AIS) and closed circuit television sites), which output their signals to a central location where operators monitor and manage*

Charts Only Work if You Use Them

Although official navigation charts are not required for recreational vessels, there are some very good reasons to have and use them. In some cases correct use of the charts could save you a lot of money.

Some years ago, one of my clients chartered a trawler for a week of cruising. I got a call from him several weeks after he returned. He had a complaint with the charter company. The deposit for his cruise was $1,500 and they refused to give it back. It seems he had encountered a bit of trouble in a shallow bay with some resulting damage to the props and one shaft. The charter company insisted the damage was his fault and forfeited his deposit to cover the repairs.

My client insisted that he did not run aground on purpose and that he was in an area with other boats and even near a state park. However, it turns out he was not using correct charts for the area even though they were on the boat at the time. He was navigating from a spiral bound collection of chart reproductions and it was difficult to read the soundings due to the small print and scale of the chart. Additionally, each page said *Not for Navigation* in block printing. Oops.

The bottom line came down to the fact that the proper charts for the area clearly showed a minimum depth of three feet and drying mudflats nearby. This was no area for a 42-foot trawler and my client should have known better.

I advised him to give up any notion of a refund and be happy that the damage to the boat was minimal. It could have been much worse. More importantly, he could have avoided the whole affair by using the correct charts that were already on the boat.

vessel traffic movement. Non-surveilled systems consist of one or more reporting points at which ships are required to report their identity, course, speed, and other data to the monitoring authority. They encompass a wide range of techniques and capabilities aimed at preventing vessel collisions, rammings, and groundings in the harbor, harbor approach and inland waterway phase of navigation. Non-surveilled systems are also designed to expedite ship movement, increase transportation system efficiency, and improve all-weather operating capability.

In locations where there is significant shipping traffic and other commercial vessels, such as ferries, in relatively confined areas, there are traffic separation lanes. These are areas where commercial shipping traffic must stay in the designated lane and move in the specified direction. These lanes are dangerous areas for recreational boats.

Are small recreational boats required to use the separation lanes?

No. Recreational boats are not required to use the lanes. In fact, recreational boats should stay out of the lanes whenever possible. When you are in a VTS area, follow these simple guidelines:

The VTS lanes in Puget Sound are clearly shown on charts.

- Recreational boaters should attempt to stay clear of the shipping lanes. A vessel not using the traffic lanes is required to avoid them by as wide a margin as possible.
- When a small vessel has to cross a lane, it should do so as quickly as possible, preferably at a right angle.
- Rule #9 of the Rules of the Road states that sailboats, fishing vessels, and any vessel less than 20 meters

Temporary Obstructions Are Dangerous

We recently completed a three week cruise of South Puget Sound in the Pacific Northwest. Before we left, I checked our collection of charts and cruising guides to see if we had enough current navigation information. Our strip charts for the area are 20 years old (but in excellent condition). We also had a set of recently purchased spiral bound official charts. Those, combined with our various cruising guides, books, and harbor charts printed from the Internet seemed sufficient for the trip through inland waters.

One portion of the cruise involved a passage through an area known as the Tacoma Narrows, which is several miles long. This area is well known for strong currents (up to 3.5 knots) and some fairly rigorous tide rips. The best plan (especially for a sailboat) is to time your passage at or near slack water. The Tacoma Narrows is also a good place to avoid when the winds are blowing against the current. Additionally, the area is narrow (thus the name) and it is also the route for all ships and other commercial traffic leaving or arriving at the busy Port of Tacoma. Finally, the

area has a famous suspension bridge over the channel. Two of the bridges' large concrete footings (on each side of the channel) are located well into the navigable area.

None of this is dangerous or intimidating if you know what to expect, and indulge in a bit of advance planning. There is plenty of room to pass safely under the bridge and keep out of the shipping lanes. However, before we began our trip I consulted the *Local Notices to Mariners*. I learned of ongoing construction for a new suspension bridge and some impediments in the channel. The blockage consisted of construction barges and submerged cables in the vicinity of the new concrete footings for the new bridge. The notice warned of the navigation hazard posed by the submerged cables and noted incidents of *severe damage* to boats that came into contact with the cables. That notice got my attention.

When we transited the passage, we stayed well clear of the construction areas. However, I could see how unaware boaters could get into trouble. We were glad to have read the notice.

(66 feet), shall not impede the passage of any vessel, which can safely navigate only within a narrow channel. Even when not in a traffic lane, small boats must yield to larger vessels in narrow or confined areas.

- Rule #10 of the Rules of the Road states that sailboats or vessels less than 20 meters, shall not impede safe passage of a power vessel following a traffic lane.

Under this rule, you are required to yield to a vessel following a traffic lane even though it may not be a narrow channel. This puts the burden on small boat owners to know when they are in a VTS area and to act accordingly. Rules of the Road (#9 and #10) are reprinted in the Appendix.

Stay Out of the Way of Ferries

There are numerous ferries that crisscross channels amid recreational and commercial boat traffic in popular cruising areas throughout North America. Ferries typically follow prescribed routes at specific times, but they may deviate depending on weather or loading delays. In areas of open waters, such as the San Francisco Bay of California, the Puget Sound of Washington, or the Gulf Islands of British Columbia, the ferries travel at 20 knots or more. They deserve your attention.

Early in our cruising lives we took a trip north from Seattle to the Canadian Gulf Islands. They are beautiful and separated from the mainland by the Strait of Georgia. One exit and entry to the Strait is aptly named Active Pass.

The pass is S-shaped and the current runs up to 7.5 knots. In the two curved parts of the S, the current backs against itself and forms large eddies and tide rips and even some dangerous whirlpools. To top it off, ferries from Vancouver go back and forth through Active Pass at top speed. Due to the shape and width of the pass, it is considered a narrow channel. Under Rule #9, small boats must yield to large vessels that have difficulty maneuvering in the confined area. This includes the big, fast-moving Canadian ferries.

We entered the pass prior to slack water, going with the current. I forgot, however, to adjust our timing for daylight-saving time; therefore, we were an hour early. *Note: The Canadian Current Tables are published using Pacific standard-time.* That meant the current still ran strong, even though it was running with us. We encountered our first ferry coming the other direction but we steered clear and passed port-to-port. Then, as we passed the halfway point, another ferry approached from behind while several oncoming boats struggled against the current toward us. We could not steer to port because of the oncoming boats

Approaching ferry.

and the nearby shoreline, and we could not steer to starboard because of a large whirlpool. We decided to speed up, hold our course, pass the oncoming boats, then steer hard to port and let the ferry pass to starboard.

With our eyes bulging, I gripped the tiller in terror, and we proceeded. A small oncoming tug was moving faster than the other boat coming at us and decided to pass everybody by crossing our bow and that of the ferry coming up behind. He passed safely ahead of us but suddenly jerked to his port and spun around helplessly in the whirlpool, belching black smoke as he powered up trying to get out. I concentrated on getting past the oncoming boats and turning to give the ferry more room. The ferry steamed by and we watched the tug still struggling in the whirlpool, as we made our way clear and headed for the opening to the Strait. We never heard any report of an incident or a sinking, so we assumed the tug escaped the whirlpool.

It was another ten years before we worked up the courage to go through Active Pass again. That time, we consulted a ferry schedule, calculated the tides correctly, went through at slack water, and had an uneventful passage. However, we have first-hand knowledge of maneuvering in narrow channels and we have never forgotten the lessons learned, the first time through.

Where are the Vessel Traffic Service Areas?

Currently, nine Vessel Traffic Centers exist, with another one in New Orleans being developed. The nine centers are Valdez, Seattle, San Francisco, Los Angeles, Houston, Morgan City, Louisville, Sault Ste. Marie, and New York. When you are traveling in one of these areas, you must be aware of the traffic lanes and be careful to avoid commercial vessels that are required to use the designated lanes. If you are unclear of the rules and regulations, or if you need information for transiting the area, contact the local VTS. Information on how to make contact with the centers is given below.

Is there VTS information available through VHF radio?

Traffic in a VTS area is coordinated by radio on specific VHF channels. If you are in such an area, you may get further information by listening on the appropriate channel. You can contact the VTS operators and get

The nine VTS areas in the United States are shown on this U.S. Coast Guard map.

information regarding the traffic situation around you. However, the system is not designated for generic or unnecessary inquiries. In most situations it is appropriate to simply monitor the correct channel and keep track

Use Common Sense Around Ships

There are a few common sense rules that apply whenever you are around large ships.

- Stay out of the way. Assume the ship does not see you. In heavy traffic areas, such as the Pacific Northwest, it is not uncommon to encounter ferries, freighters, tugs, barges, or oil tankers. It is far safer and much less stressful to simply steer clear of commercial vessels. If you see any of these large ships several miles away, consider estimating its course and speed and adjusting your course to safely pass its stern. Or simply slow down or steer away from the vessel. Never attempt to cross the bow unless it is obviously safe and easily done.

- Assume a ship is moving much faster than you think. I am constantly amazed at how quickly a freighter goes from being three miles away to being 500 yards away. If your boat is three nautical miles ahead of a freighter coming at you at 20 knots it will be at your location in just nine minutes. Additionally, it will take a huge distance for it to come to a complete stop. Consider powering-down and putting-along slowly to go behind a ship whenever it is prudent, as you will rarely lose more than about ten minutes time to your destination. The stern of

a ship moving away is a far more pleasant sight than the bow bearing down on you like a behemoth.

- Except when it is completely impossible due to an obstruction like a reef or island, yield the right of way. Additionally, the best way to avoid being pinched between an obstruction and a ship is to be alert. In our favorite cruising grounds, there is an area where we have a blind corner near popular Stuart Island in the San Juan Islands in Washington State. When we sail past the south side of Turn Point on Stuart Island, we remain alert for fast moving southbound freighters coming around from the north. It is not really a tight spot, but the current runs fast, and there can be some unpleasant tide rips. If a ship is coming around the bend it is best to wait patiently in calm water rather than sprint into a tide rips and risk an unpleasant or harrowing experience.

- Fourth, be predictable when you are near the shipping lanes. Try to stay out of the lanes, cross at right angles as quickly as you can, and never do something stupid, such as stop in front of a ship during limited visibility conditions. Make your course adjustments early, and obvious, so the ship can easily tell what you are doing.

of what is going on around you. If you need to contact traffic operators through VHF for further information, be as specific as possible about the information you need and ask your questions succinctly and clearly.

How do I know whom to call or what channel to use?

If you are in a VTS area, it will be shown on your charts and mentioned in any good cruising guide. The cruising guide may also have the correct VTS radio channel, but if you do not know it, you can call the U.S. Coast Guard and get the information. A guide to VTS radio frequencies is available on the Internet and the 2004 guide is reprinted in the Appendix. Remember that the VTS lanes are not for recreational use and the operators have far better things to do than chat. However, if you have questions, or if you are in any sort of trouble or difficulty in a shipping lane, make the call and let them know.

Should ships yield to sailboats not under power?

No. The big ships do not yield to sailboats. Recreational vessels under sail or under power do not have prevailing rights over ships in the VTS lanes or in narrow channels. Furthermore, the ships are often traveling deceptively fast and they will maintain their course. They must maintain speed to keep steerage and stay within the designated lane. They do not dodge and weave because to do so would make their course unpredictable and endanger other vessels. Many sailors operate under the mistaken impression that whenever they are under sail, they have the right of way. However, under Rules #9 and #10, this is not true.

F. Penalties and Fines

Are there penalties for violating the navigation rules?

Substantial fines may be levied in cases of violations. Negligent operation may result in fines of $1,000, while gross negligence may bring a fine of $5,000. A person who fails to give assistance when required may be fined up to $1,000 or imprisoned for up to two years. Intoxicated operation is subject to fines up of $1,000 (first violation) and $5,000 (subsequent violation). Additionally, operation of your boat in violation of the right of way rules can result in a personal fine up to $5,000 and a fine against your vessel up to $5,000. The penalty provisions are reproduced in the Appendix. More information about penalties and enforcement is included in Section 13.

G. Security Zones and Restrictions

What are Security Zones?

For security reasons, you must obey special rules applicable to passing U.S. naval vessels, cruise ships, and passenger ferries. *Do not approach within 100 yards of such vessels.* If you need to pass within 100 yards to ensure a safe passage, in accordance with the Navigation Rules you must contact the vessel or its escort vessel on VHF-FM Channel 16. *If you are within 500 yards of a U.S. naval vessel you must operate at minimum speed* and proceed as directed by the Commanding Officer of the vessel. Be very careful around naval vessels. Violations of the protection zone are a felony offense and can be punished by up to six years in prison and/or up to $250,000 in fines.

H. Port Closures and Restrictions

Which areas are closed to recreational boats?

If you are boating on the Mississippi River, the Atlantic Coast, or the Gulf Coast, you can contact a U.S. Coast Guard Maritime Safety Line 800-682-1796 for information on closures. The Maritime Safety Line provides information for the following five regions:

- The Northeast Region, including most of New York, Rhode Island, Maine and Massachusetts.
- The Mid-Atlantic/Southeast Region, comprised of eastern and southern Florida, Georgia, South and North Carolina, Virginia, Maryland and eastern Pennsylvania.

WARNING!

Do not approach within 100 yards of any U.S. naval vessel. If you need to pass within 100 yards of a U.S. naval vessel in order to ensure a safe passage in accordance with the Navigation Rules, you must contact the U.S. naval vessel or the Coast Guard escort vessel on VHF-FM channel 16.

500 Yards

KEEP OUT!

OPERATE AT MINIMUM SPEED

You must operate at minimum speed within 500 yards of any U.S. naval vessel and proceed as directed by the Commanding Officer or the official patrol.

Violations of the Naval Vessel Protection Zone are a felony offense, punishable by up to 6 years in prison and/or up to $250,000 in fines

One-hundred yard approach.

- The Gulf Region, made up of Northwest Florida, Alabama, Louisiana, and Texas.
- The Great Lakes Region, including western New York, Ohio, Michigan, Illinois, Wisconsin and Minnesota.
- The Mid-West Rivers Region, including Missouri, West Virginia, Western Pennsylvania, Kentucky and Tennessee.

If you intend to go boating on the Pacific Coast, Alaska, or Hawaii, call the unit nearest to your intended boating area. Normal working hours for these offices are from 8:00 a.m. to 4:00 p.m. (local time) Monday through Friday. Additional information about security zones and port security is available on the U.S. Coast Guard web site.

Changing Aspects of Boating

In times of heightened security, boaters should pay special attention to various restrictions and a few simple rules. At best, our attention to some simple rules may help avert a mishap. Even at the worst, it will help make the jobs of security officials easier and allow them to concentrate their energies on persons who might intend harm without diverting their attention to harmless, but careless boaters.

1. Observe and avoid security zones. These include military vessels, cruise vessels, large ferries, tankers, and petroleum facilities.

2. Observe restricted areas such as those around dams, power plants, etc.

3. Do not stop or drop your anchor underneath bridges.

4. Keep an eye out for suspicious activity by other persons. There is a National Response Center terrorist hotline at 800-424-8802. It is designed to make it easy to report suspicious activity such as:

- Unusual activity near bridges, or high-security facilities.
- Roadside stands next to large marine facilities.
- Unknown persons photographing or creating diagrams of structures or facilities such as: the underside of bridges, power plants, or waterfront facilities near military installations, cruise ships, or commercial vessels.

Operation and Safety Requirements

As with all aspects of modern life, the legalities of boat ownership, no matter what size, are becoming more complex every day. There are many things you need to know and many rules to follow. The information that follows is not an exhaustive explanation of the all safety laws, rules, and regulations. We have attempted to give you the basics and the resources to get more information, if necessary.

The discussion is focused on vessel requirements under U.S. laws and regulations. Other countries have different requirements, particularly for commercial vessels. Generally, if your boat is equipped to satisfy the requirements of U.S. laws, and your visit to another country is temporary, then you will not be required to meet the other country's different equipment requirements. However, this is not always the case. For example, overboard discharge rules and other environmental regulations vary from one country to another. Additionally, you must be aware of different requirements for operator age and even competency requirements. For example, Canada is now implementing rules to require proof of competency for all boat owners and operators. Visitors to Canada who are staying less than 45 days are exempt, but if your stay will exceed 45 days you must comply with the new regulations.

Before you visit another country, particularly for an extended stay, be sure to learn the equipment and safety requirements that are applicable during your visit.

Local Restrictions and Regulations Are Important

In addition to federal and state regulations, it is also necessary to know about local requirements and restrictions before you visit an area. For example, the San Juan Islands in Washington State are governed by San Juan County. About 10 years ago, the county responded to petitions from its citizens and banned operation of personal watercraft and jet-skis in all areas of the county. It is not uncommon to see a large powerboat with a personal watercraft or jet ski tied aboard, but we never see them buzzing around the harbors, bays or inlets. However, San Juan County is surrounded on all sides by jurisdictions that allow such crafts and boaters need to know about the restriction and when they have crossed the line.

Good examples of local restrictions are *no discharge* zones. In Canada, it is not illegal to pump sewage waste overboard. However, a growing number of Canadian parks and bays are designated *no discharge* zones due to environmental concerns. These zones also exist in most lakes and many other confined bodies of water in the United States. Every boater is responsible to know where these areas are and to obey the regulations.

Another good example of important local rules is the protection of Manatees in various counties in Florida. These include some of the largest Florida counties (such as Brevard, Broward, Dade and Palm Beach). Protective measures include speed limits and restricted access areas. Every boater must understand and obey these local regulations. For more information on Manatees, see page 66.

It is not enough anymore to just have the correct number of lifejackets, flares, and other equipment aboard. Before you go boating in a new area, check the local regulations and restrictions.

A. U.S. Requirements for Safety Equipment on Your Boat

Federal laws governing operation of recreational vessels are contained in USC Title 46. The federal regulations (rules written by federal agencies) are contained in the Code of Federal Regulations, Title 46 and Title 33. Congress authorizes the regulations as the means by which agencies enforce the laws. Although Congress does not pass the regulations, they have the full force and effect of law, with substantial penalties for violations.

What safety equipment is required?

United States statutes contain requirements for basic safety equipment on boats of various sizes. Of course, there is no prohibition against exceeding the minimum requirements. For example, it is a good practice to have more than one signaling device (air-horn), extra life preservers, more than one fire extinguisher, and extra aerial and hand-held flares. The U.S. Coast Guard has produced quick reference guides that summarize the safety equipment requirements. Copies of the guides are reproduced in the Appendix.

How important are these requirements?

It is very important that your vessel carry all the required equipment. When your boat is inspected, local, state, and federal authorities can levy fines for non-compliance. Furthermore, some violations may result in termination of your trip and an order that you immediately return to port. If you are in an accident caused by your failure to carry required equipment, your negligence may be easier to prove

These small-size disposable fire extinguishers are ideal to have in the event a small fire flares up that does not require a U.S. Coast Guard approved full-size extinguisher.

or even presumed. Additionally, if your insurance requires particular equipment (such as an electric bilge pump), failure to satisfy the requirement can affect your policy renewal. If your insurance requires specific equipment, and your failure to have it causes an insured loss, the company will have a justifiable reason to deny your claim. A simple equipment checklist is included in the Appendix.

Should I have other safety gear, even if it is not required?

The simple answer is yes. In the last 20 years, cruising boats have become larger, heavier, and faster. Used boats are available at prices that allow more and more people to participate in the sport of boating. Inland waters and popular cruising grounds are increasingly crowded, and safe boating requires more skill and better equipment.

Additionally, some very useful pieces of equipment are now available at very attractive prices and should be on every cruising boat, even though not legally required. Some examples are:

- **A Global Position System (GPS).** The GPS is not a substitute for good charts and the ability to navigate using traditional tools and devices. However, a proper-functioning GPS will pinpoint your location and make it easier to plot your position and course. A GPS with chart-plotter software will even show an icon of your boat superimposed over an electronic chart. Small hand-held GPS devices can be an excellent back up to a full-sized unit mounted at the chart table, as they are capable of displaying latitude and longitude and include chart-plotter capabilities.

- **Very High Frequency (VHF) radio**. VHF radios are small and inexpensive. Some new models include the ability to interface with a GPS and transmit a signal that pinpoints your location at the press of a single button. This is called Digital Selective Calling (DSC). A DSC requires registration with the U.S. Coast Guard, but these new radios can transmit your vessel's unique identification number, and if coupled with the GPS, your exact location. The DSC capability can help overcome radio ignorance or panic and facilitate assistance or rescue when necessary. A child or guest can be easily and quickly taught how to operate the DSC capability in the event of an emergency.

- **Radar units.** Larger recreational vessels should consider having a radar unit as well. Although it takes some effort and experience to properly use radar, it is well worth the time and money, especially for cruising in areas prone to fog or heavy traffic. A slightly foggy day is a perfect time to practice using radar.

- **Emergency Position Indicating Radio Beacon (EPIRB).** Another useful electronic device for cruising offshore is an EPIRB. You must register your EPIRB with the National Oceanographic and Atmospheric Administration (NOAA). Once activated, either automatically or manually, an EPIRB will transmit a distress signal to orbiting satellites that relay the signal to NOAA. The satellite can pinpoint the position of the signal and NOAA notifies the U.S. Coast Guard. These devices are very useful and can be rented. BoatU.S. offers low cost daily or weekly rental of EPIRB units along the Atlantic Coast. These rental units have been instrumental in several emergency rescues at sea. For more information about the BoatU.S. EPIRB Rental Program for units such as the one shown here, call (888-663-7472) or reserve on the BoatU.S. web site.

- **Spares.** All cruising boats should, at a minimum, have an extra anchor and rode, spare engine parts along with important electrical parts, electric bilge pump (and at least one manual bilge pump), extra prop, a complete first aid kit, and a complete tool kit.

Safety related electronic devices (such as a GPS and radar) might prevent accidents due to adverse conditions or other

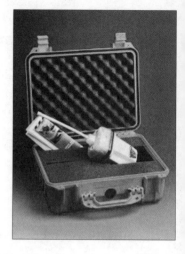

An EPIRB kit.

causes. A properly used VHF radio and an EPIRB will significantly enhance assistance or rescue.

Can I have my boat checked to see if it complies with the safety and equipment rules?

Yes. The U.S. Coast Guard Auxiliary provides free, voluntary inspections. You will not be fined or punished for any violations. The free inspection is an excellent opportunity to make sure your boat satisfies the safety and equipment requirements. A copy of the inspection form is reproduced in the Appendix.

Knowing the Rules Can Save You Money

Your knowledge of the various safety equipment requirements may come in handy the next time you visit the marine store. It could even save you some money.

On our last trip to British Columbia, we stopped at a local marine store to buy updated charts for the areas we would visit. The fellow in line in front of me was buying new flares for his 36-foot sailboat and spending a fair bit of money. The salesman informed him that the Canadian regulations required 12 flares, six of which could be smoke flares.

When it was my turn, I asked about the previous sale. I got the same sales pitch (i.e., I should buy 12 new flares). However, since ours is a U.S. vessel, compliance with U.S. regulations, which require three flares, would satisfy Canadian regulations during our trip.

I remarked that twelve flares seemed a bit many compared to the U.S. regulations. The enthusiastic clerk told me that as long as we were in compliance with U.S. rules we would be OK. "But," he said, "I don't think the regulations are that much different. Maybe you should buy some additional flares just to be safe."

To save an argument or any further discussion, I bought three hand-held aerial flares to add to my kit, even though we did not need them. They are good for several years and it is never bad to have a few extras. Now we have a full complement of nine 12-gauge style aerial flares, six hand-held aerial flares, and three smoke flares, all of various vintages. At least I got off spending a bit less than the guy in front of me.

A VHF radio is one of the most valuable safety devices for your boat. Small and inexpensive hand-held units are great for a back up on larger boats and as a primary unit for smaller boats.

B. VHF Radio Regulations

Do regulations require carrying a two-way radio?

Federal laws do not require recreational vessels under 65.5 feet to carry a marine radio. However, as mentioned previously, a VHF radio (even a small hand-held unit) is a valuable piece of safety equipment. Prices begin under $100 and there are plenty of good reasons to have one. Recreational vessels with a VHF do not need a license, but users of the radio must follow FCC rules. For example, you must identify your station (vessel name or number).

VHF Channel 16 is for emergency use but is also often used as a hailing channel. However, Channel 9 is also available for this use. The best practice is to reserve use of Channel 16 for emergencies only and make contact by using Channel 9. Once contact is made, you should switch to one of the channels designated for non-commercial, vessel to vessel, communication. A copy of the FCC chart showing various VHF channels and their proper use is in the Appendix.

What should be transmitted in the event of an emergency?

The VHF radio is the primary tool to use for emergency assistance. The U.S. Coast Guard monitors VHF Channel 16. A radio is useless if the operator is not familiar with its operation and basic radio procedures. Before leaving port, instruct everyone aboard how to use the radio. Additionally, it may be very useful to post instructions on basic procedures to call for help. The following chart is a guide for how to send a MAYDAY call for help. However, it is important to remember that a MAYDAY call should only be used in emergency situations. False MAYDAY calls are a crime and will be investigated and prosecuted.

What other safety related messages should I know?

There are two additional types of signals used on the radio to transmit safety related messages. The first of these is the "Pan, Pan" (pronounced "pahn") alert. This signal is used when a person or vessel is in danger and requires assistance, but the situation is not an emergency that requires a "MAYDAY." An example would be a man overboard situation or a vessel grounding. The second of these is the "Securite" transmission (pronounced "say-cure-e-tay"). It is used to give notice of hazardous navigational information such as obstructions or weather related conditions.

C. Alcoholic Beverages and Vessel Operation

Is it illegal to drink alcohol and drive a boat?

It is not illegal under U.S. law to drink alcohol while driving a boat, but different states and other countries have various statutes and regulations. Both federal and state law, however, prohibit operation of a vessel while intoxicated. Although consumption of alcohol while operating a vessel is not prohibited, if the blood alcohol level is .08 percent or higher (.10 percent in some states), fines and penalties can be imposed. It is increasingly common for the U.S. Coast Guard to terminate a cruise and order a boat back to port when the operator is intoxicated.

What penalties do drunken drivers face?

Illegal blood alcohol levels may result in a civil penalty of up to $1,000, or a criminal penalty of up to $5,000, and one-year imprisonment. Additionally, if an accident occurs due to intoxication, other civil damages may accrue. If an injury occurs, additional criminal penalties are possible. Furthermore, negligent operation of a vessel or interference with the safe operation of a vessel, which endangers life or property is prohibited. Intoxication is considered negligent operation. The Coast Guard may impose a civil penalty for negligent operation and up to a $5,000 criminal fine for gross negligence. Other examples of negligence include excessive speed around other boats, operating a boat in a swimming area, and bow riding.

Emergency MAYDAY Calls

In the event of an emergency, your VHF radio may be the most important piece of safety equipment on your boat. But you must know how to use it. Read the operator manual and practice using the radio when possible. Just as importantly, other persons aboard must also know how to use the radio. On the VHF radio, there is a squelch control. It blocks static and interference and allows strong voice signals through when properly adjusted. When set too low, there will be static or hissing whenever the radio is on. When set too high, the squelch will prevent the user from hearing replies.

In one instance, a man fell overboard and drowned next to the boat while his wife called for help on VHF Channel 16. The U.S. Coast Guard could clearly hear her, however, the squelch control was set too high, which prevented her from hearing their questions or instructions.

VHF Channel 16 is the distress channel and must not be used for chatter or routine communications, as the U.S. Coast Guard monitors it. In the event of a serious emergency, use VHF Channel 16. Here is a guide for what to say:

SPEAK: SLOWLY — CLEARLY — CALMLY

1. Turn VHF on and select Channel 16 (156.8 MHz).

2. Press and hold microphone button and say: "MAYDAY—MAYDAY—MAYDAY."

3. Say: "THIS IS: _____."
   Your boat name and call sign or registration number repeated three times.

4. Say: "MAYDAY _____ (your boat name)"

5. TELL WHERE YOU ARE. (What navigation aids, landmarks or other vessels are near?)

6. STATE THE NATURE OF YOUR DISTRESS. (Taking on water, fire aboard, etc.)

7. GIVE NUMBER OF PERSONS ABOARD AND CONDITIONS OF INJURED.

8. ESTIMATE PRESENT SEAWORTHINESS OF YOUR BOAT.

9. BRIEFLY DESCRIBE YOUR BOAT: Length? Type (sail/power)? Hull color? Trim color or style? Mast style or number? Other distinguishing items? (Anything else you think will help rescuers find you.)

10. SAY: "THIS IS _____ (call sign, boat name)---- OVER."

11. Release microphone button and listen. Someone should answer.

IF NO ONE ANSWERS, REPEAT YOUR CALL, BEGINNING AT ITEM NUMBER TWO ABOVE.

If there is still no answer, try switching to another channel and begin again. Have everyone put on their PFD. If you are drifting without power, putting your anchor out may keep you off the shore. Have your flares or other visual signaling items available for use.

U.S. Coast Guard Blood Alcohol Chart

Drinks	APPROXIMATE BLOOD ALCOHOL PERCENTAGE								
	Body Weight in Pounds								
	100	120	140	160	180	200	220	240	
1	0.04	0.04	0.03	0.03	0.02	0.02	0.02	0.02	RARELY
2	0.09*	0.07*	0.06*	0.06*	0.05*	0.04	0.04	0.04	
3	0.13	0.11	0.09*	0.08*	0.07*	0.07*	0.06*	0.06*	
4	0.18	0.15	0.13	0.11	0.1	0.09*	0.08*	0.07*	POSSIBLY*
5	0.22	0.18	0.16	0.14	0.12	0.11	0.1	0.09*	
6	0.26	0.22	0.19	0.17	0.15	0.13	0.12	0.11	

D. Accident Reporting

Am I required to report boating accidents?

The U.S. Coast Guard requires accident reports under specific circumstances. The owner or operator must file a boating accident report if the accident involves loss of life, personal injury with medical treatment, damage greater than $2,000, or complete loss of a vessel. If a person is killed or lost, accident reporting must be immediate and must include date, time, location, name of the fatality victim, name and number of the vessel, as well as the name and address of the owner and operator. Information about all accidents should be contemporaneously recorded in the vessel logbook.

To whom do I report accidents?

Reports must be made to local authorities. Some state laws require the use of a specific accident report form. Generic information about accident reporting may be obtained by

Accident Reporting Requirements

Who: The boat operator usually makes the report, unless he is physically unable to do so. In that case, the boat owner must submit the report.

When: Make the report when a vessel is damaged, there is injury or loss of life, or a person disappears. Report within 48 hours if there is loss of life, significant injury, or disappearance. Report within 10 days if there is only damage to the vessel or to property.

What: Examples of reportable accidents include grounding, capsizing, collision, sinking, flooding, fire, explosion, disappearance, and falls overboard.

How: Call your local law enforcement authorities to report an accident. You may also need to call the applicable state agency for state reporting requirements and/or forms.

Why: Information from accident reports is used to help develop safety regulations and manufacturing standards. The information is also used in boating safety education programs.

calling the U.S. Coast Guard information line at 800-368-5647. To find out if your state has a required accident form, call your applicable state agency or visit its web site. The table of state information in the Appendix has a list of Web addresses to get more information about your state's requirements. If you have an accident and are in doubt, call your local law enforcement agency.

E. Personal Flotation Devices (Life Jackets)

What are the requirements for life jackets?

Laws and regulations refer to life jackets and life vests as Personal Flotation Devices (PFDs). The U.S. Coast Guard divides PFDs into five types. Every boat must have at least one Type I, Type II, or Type III PFD for each person aboard; if your vessel is over 16 feet, there must also be a throwable Type IV PFD. Some states require that children wear a PFD at *all* times while on a boat. The U.S. Coast Guard regulations for PFDs are very detailed

---

Do Not Be an Accident Statistic

Between September 2001 and September 2002, the Strategic Research Group of Columbus, Ohio analyzed more than 25,000 completed boating questionnaires. The complete 154-page report is available from the U.S. Coast Guard Office of Boating Safety.

Some highlights of the survey are as follows:

Safety:	Operators who have never taken a safety course – 65%
	Operators who have taken a course within past two years – 2%
	Most popular classroom course: U.S. Coast Guard Auxiliary – 34%
	Minimal exposure to safety information: (TV & magazines) – 58%
Enforcement:	Favor more enforcement of alcohol laws – 92%
	Favor more enforcement of reckless boating laws – 90%
	Favor boating competency tests – 74%
	Favor mandatory life jacket use – 43%
	Favor mandatory life jacket use for children under 13 – 86%
Activities:	Recreational fishing – 51%
	Cruising – 44%
	Swimming from the boat – 29%
	Primary areas of use: Lakes, ponds, reservoirs, gravel pits – 52%
Accidents:	Largest cause of injury: Action by operator or passenger – 43%
	Largest cause of property damage: Action by operator or passenger – 26%
	Injury accident caused by another boater – 18%
	Boats most often involved in damage accident: Open motorboat – 49%
Life Jackets:	Operators carrying enough PFDs – 95%
	Operators who always wear a PFD – 34%
	Operators who never wear a PFD – 20%
	Most likely use of a PFD: water skiing or tubing – 82%
	Other PFD use: Rough water – 65%: Strong currents or winds – 62%

These Type III PFDs are clearly visible and easily accessible in a hanging locker and Type II PFDs are stored directly below in the locker.

and specific, with definitions and descriptions for various life jackets. For example, PFDs must be U.S. Coast Guard approved, readily accessible, in good condition, and the right size. The U.S. Coast Guard requires that all children under 13 years of age wear U.S. Coast Guard approved life jackets while aboard recreational vessels under way, except when below decks or in an enclosed cabin. The U.S. Coast Guard regulation affects only states that do not require children to wear life jackets. For other states, the U.S. Coast Guard regulation supersedes a state rule that is less stringent.

F. Fire Extinguishers

Do U.S. Coast Guard regulations require a fire extinguisher?

Fire extinguishers are required on boats when any of the following conditions exist:

- An inboard engine is installed.
- There are closed compartments and compartments under seats where portable fuel tanks may be stored.
- There are double bottoms not sealed to the hull or not completely filled with flotation materials.
- There are closed living spaces.
- There are closed stowage compartments in which combustible or flammable materials are stored.
- There are permanently installed fuel tanks. Fuel tanks secured so they cannot be moved in case of fire or other emergencies are considered permanently installed. There are no gallon capacity limits to determine if a fuel tank is portable. If the weight of a fuel tank is such that persons aboard cannot move it, the Coast Guard considers it permanently installed.

How should the extinguisher be installed?

Your fire extinguisher will not satisfy the regulations if it is still in its box and stored under a seat or berth in an inaccessible location. The fire extinguisher should be mounted in a readily and easily accessed place. It should also be mounted away from the source of a possible fire. For example, do not mount the fire extinguisher above a stove where it may be impossible to reach if a fire is

PFD Designations

- A Type I PFD is an offshore life jacket designed to turn most unconscious wearers to a face-up position. A Type I PFD may be inherently buoyant (foam or other material) or inflatable.
- A Type II PFD is a near-shore vest. It is designed for situations where there is a good chance for quick rescue. It will not work as well as a Type I PFD to turn the wearer face up. A Type II PFD may be inherently buoyant (foam or other material) or inflatable.
- A Type III PFD is also designed for situations where quick rescue is likely. It is designed for conscious wearers who

can turn themselves face up. A Type III PFDs may be inherently buoyant (foam or other material) or inflatable.
- A Type IV throwable PFD is required on all boats over 16 feet in length. It is designed to be thrown to the person in the water. It is not designed to be worn.
- A Type V Inflatable PFD with Safety Harness is designed to prevent falls overboard. The safety harnesses are designed to be worn at the chest area. Some inflatable PFDs automatically inflate when a person falls into the water and others inflate when a strap or cord is pulled to activate the gas cartridge.

burning. Do not mount the fire extinguisher inside the engine compartment where it will be engulfed in flames or smoke (unless it is self activating and designed for engine compartment mounting).

Do I need a specific type of fire extinguisher?

Yes. Fire extinguishers must be U.S. Coast Guard certified. Make sure Type B is indicated. The chart below summarize the different types of fire extinguishers.

G. Other Equipment Regulations

What are there other equipment requirements?

There are various other important equipment requirements to note for recreational vessels, including regulations for propane tanks, engines and ventilation, sound signals, distress flags, and flares.

Propane tanks must be securely mounted in an enclosed locker that drains overboard. These tanks will not move about when the cover is closed and latched. The spare tank is not hooked up until needed. There is an electric shut off valve that is controlled by a lighted switch in the galley.

• **Propane Tanks.** United States Federal Regulations for portable propane tanks have changed. Tanks must have an Overfill Protection Device (OPD) inside the tank. A three-pronged valve handle on the tank identifies those with OPDs. Recertified horizontal-type tanks are exempt from the OPD requirement. Only a licensed propane dealer can recertify a tank, and the recertification must be stamped into the metal of the tank. Tanks that comply with the regulations may be refilled.

Even an older tank that appears to be in excellent condition may not be refilled if it does not have an OPD valve. In most cases, it is relatively inexpensive to replace older tanks with the newer tanks and it is worth doing to avoid refilling difficulties and possible leakage from an old tank. Propane gas contains

water vapor and tanks may rust from the inside to the outside. An old tank may appear to be in good shape but still develop a leak. Propane regulations vary in other countries, so if you plan on crossing a border, it is a good idea to know the regulations for the countries you intend to visit. Additionally, it may be difficult to refill tanks in some countries due to differences in the refill valves or the threads on the refill equipment. If you are traveling outside the U.S., it is advisable to have spare fittings and adapters for different situations.

• **Engines and Ventilation.** Post 1940 gasoline engine vessels must have at least two natural ventilation ducts; post 1980 gasoline engine vessels must have a power blower.

Fire Extinguishers

Classes	Foam (Gals)	CO_2(lbs)	Dry Chemical (lbs)	Halon (lbs)
B-I (Type B, Size I)	1.25	4	2	2.5
B-I (Type B, Size II)	2.5	15	10	10

Minimum number of hand portable fire extinguishers required		
Vessel Length	**No Fixed System**	**With approved Fixed Systems**
Less than 26 feet	1 B-1	0
26 to less than 40 feet	2 B-1 or 1 B-II	1 B-I
40 to 65 feet	3 B-I or 1 B-II and 1 B-1	2 B-1 or 1 B-II

- **Sound Signals.** Vessels less than 39.4 feet must have a sound signal device (such as an air horn), while vessels more than 39.4 feet must have both a sound device and an eight-inch bell with a clapper.
- **Distress Lights and Flares.** Vessels over 16 feet must have one of the three options below:
  - an orange distress flag and an electric distress light
  - three hand-held flares and one electric distress light
  - three combination (day/night) red flares that are either hand-held, meteor, or parachute type.

Basic Facts About Fuels

There are some important things to understand regarding fuels that are used for purposes other than running your boat's engine.

Propane, natural gas, and alcohol are the three basic fuels that are used for purposes other than running the engine. Primarily, these are used for cooking and for cabin heaters. On many larger boats, a diesel furnace that blows warm air through ducts heats the cabin areas. The use of diesel for cabin heating is not part of this discussion.

Propane is a very popular fuel for cooking and heating. It is inexpensive, easy to find and buy (even in remote areas), and easy to transport inside a standard tank. However, propane releases water vapor when it burns, so it can contribute to humidity in an enclosed area. The most important thing to remember about propane is that it is heavier than air. If you have a propane leak in your boat it will move to the lowest point (usually the bilge) and can present a real danger of explosion triggered by a bilge pump or other electrical spark. Propane has a distinctive rotten egg smell, so a leak is usually easy to detect. The best propane installations have a remote controlled switch in the propane locker that can be turned off from inside the boat (usually in the galley). The propane locker must be sealed off from the rest of the boat and have an overboard drain in case a tank or connection leaks.

Natural gas is also popular, and arguably safer, than propane because it is lighter than air and will safely dissipate in an event of a leak. Natural gas is a popular fuel on newer boats, particularly larger vessels. However, it has not gained the same widespread acceptance and use as propane.

Alcohol is used on many small boats for cooking. However, since alcohol is a liquid, it is not as safe as propane or natural gas. The liquid must be stored in a portable jug or tank somewhere in a safe place. Alcohol burners can flare-up if not hot enough, and the fuel can be spilled on the stove top or around it and ignited. A flare-up on an alcohol burner can send flames up to 12 or more inches, but will usually burn out quickly. You should never have flammable decorations (such as curtains) above an alcohol stove. The best way to quickly and safely extinguish a flare-up is to put a non-flammable cover over the flame. Alcohol is also inexpensive and readily available in most places.

During our many years of cruising we have used all three of the above fuels at various times. All things considered, our preference is for propane. We regularly check all the connections for leaks and are always very careful when cooking with our propane burners and oven.

SECTION 8

Crossing the Border

For most boat owners and operators, international means a trip to Canada, Mexico, the Bahamas, or another spot close to the United States. Very few cruisers actually cross the oceans to more distant nations. The following discussion assumes that simple border crossings are the most prevalent occurrence and the next several paragraphs will give you some general information about crossing the border. Then we will specifically discuss entering the United States, Canada, Mexico, and the Bahamas.

A. General Considerations for Border Crossings

Each country you visit will have different requirements for entry and exit. It is important to obtain and study the relevant rules before you leave the United States. There are many important regulations. For example, vessels entering Canada and Mexico must comply with strict firearms restrictions and regulations, various fruit and vegetable restrictions, pet regulations, length of stay, and insurance requirements. Failure to comply may result in seizure of offending items, civil penalties, and even arrest.

Do I need to carry identification and proof of citizenship?

Before you leave the U.S., you must be sure you can prove your identity and citizenship and that of everyone aboard. You must also be able to prove the ownership and legal registration of your vessel. A documentation certificate is proof that your vessel is a U.S. craft. You should carry acceptable picture identification, such as your driver's license. It is also advisable to carry passports or copies of birth certificates. When entering Canada, one piece of photo identification and a copy of a birth certificate or even a copy of a passport will usually suffice. A good

practice is to put copies of passports and birth certificates in your *Keeping Your Boat Legal* binder, along with other important information and documents. Do not rely on your voter's registration card to prove your citizenship. Some election districts in the U.S. now allow non-citizens to vote, so a voter's registration card is no longer considered proof of U.S. citizenship.

Do I need a visa to enter another country?

Prior to crossing into another country you must determine whether you need a Visa. When U.S. citizens visit countries such as Canada, Mexico, or the Bahamas, no visa is required. However, other countries will have different requirements and it is up to you to know the rules before you leave. You may contact immigration authorities for the countries you intend to visit or you can contact U.S. authorities to find out what requirements apply or how to get further information.

What are the general rules for entering another country?

In addition to the specific laws for each place that you visit, there are some general rules to always remember.

- When you visit another country by boat you should properly show the flag of the country you are visiting, along with your U.S. flag. *Do not neglect to display these flags.*

- When you arrive in another country, remember that the customs and immigration officials have a serious job to do. Being flippant or disrespectful is not advisable. In most situations you will be treated with more respect if you show respect. It does not hurt to wear nicer clothes in lieu of very informal cruising attire.

- If possible, check in at locations that deal primarily with visiting vessels. Find out the office hours and procedures in advance.

- Only the skipper of the vessel may leave the boat before check-in is completed; other persons may not board the vessel until check-in is complete. Check-in may include an inspection of the vessel. Until completion of check-in, passengers and crew on your boat must stay put.

- After arrival at a port of entry, tie up at the designated area and proceed directly to the customs or immigration office with your papers and information. Sometimes the port will have a telephone check-in facility. In that case, go directly to the phone and talk to the appropriate official. Assume you are being watched, either visually or by camera.

- Be aware of terror alerts, special events, or circumstances that may be present when or where you cross the border. Terror alerts or international meetings will mean greater scrutiny for everyone.

- Know in advance what items may be restricted, regulated, or prohibited. Fines and penalties for bringing along prohibited items can be substantial.

Are there restrictions on taking food across the border?

Many countries prohibit the importation of certain fruits and vegetables. You will be asked about items that are prohibited and you will not be permitted to bring such items with you. For example, when entering Canada, you may not bring in certain fruits with pits (such as peaches or plums), corn, and certain other vegetables. The list changes over time and is periodically revised. It is your responsibility to know which items are prohibited. If you have a food item that is not allowed, tell the customs officer about it. In most cases, you will be asked to dispose of it at the check-in station. In some situations you will be allowed to bring in prohibited fruits if the pits are removed and disposed of (usually in a bin or other container at the check-in office). Remember also to check before you leave to make sure there are not any temporary, special restrictions in effect.

Are there restrictions on firearms?

Fruits and vegetables are one thing, but firearms are another situation altogether. Canada and Mexico (and many other countries) have stringent restrictions on

Double-Checked in Canada

It is very important to follow the proper procedures when crossing a border and entering another country. In most cases you will only be asked some simple questions and asked to produce basic documents for you, your crew, and your boat. In some situations your vessel may be inspected. Regardless of the usually quick and simple process, do not assume that you can be less than completely truthful or that you can violate some of the rules. As a visitor to a foreign country you are subject to continued scrutiny and the check-in process may not be your only contact with enforcement authorities.

Once while taking our annual cruise to the Gulf Islands of British Columbia, it just happened to be the same week that a large international conference was being hosted in the nearby area. We crossed the border and cleared customs without any problems and cruised north. On our third day in Canada, we stopped for the night at a local marina. That afternoon, a group of Royal Canadian Mounted Police

(RCMPs) visited the marina. One plain-clothed officer accompanied two uniformed officers.

They contacted persons aboard all the foreign flagged vessels, including ours. Their questions were simple and quick and just reiterated the items covered at our initial check-in. However, they also asked for identification of all persons aboard and visual confirmation of information they had on their clipboard.

Since the process was new to me, I asked what was going on. One officer informed me that they were just double-checking and confirming information previously given and checking for any discrepancies. The process appeared to be an effort to increase security, in light of the international conference.

The point here is that crossing the border is usually simple and sometimes seems like just a formality. However, do not be tempted to cut corners or give inaccurate information.

Certain firearms may be completely prohibited.

firearms and even ammunition. Certain firearms may be allowed but usually only if prior registration and licensing requirements are completed. Other firearms (handguns, automatic weapons or semi-automatic weapons) may be completely prohibited. Never attempt to bring a firearm or ammunition into another country unless you are completely sure about the applicable regulations and unless you have made arrangements in advance. The penalties for violating firearm laws can be severe, including substantial fines and prison sentences. Simply bringing a bullet along on your trip to Mexico can result in a jail sentence.

We Ate The Forbidden Fruit

On one of our cruises to Canada we remembered some fresh plums about an hour before we crossed the border. Knowing they would not be allowed we decided to eat them along the way. There were not too many but it was still a bit of a challenge. When we arrived at the check-in port I went to the office, documents in hand. At the standard question, "Do you have any fruit or vegetables aboard?" I volunteered that we ate the plums along the way. The officer then asked, "What did you do with the pits?" I confessed that we spit them overboard. Then she said, "Do you realize those could wash ashore on Canadian territory?" Oops! But some quick thinking kicked in and I pointed out that the tide was ebbing and the current flowed to the United States. She smiled and gave me our clearance number. *Despite this story, do not spit pits overboard, as it is illegal to discharge garbage.*

B. Navigating U.S. Immigrations and Customs Upon Returning to the United States

The agencies that enforce U.S. customs and immigration laws and regulations have changed. There used to be separate agencies for customs inspections and for immigration. When a boater checked in at a designated port of entry the skipper met with a customs officer who also had limited training to handle basic immigration functions. However, with the creation of the Department of Homeland Security, the old agencies have been reorganized. The U.S. Customs and Border Protection (CBP) within the Department of Homeland Security brings together the enforcement and investigative arms of the Customs Service, the investigative and enforcement functions of the former Immigration and Naturalization Service (INS), and the Federal Protective Service (FPS). Within CBP, three different inspector occupations — the customs inspector, the immigration inspector, and the agriculture inspector — are joined at the nation's ports of entry. A new CBP Officer position unifies duties and responsibilities, presenting one face at the border to travelers.

Although the agency reorganization strives to make the process more efficient and effective, returning to the U.S. by boat has become more formal since the September 11, 2001 terrorist attack. It is still not an onerous situation in most cases, but we must all recognize that the United States now operates under a system with various levels of terrorism alerts. When the levels are elevated, procedures change and requirements will be more strictly enforced. Always be aware of the current level of terrorism alert and always be prepared to provide all necessary information.

How do I re-enter the U.S.?

Returning to the United States is normally not a big problem for recreational boaters. Detailed information may be obtained from U.S. Customs and Border Protection. The CBP provides excellent information in various publications, and the CBP web site is also very useful. A summary of some of the requirements, as well as a list of helpful CBP Web pages is also included in the Appendix.

Must I report in person to an immigration officer?

Current immigration regulations require every person crossing the border into the U.S. to make application for entry. Essentially, the law requires that every person entering the U.S. make personal contact with an immigration officer at a port of entry at a time when the port is open for inspection. However, that is not always practical and the actual procedures vary, depending upon where you are when crossing the border back into the U.S. For example, in the Pacific Northwest, it is physically and financially impossible for an officer to make personal contact with every individual on every boat. In the past, a different process was used to expedite check-in and entry. Under the Canadian border Small Boat Program, if you had a PIN (Personal Identification Number) for reporting to U.S. Customs, you could call in prior to crossing the border, answer a few simple questions, and obtain a reentry number. If you did not have a PIN you reported to a U.S. CBP Office at a designated re-entry place. However, the PIN system has been discontinued. It is being replaced by a check-in process at ports of entry with video

If You Have a Question, Just Ask

When preparing for a trip to Canadian waters a couple years ago, I left my passport behind on my desk, instead of including it with all the usual items like vessel documents and photo identification. Somewhat in a panic, I stopped in at the Customs and Immigration office at our marina. I asked the officer there if I would have difficulty returning home with just my photo identification and no real proof of citizenship.

He asked me a few quick questions, then remarked that I should not have any difficulties since we had crossed the border many times and our personal information and boat information was in their computer database.

However, he also said that if the terror alert level became elevated before our return things would get much more formal. In that case, the local phone check-in procedure would be inactive and everyone would have to check in personally and be questioned. I decided not to take any chances. I called my office and had my secretary make a copy of my passport and fax it to a friend's office near the marina. The facsimile copy was not great, but I felt better knowing that at least I had something, if worse came to worse.

Thankfully, we returned home several weeks later without incident.

document scanners on the docks to allow ABP officers to remotely view individuals and documents.

Are there other alternatives to personally reporting every time?

The Canadian Border Boat Landing Program (I-68 Permit Program) also provides an exception to the rule that every entry into the U.S. must be made in person to an immigration office. The I-68 Permit Program allows certain persons entering the U.S. by small boat to be inspected once per year. Once a permit is received, persons may enter the U.S. for recreational purposes without further inspection. The I-68 Permit Program initial inspection involves an interview, a check of the individual in the Interagency Border Inspection System (IBIS) and other law enforcement databases, three photographs, fingerprinting and payment of a fee. More detailed information about the I-68 Permit Program is available from the CBP and on the Internet. Recently the author and his wife each applied for and received I-68 permits at a local CBP office. We presented our passport sized photos, our U.S. passports (for proof of citizenship) and received the permits in less than 20 minutes. The CBP personnel were friendly, professional, and efficient. The cost was just $32.00. The I-68 Permit Program allows us to simply call the toll-free number to re-enter the U.S. When we last crossed the border our call-in procedure (by cellphone) took less than five minutes.

How do I report in person for my entry into the U.S.?

When you return to the U.S., you can physically check in at numerous locations. Cruising guides and visitor or travel brochures often list the various ports where you may land and check in upon your return. Be sure you know where to go and plan your return accordingly. Large fines and vessel seizure may be imposed for improperly reporting your arrival back in the United States.

Who may leave the boat after you tie up?

Except for safely landing the boat, no one but the captain or skipper is allowed to leave the vessel. Assume you are being observed. Once you are safely tied up at a designated reporting station immediately go to the CBP Office and be sure to have all your paperwork with you and in order. Persons aboard the vessel must stay aboard. Usually, the correct space to tie up is clearly designated by signs or special paint on the edge of the dock.

May anyone else come aboard the boat during the check-in process?

No one else is permitted to come aboard until the check-in is complete. It is not OK to go visit a friend on the other side of the dock, and it is not OK to invite a friend aboard, during the process. If you see someone you know or want to talk to, wait until the check-in process is complete. Doing otherwise makes the process more difficult for everyone.

May I tie up anywhere and go to the check-in office?

If you land at a port that has a designated dock, do not tie up to a dock not within the designated landing. Although it is technically legal to tie up at a slip or dock outside the designated area, the CBP officer has the authority to require you to move so he can conduct an inspection. If there is not space at the designated area, wait until sufficient room appears. According to U.S. Customs requirements, "When a yacht or any other type of pleasure boat arrives in the United States, the first place it docks must be at a Customs port or other place where Customs service is available."

What information should I have for re-entering the U.S.?

It is very important that you have the right information with you when you check into the United States. You may not always be asked for everything, but the following is a list of the items you should always have with you.

- **Vessel information**. You must have your vessel documentation or state registration.
- **When and where you left the foreign country**. You may be asked the time and place you left for return to the U.S., so be prepared to answer.
- **Your foreign clearance number**. When you enter a foreign country you will be given a clearance number to display on your boat. When you re-enter the United States the U.S. official will ask you for that number.
- **The names and birthdays of everyone aboard.** You will be required to answer some simple questions, such as your name and birth date and the name and birth date of every person aboard. It is helpful to write this beforehand, so you can answer easily. Copies of passports make this process simple. The *Keeping Your Boat Legal* binder has blank forms and space you can use to record this information.

Display your CBP sticker prominently.

- **Identification and proof of citizenship.** Make sure you have proper identification and proof of citizenship for everyone aboard. If requested, you must be able to prove that everyone aboard is a U.S. citizen or documented alien.
- **Information for any purchases of goods that you are bringing back.** You will be asked about purchases, whether you have any Cuban cigars, and whether you have cash or instruments in excess of $10,000. If you have any purchases, you will have to declare them. The best and simplest practice is to limit your spending in foreign countries to consumables such as food, fuel, etc. Alternatively, just come back into the U.S. with simple miscellaneous purchases such as a few souvenirs. U.S. citizens are allowed an $800 exemption once every 30 days to bring goods into the country, and family members who live together may combine their exemptions. When re-entering the U.S. you must declare certain items that you purchased or received abroad and are bringing back. These are items you purchased, received, or inherited; repairs or alterations on your vessel; and items you intend to sell or use in your business. You must state the price you paid or the retail value if the item was a gift.

Will I have to prove I did not purchase things outside the U.S.?

It is possible that your boat will be boarded and inspected upon re-entering the United States. It is also possible you will be asked about items aboard that appear new and could have been purchased abroad (such as electronics, cameras, etc.). Normally, your honest answer is all that is required. However, if you have new items on your boat or in your possession, it is not a bad idea to bring proof of purchase in the U.S or ownership prior to your trip. Documents that fully describe the item — for example, sales receipts, insurance policies, or jeweler's appraisals — are acceptable forms of proof. You will be able to eliminate any questions and make the officer's job that much easier.

What items am I prohibited from bringing into the U.S.?

The CBP Service enforces about 400 laws for 40 other government agencies, such as the Fish and Wildlife Service and the Department of Agriculture. There are numerous items that are prohibited to bring into the U.S. or that are restricted. Some examples are cultural artifacts, drug paraphernalia, firearms, certain fish and wildlife products, game and hunting trophies, and designated fruits and vegetables. For casual travelers and recreational boaters these restrictions are usually not any problem. However, you must know the rules and abide by them.

Do I have to pay to re-enter the U.S.?

There is no specific fee charged to cross the border back into the United States. However, when you travel by boat and your boat is over 30 feet long, you must pay a $25 U.S. Customs User Fee each year and display a User Fee Decal on your boat. The decal should be obtained in advance each year. When you receive the decal, put it on the side of your boat. Keep a copy of your Customs Decal and the Decal Request Form in your *Keeping Your Boat Legal* binder. Call 317-298-1200 ext. 1245 for an application or get the decal by applying online with the CBP. Information for applying online is in the Appendix (see page xx). You may also purchase the customs decal the first time you re-enter the U.S., but the best practice is to get the decal in advance.

Are there specific things I can do to make it easy to report in and get clearance?

There is extensive information on the Internet; you may also wish to examine the *Know Before You Go* brochure online. The tips below from U.S. Customs will make travel easier.

Ten Tips for Re-entering the United States

10. Do not rely on friends and shopkeepers for advice on what items will clear U.S. Customs; instead, obtain this information directly from the U.S. Customs Service.

9. Declare *duty-free goods*, even if purchased in duty-free stores.

8. Do not attempt to bring unauthorized fruits, meats, and dairy products into the United States without first checking whether they are permitted.

7. Know the difference between goods for personal use vs. commercial use.

6. Know the difference between prohibited merchandise (such as ivory, tortoise shell products, absinthe, and counterfeit items) and restricted merchandise.

5. Be aware that many foreign manufactured medications are not FDA-approved and, consequently, cannot be brought into the United States. Also when traveling abroad, bring only the amount of medication you will need during the trip.

4. Do not attempt to return with Cuban cigars unless they were purchased in Cuba while on authorized travel.

3. Know the rules governing the $800 exemption on goods brought back from abroad.

2. Understand that Customs officers have the authority to conduct enforcement examinations without a warrant, ranging from a single luggage examination, up to and possibly including, a personal search.

1. Be sure and read *Know Before You Go* brochure (available online from the CBP).

C. Visiting Canada by Boat

There are two situations involved with any border crossing. First, the entry of a non-citizen into another country, and second, the return of a citizen to his own country. The discussion below is focused on the requirements for a U.S. citizen to enter Canada by boat.

What is CanPass?

Canada has simplified entry for recreational boaters by setting up a program known as CanPass. In effect, a U.S. citizen may register in advance with Canadian authorities by providing the necessary citizenship documents and information. The CanPass system can be a real timesaver, but the fact that one person on your vessel has a CanPass does not suffice for others aboard. Everyone aboard must have his or her own CanPass. If you have a CanPass but still choose to check-in and get clearance at a designated point of entry, you may find the process simpler and less time consuming because you will already be present on the computer database. However, you should still carry all the necessary information and identification documents suggested above. Directions to get more information about CanPass are in the Appendix.

What are the proper procedures for crossing into Canada by boat?

Detailed information for visiting Canada is available from the new Canada Border Services Agency. Because the procedures and requirements change fairly frequently, you should check for up-to-date information before you travel. If everyone aboard has a CanPass, you may call in your estimated arrival time in Canada up to four hours in advance. You will be requested to report to an entry point where your boat may or may not be inspected. If you are not using CanPass, then proceed as follows:

- Report to a designated Canadian Customs entry point.
- Tie up at the designated area. The captain or skipper must immediately report to the office and receive clearance to proceed.
- In some areas, there will be a phone available to call in and give the appropriate information. Assume that you are being observed. Other persons may not enter or exit the boat during this period.
- You will be asked to present your vessel documentation or registration and identification for every person

aboard. You will be asked where you arrived from and the length of your stay in Canada. You will be asked questions regarding prohibited or restricted items (such as tobacco, alcohol, firearms, and other weapons).

- At the end of the clearance process you will be given a clearance number that you must visibly display aboard your boat. A good way to do this is to buy a small hook on a suction cup (similar to those you might use around the house) and stick it to the inside of a window on your boat. Then you just hang a piece of paper with the clearance number from the hook.
- Once back aboard, make an entry in your logbook of the time and location of your clearance and the number.

What information should I bring with me?

The following items are important to carry with you:

- Have your boat license or registration information with you, as well as the full names, citizenship, birth dates, and addresses of all persons aboard.
- Have valid photo ID and proof of citizenship (*birth certificate, citizenship certificate, or passport*) for every person aboard.
- If you are traveling with minors who are not accompanied by *both* their parents, you must have written, notarized authorization from the parents for each child to cross the border. The authorization should also specify the dates of travel.
- If you are traveling with a pet (12 weeks or older), you must provide proof of a current rabies vaccination. If you do not have the proof of vaccination, you may not be allowed to cross the border with your pet.

Are there special equipment or operation requirements for boats in Canada?

Every country has different laws and regulations governing boats and their operation. In the United States and Canada, the regulations may vary from state to state or province to province. If your stay in Canada will be less than 45 days, and your vessel complies with U.S. equipment requirements, it will be acceptable in Canada. However, you must still comply with Canadian federal, regional, and local *operational* requirements at all times. For example, you must comply with speed limits, zero discharge rules, age requirements, etc. Additionally, if you want to catch fish or collect shellfish you must have a Canadian fishing license.

May I use my marine VHF radio while I am in Canada?

You may use your VHF radio in Canada just as you would use it in the United States. No license is required if the vessel is not operated in foreign waters other than the U.S., and the radio operates only on frequencies allocated for maritime mobile communications or marine radio navigation. For a call sign, use your name, boat name, or your vessel identification number.

Are there restrictions on alcohol consumption in Canada?

Just as in the U.S., operation of a vessel while intoxicated is prohibited and subject to fines and/or arrest. In some provinces, no alcohol may be consumed by anyone while the vessel is under way. In Ontario, for example, it is unlawful to transport beverage alcohol in a motor vehicle or boat unless the beverage is unopened and the seal unbroken. In a boat, the beverage must be stored in a closed compartment. Furthermore, there are strict limits on how much duty-free tobacco, beer, wine or spirits you may bring with you across the border.

> *"If you meet the age requirements of the province or territory where you enter Canada, you are allowed to bring in, free of duty and taxes, either 1.5 litres of wine, or 1.14 litres (40 ounces) of liquor, or 24 x 355 millilitres (12 ounces) cans or bottles (8.5 litres) of beer or ale. If you meet the age requirements of the province or territory where you enter Canada, you are allowed to bring the following amounts of tobacco into Canada without paying duty: up to 200 cigarettes, 50 cigars or cigarillos, 200 grams (7 ounces) of manufactured tobacco and 200 tobacco sticks."*
> (Source: Canada Border Services Agency)

Do Canadian laws and regulations vary among the Provinces?

As in the U.S., the laws regarding recreational boating will vary within Canada. When you visit Canada by boat it is important that you be aware of local rules and regulations. For example, unlike the U.S. it is not illegal per se to discharge sewage in Canadian waters. However, Canadian federal law mandates that any pleasure craft with toilet facilities have sewage retention capabilities (holding tanks) to prevent sewage discharge when operating in designated bodies of water. Individual provinces designate *no discharge* zones within their jurisdiction. Before you visit a province in Canada you must be aware of those no discharge areas. Directions for researching provincial requirements are in the Appendix.

D. Visiting Mexico by Boat

Thousands of U.S. citizens visit Mexico on their boats each year and the procedures are fairly simple and straightforward. However, careful adherence to rules and regulations is a must. Information is available from Mexican Consulates in the United States. Directions to obtain a list of Consulates are in the Appendix. The Mexican government (Secretaria de Turismo) has published a detailed guide entitled, *The Manual of Tourist Entry.* The manual is available for free on the Internet in PDF format. Visit the Ministry of Tourism web site referred to in the Appendix.

What are the proper procedures for entering Mexico?

Plan your time of arrival at a Mexican port during normal business hours. Normal hours are 8 a.m. to 3 p.m., Monday through Friday, but irregular hours or absent officials may cause difficulties. It is best to ask other cruisers or listen to cruiser radio nets for information.

- When you arrive at your first Mexican port, go to the Immigration Office and obtain a Tourist Migratory form (FM-T) for every person aboard. (You can get the forms prior to arrival from a Mexican Consulate or Mexican Government Tourism Office. Some travel agencies also carry these forms. This is often referred to as a Tourist Card. It is good for 180 days. If you decide to extend your stay, be sure to request an extension prior to the expiration.

- You must also check in with Mexican customs officials and fill out one Customs Declaration Form per family. Random searches are possible, so be sure to fill out the form accurately.

- Along with your personal entry into Mexico you must make a provisional importation of your vessel. Marina staff at your port of entry may assist with this step along with the other steps for entry. The form for your vessel is called an Application for Provisional Importation of Ships. Once stamped and signed, the provisional importation license allows your vessel to stay in Mexico for a maximum of 10 years. Keep the license aboard at all times.

- Along with the vessel, you must also import spare parts and equipment that are aboard. There is another form for this called the Application for Authorization of Provisional Importation of Goods Meant for the Maintenance and Repair of Goods Provisionally Imported. This application is also submitted to customs and describes in detail the merchandise designated for maintenance or repair. It is useful to have brand names, model numbers, serial numbers, or technical specifications to identify items.

What information and documents are required to obtain the FM-T?

As in other countries, the requirements to enter Mexico differ based upon your nationality. Visitors from some countries must obtain a visa. Visitors from the United States and Canada may obtain the FM-T by presenting either a current passport, certified copy of a birth certificate accompanied by photo identification, or a voter registration card accompanied by photo identification. Minors must be accompanied by both parents or have a notarized letter from the absent parent. The letter must authorize the minor person to leave the country of origin.

Is there a fee for entry to Mexico?

Mexico charges a fee for non-immigrants who are visiting. The fee is updated annually. Recently the fee was $210. Check with the Ministry of Tourism web site for the latest fees.

What information do I need for my boat and crew?

- **Vessel Documents.** You must be able to prove the ownership of your boat. If your boat is documented, you must have the documentation proving ownership and homeport. If not documented, you must have the title or registration information for the vessel (or a lease agreement in your name if the vessel is rented) and proof that the owner resides outside Mexico. If you are the owner, your tourist card is sufficient for that purpose.

- **Crew Documents.** You must also have proof of citizenship for every person aboard and a notarized letter of authorization for any children who are not accompanied by both parents. Passports are not required *but highly recommended.*

- **Crew List.** Have at least five copies of your crew list. If your crew changes at any time while you are in Mexico, you need to repeat the entry procedures. When you are at sea, the crew list must match the persons aboard. Your crew list will be used whenever you leave or arrive at a Mexican port or marina.

Are there special requirements for boats in Mexico?

There are some special considerations for cruising in Mexico. For the latest information, check with a Mexican Consulate. A list of consulates is available on the Internet (see Appendix).

- **Insurance.** You should already have insurance to cover possible damage to your boat. Contact your insurer about adding a rider for cruising in Mexico. You should also have Mexican Liability Insurance to cover any damage you might cause to someone else. A list of insurance agencies and contact information is available on the Internet (see Appendix).

- **Fishing licenses.** If you have any fishing gear aboard, you must obtain fishing licenses for every person aboard and for your vessel and dinghy. In Mexico, a few fishing hooks qualify as fishing gear. The test is whether you have *any* fishing gear aboard, not whether you are actually trying to catch fish. Fines are substantial if you get caught without a license. Obtain fishing licenses before you enter Mexico.

- **Cruising in Mexico.** Prior to 2005, cruisers in Mexico needed to check in and check out from each port visited. In some situations this meant visiting multiple offices and presenting papers to various officials. However, the regulations are changing and being simplified. Visitors are no longer required to obtain clearance at every port and several cities have established *one-stop* offices where you can contact all the various officials and pay all the necessary fees. The new rules will vastly simplify traveling in Mexican waters. Nevertheless, be sure to check on the latest requirements before you travel to Mexico and find out what services are available for the areas you expect to visit. Always be prepared to present your crew list. If you are leaving Mexico you must have authorization to depart from the Mexican marina or port. Departure entails re-visiting the harbor master and the officials in charge and receiving a *dispatch* form for clearance.

- **Weapons.** Do not bring any firearms or ammunition into Mexico.

- **Marine radios.** Many cruising boats have HAM (hold-and-modify) radios and SSB (single-sideband modulation) radios aboard. For radios that require a U.S. license, you can obtain a reciprocal Mexican license from the Secretaria de Communicationes y Transportes.

- **Navigation and charts.** Many cruising boats now have electronic navigation equipment built around a GPS. However, while the GPS is highly accurate, most Mexican charts are not. In some places, your GPS may show your location on the chart as a spot high-and-dry or well inland. It is necessary that you have basic navigation skills beyond reading from the screen of an electronic device.

E. Visiting the Bahamas by Boat

The islands of the Commonwealth of the Bahamas are a popular cruising destination for cruisers from the Southeast United States. Immigration and customs requirements are relatively simple.

What are the proper procedures for crossing into the Bahamas by boat?

Once you cross into Bahamian waters you must fly a yellow quarantine flag from your starboard spreader or the equivalent position for a powerboat. This flag must fly until you have cleared immigration and customs. Report to a designated port of entry. You have 24 hours from arrival to clear and only the captain is allowed to leave the vessel. The Appendix has a list of authorized ports of entry for the Bahamas.

What information do I need to enter the Bahamas?

You must have your vessel documentation or title and registration. All persons entering the Bahamas must have passports except for citizens of the United Kingdom and Canada who are staying less than three weeks and citizens of the U.S., who are genuine tourists for less than eight months. Persons who do not have a passport must have other proof of citizenship (birth certificate) and photo identification (driver's license). Additionally, U.S.,

Canadian, and UK citizens do not need a visa if they are staying for those same short time periods. You will need a full list of your crew and passengers (including addresses and nationalities), and you must fill out a Maritime Declaration of Health to account for the health of every person aboard. Regular business hours are weekdays from 9 a.m. to 5 p.m. with officers on-call during weekends and holidays.

Are there special requirements for boats in the Bahamas?

- **Entry-cruising fee.** You will be charged a cruising fee, currently $150 for boats up to 35 feet and $300 for larger vessels. This fee includes the cruising permit, fishing permit, and departure tax for up to four persons. If there are more than four persons, each of them will have to pay an additional departure tax. This fee allows two visits within a 90-day period.

- **Bahamian flag.** Once you have cleared immigration and customs, take down the yellow quarantine flag and replace it with a Bahamian courtesy flag.

- **Arrival/departure card.** When you check in you will receive an arrival/departure card that you keep aboard until departure from the Bahamas.

- **Departure fee.** Each person entering the Bahamas must fill out an arrival/departure card. When you leave the Bahamas you must pay a departure fee (unless it was part of the entry fee), which is currently $18. You also surrender your arrival/departure card.

- **Weapons.** Firearms are not prohibited, but you must provide the serial number and manufacturer and an exact ammunition count. Firearms must be kept under lock and key and may not be removed from the vessel without a special permit from the Bahamian Police.

Check the Internet for the most up-to-date information before visiting the Bahamas by boat.

United States Pollution Regulations

Is it illegal to dump or spill oil overboard?

YES! This is one of the most stringent pollution restrictions under U.S. law. You must never discharge or spill oil overboard. The federal Water Pollution Control Act prohibits the discharge of oil or oily waste into any navigable U.S. waters. You may not cause a film or discoloration of the water surface, or sludge or emulsion under the surface. If oil or fuel gets into your bilge, you must manually remove it and clean the bilge. Violations are subject to substantial civil and criminal penalties, including large fines and/or imprisonment. All vessels with an engine must have some means to retain oily mixtures onboard and then transfer the mix to a shore-side facility. For recreational vessels, carrying a bucket, oil absorbent pads, or just a heavy plastic bag may satisfy this requirement. In the event of an accident you must take measures to prevent fuel spills into the water.

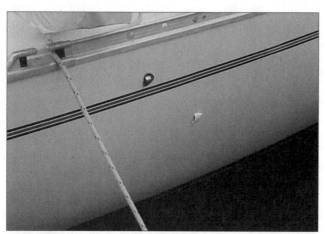

The vent for your fuel tank is a likely source for an unintended spill overboard. Air exits from the fuel tank while filling, but if you put in too much fuel it can spill out of the vent into the water. Be careful not to top off your tank. Marine stores sell cups that fasten over the vent and catch fuel if it leaks.

What happens if there is an oil or gas spill?

The National Oil Pollution Act states that a person responsible for an oil spill can be held financially accountable for cleanup costs and for damage to the environment. In addition, you are required to immediately notify the U.S. Coast Guard if your vessel discharges oil or hazardous substances in the water. Civil penalties can be imposed against an individual for failing to make such

Be Careful When Filling Your Fuel Tank

One of the most common sources of fuel spills is the process of filling your gas or diesel tanks. Here are a few tips to avoid problems.

1. When the attendant hands you the nozzle, keep it pointed up. That way no fuel will run out of the hose onto your boat or into the water.

2. When you are filling the tank, pay attention. Do not leave the area to do something else.

3. Listen to the sound of the tank filling. You will be able to hear the pitch change as the tank nears full. Don't wait for an automatic shut off in the nozzle. If possible, keep an eye on your fuel gauge or have someone else do so. Stop filling before the tank is absolutely full. If you overfill the tank, fuel might leak out of the vent on the side of you boat and enter the water.

4. Have some rags or towels nearby while you are filling. If fuel spills or drips on your boat, wipe it up immediately, before it drains overboard.

5. When you finish, wipe the nozzle with your rag or towel and then carefully hand it back to the attendant. Again, keep the nozzle pointed up.

a report. Call the U.S. Coast Guard toll-free 800-424-8802 or locally in the District of Columbia 202-267-2675. Be prepared to report the following information:

- Your name and address.
- Location of the incident.
- Description of the spill material.
- Suspected source of the material, suspected cause of the spill, and suspected responsible party.

What are the restrictions on overboard discharge from toilets?

Most cruising vessels and many small recreational boats have toilets onboard. The federal Water Pollution Prevention and Control Act requires all boat owners with an onboard toilet to install and use a marine sanitation device. The simplest of these are portable toilets that have a built-in holding tank that can be carried ashore and emptied. The most complicated are devises that actually treat sewage or incinerate it prior to discharge, meeting specified health standards. These devises are high consumers of power and are typically present only on larger vessels.

Marine Sanitation Devices (MSD)

Type I. A Type I device treats sewage and then discharges into the water. It discharges effluent having a fecal coliform bacteria count not greater than 1,000 per 100 milliliters and no visible floating solids.

Type II. Similar to Type I, but meets a higher level of treatment. Fecal coliform count is not greater than 200 per 100 milliliters and suspended solids not greater than 150 milligrams per liter. These typically use a combination of chemical, biological, electrical, or incinerating methods. Many use chlorine or other disinfectants.

Type III. When emptied at a shore-side pumpout station the Type III is the most environmentally friendly system, since there is no discharge into the water. This type is the familiar holding tank present on most recreational boats. The Type III is the only legal system in no discharge zones.

Portable Toilets Are An Alternative for Some Boats

Many small boats have a portable toilet instead of a marine sanitation system with a toilet and holding tank. Owners of smaller cruising boats (particularly sailboats) are turning to these as an alternative to extensive hoses and plumbing, through-hulls and valves, and holding tanks.

Instead of taking up space with all the hoses, valves and a holding tank, the portable toilet is securely mounted in an accessible spot, with quick detachment for easy removal. The portable tank can be taken ashore and dumped at a pumpout station or a suitable restroom facility. Pumpout stations usually have a water hose and nozzle so the portable tank can be washed clean and placed back onboard.

The clean portable tank, without hoses or valves that accumulate debris and cause odors, is an advantage on a smaller vessel. This solution is not suitable for offshore cruising or larger boats with family and friends onboard

but it may be perfect for smaller cruisers that do not stray far from pumpout facilities.

Marine toilets used to be relatively simple devices; now, larger recreational cruisers often have electric toilets that work at the push of a button. Nevertheless, all of them must comply with federal and state laws and regulations. Overboard discharge of untreated sewage is prohibited in U.S. waters. Any vessel that has an installed toilet must have a holding tank or an approved sewage treatment device. Devices that treat sewage with chemicals or with heat may not be used in certain no discharge zones. You must be aware of such zones if you have a sewage treatment system and make sure it does not discharge overboard in such zones. The holding tank may have an overboard discharge for use when outside U.S. waters but the overboard discharge valve must be secured in the closed position while in U.S. waters.

What are the restrictions on overboard discharge from sinks or other non-sewage sources?

More and more states are designating certain areas as *zero discharge* zones. Freshwater lakes and reservoirs fall into this category. Individual states may establish *no discharge* zones within their waters; at this time the following have done so: California, Florida, Massachusetts, Michigan, Minnesota, Missouri, Mississippi, New Hampshire, New Mexico, New York, Rhode Island, Texas, Vermont, and Wisconsin. Special precautions may be necessary when you are in a no discharge zone. Check with the appropriate state or local authorities for more specific information on no discharge zones. The best practice is to know the rules in advance and modify your behavior accordingly.

Is it illegal to throw garbage, bottles, cans or food overboard?

Federal law (The Refuse Act of 1899) prohibits throwing garbage overboard. No refuse of any kind (including trash, garbage, oil and other liquid pollutants) may be dumped into the water. It is illegal to operate a garbage disposal that discharges overboard. Specific U.S. Coast Guard regulations prohibit dumping of plastic refuse, and garbage mixed with plastic, into any waters. Additionally, State and local regulations may further restrict the disposal of garbage. Make sure you know about any local regulations.

What is a waste management plan?

If your boat is over 40 feet long, equipped with a galley and berthing, and certified to operate beyond three miles offshore or actually operated past three miles, federal regulations require that it have a Waste Management Plan. The plan must be in writing and describe procedures for collecting, processing, storing and properly disposing of garbage. It must also designate the person who is in charge of garbage.

THE DISCHARGE OF PLASTIC OR GARBAGE MIXED WITH PLASTIC INTO ANY WATERS IS PROHIBITED. THE DISCHARGE OF ALL GARBAGE IS PROHIBITED IN THE NAVIGABLE WATERS OF THE UNITED STATES AND, IN ALL OTHER WATERS, WITHIN THREE NAUTICAL MILES OF THE NEAREST LAND.

| THE DISCHARGE OF DUNNAGE, LINING, AND PACKING MATERIALS THAT FLOAT IS PROHIBITED WITHIN 25 NAUTICAL MILES FROM THE NEAREST LAND. | OTHER UNGROUND GARBAGE MAY BE DISCHARGED BEYOND 12 NAUTICAL MILES FROM THE NEAREST LAND. | OTHER GARBAGE GROUND TO LESS THAN ONE INCH MAY BE DISCHARGED BEYOND THREE NAUTICAL MILES OF THE NEAREST LAND. |

A PERSON WHO VIOLATES THE ABOVE REQUIREMENTS IS LIABLE FOR A CIVIL PENALTY OF UP TO $25,000, A FINE OF UP TO $50,000, AND IMPRISONMENT FOR UP TO FIVE YEARS FOR EACH VIOLATION. REGIONAL, STATE, AND LOCAL RESTRICTIONS ON GARBAGE DISCHARGES ALSO MAY APPLY.

This photo shows a plaque like those available at most marine stores.

Tips for Environmentally Safe Boating

- Observe the rules regarding overboard discharge. No discharge of sewage, garbage, or trash. Use restrooms and facilities ashore when at the dock.

- When you clean your boat, use biodegradable soaps and cleaners. Limit the amount of soaps and cleaners to the minimum needed. Wash your boat frequently with fresh water only. Do not use any toxic chemicals or cleaners (bleach, teak cleaners, etc.) to clean your boat, except when your boat is out of the water and then rinse it thoroughly.

- Keep your engine properly maintained and tuned. Inspect fuel lines and clamps regularly.

- Control discharge from your bilge. Place an absorbent mat or cloth at places where oil or fuel might make its way into the bilge. Place an oil absorbent pad or cloth in the bilge to soak up any oil which ends up there. Avoid the use of toxic cleaners in your bilge.

- Choose the least toxic bottom paint that is appropriate for your area and your circumstances. When removing or applying bottom paint always follow the *Best Practices* posted at your boatyard.

Summary of Federal Discharge Laws Relevant to Recreational Boats

	Sewage	Oil & Fuel	Garbage (food waste)	Plastics	Trash
Distance from U.S. Coast					
0 - 3 nautical miles	No discharge except for approved MSD	<15 PPM, no visible sheen	No discharge	No discharge	No discharge
3 - 12 nautical miles	No Prohibition	< 15 PPM, no visible sheen	OK if ground to < 1 inch	No discharge	OK if ground to < 1 inch

What needs to be in the waste management plan?

The following language will constitute a satisfactory waste management plan. The *Keeping Your Boat Legal* binder includes a full-size plan for use on your boat.

Do I have to post legal notices or placards on my boat?

Federal law requires several placards. Boats over 26 feet in length with an engine compartment must have an oil pollution placard at least 5 by 8 inches and place it in the machinery area or bilge. There must also be a garbage notice Save Our Seas (SOS) placard at least 4 by 9 inches that is in a conspicuous place. The SOS placard outlines the rules of dumping waste offshore. These placards may be purchased from local marinas, boat dealers, and marine equipment suppliers. Samples of these placards are in the Appendix.

Waste Management Plan

Vessel Name _____

1. This plan describes policy and procedures for handling this vessel's garbage according to MARPOL Annex V and 33 CFR Subparts 151.51 through 151.77. As Captain, I am responsible for carrying out this plan. All crew members and embarked persons shall follow the instructions in this plan. **It is the general policy of this vessel that all food waste and garbage will be retained onboard for proper disposal ashore.**

2. Waste for this vessel is collected _____ (where) and stored _____ (location). When moored, all waste will be carried from the vessel and disposed of _____ (location of dumpster, etc.). **Plastics and waste containing plastic materials will never be discharged into the water from this vessel regardless of location.**

3. When sailing on inland waters or at sea within 12 nautical miles of land, no food, garbage, or waste of any type will be discharged. When on an extended voyage, beyond 12 nautical miles from land, certain non-plastic and non-floating waste may be discharged if storage space is not available. In this case, all plastics (including foamed plastic) are to be segregated from other wastes and stored onboard for proper disposal ashore. Only those materials permitted for discharge according to the MARPOL Annex V placard may be discharged in the water. **In no case will waste of any kind be discharged into the water without my prior inspection and explicit permission.**

4. If you have any questions about this plan, waste handling procedures, or materials that may be discharged, please consult me.

_____   _____
Captain   Date

Marine Mammal Protection And Other Wildlife

Although consideration of protected wildlife is not high on the list of boater concerns, there are federal laws that impact boaters and how we use our vessels. Two of the most important laws are the Marine Mammal Protection Act (MMPA) and the Endangered Species Act (ESA). Between these two laws, all marine mammals (seals, porpoise, whales, manatees, polar bears, dolphins, etc.) sea turtles, salmon in some areas, and many other species of fish are protected. Additionally, under the ESA there is specific protection for the habitats of threatened and endangered species. Since boaters may come into contact (near or far) with protected animals, and since we interact with their habitats while boating, some knowledge of these laws is important.

Orca (killer whales) in Washington State are under consideration as a threatened species.

A. Marine Mammals

What is the MMPA?

The Marine Mammal Protection Act protects marine mammals from harm or harassment. The protected animals include large cetaceans such as gray whales and humpback whales, and smaller animals such as orca, manatees, dolphins, porpoise, seal lions, and seals. Under the Act, it is illegal "to harass, hunt, capture, or kill, or attempt to harass, hunt, capture or kill, any marine mammal." In 1994, Congress defined the term *harassment* to mean any act of pursuit, torment, or annoyance.

1. Level A Harassment. Has the potential to injure a marine mammal or marine mammal stock in the wild.

2. Level B Harassment. Has the potential to disturb a marine mammal or marine mammal stock in the wild by causing disruption of behavioral patterns, including, but not limited to, migration, breathing, nursing, breeding, feeding, or sheltering.

Is it legal to observe or follow marine mammals?

Observing marine mammals is popular and many areas have commercial whale watching cruises. Boaters are allowed to view marine mammals but must do so in a manner that does not endanger the animals and does not substantially disrupt normal behavior.

What is the best way to observe marine mammals from a boat?

The best method for observing swimming marine mammals (such as whales and orca) is unclear. There is some scientific evidence that loud engine acceleration noise is disruptive, yet there also is some evidence that sitting in one place is disruptive. More studies are under way. Nevertheless, the vessel must be operated slowly and predictably. Avoid positioning in a way that restricts or modifies the animals' normal movement.

How close may I approach a marine mammal?

A vessel or person should not approach closer than 100 yards. Being closer than 100 yards requires caution and being closer than 50 yards involves a high risk of harassment. It is strictly forbidden to touch or feed any marine mammal.

Are there specific local protections for marine mammals?

Yes, there are local areas with specific protections for marine mammals. In the Pacific Northwest and California, some islets and rocks are protected as wildlife reserves for seals and sea lions. In Florida, state statutes allow for manatee protections, and numerous counties have specific ordinances regarding manatees. The manatee protections include speed limits and restricted entry in certain areas. Protections for manatees are implemented by the Florida Fish and Wildlife Commission and by local governments (subject to FWC approval). It is every boat owner's responsibility to know and follow the local restrictions.

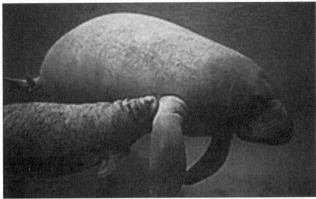

West Indian Manatees are protected species under the MMPA and under the ESA. Their protection in Florida is coordinated between the U.S. Fish and Wildlife Service, the Florida Fish and Wildlife Commission and local governments in various Florida counties.

Operational Guidelines When Spotting Whales

From two miles to one mile away:

- Reduce speed to 13 knots.
- Post a dedicated lookout to assist the vessel operator in monitoring the location of all marine mammals.
- Avoid sudden changes in speed and direction.
- Aircraft observe the FAA minimum altitude of 1,000 feet over water.

From one mile to one-half mile away:

- Reduce speed to 10 knots.

From one-half mile to 600 feet away:

- Reduce speed to 7 knots.
- Maneuver to avoid head-on approach.

Close approach procedure 600 feet or closer:

- Parallel the course and speed of moving whales up to the designated speed limit within that distance.
- Do not attempt a head-on approach to whales.
- Approach and leave stationary whales at no more than idle or *no wake* speed, not to exceed 7 knots.
- Do not intentionally drift down on whales.

Vessels in multi-vessel approaches should maintain communication with each other (via VHF channels for hailing) to coordinate viewing.

Take into account the presence of obstacles (vessels, structures, fishing gear, or the shoreline). All vessels in close approach must stay to the side or behind the whales so they do not box in the whales or cut off their path.

Stand-by Zone - From 300 feet to 600 feet away:

- Two-vessel limit within the 300- to 600-foot Stand-by Zone at any one time.

Close Approach Zone - From 100 feet to 300 feet away:

- One vessel limit.
- Other vessels stand off. (up to two vessels in the Stand-by Zone – others outside 600 feet).
- If more than one vessel is within 600 feet, the vessel within 300 feet should limit its time to 15 minutes in close approach to whales.

No Intentional Approach within 100 feet:

Do not approach within 100 feet of whales. If whales approach within 100 feet of your vessel, put engines in neutral and do not re-engage propulsion until whales are observed clear of harm's way from your vessel.

Additional information is available from the Florida Fish and Wildlife Conservation Commission and from its Internet web site at www.floridaconservation.org.

The Appendix contains additional information for observing marine mammals.

B. Other U.S. Environmental Regulations

What is the ESA?

The Endangered Species Act is a law protecting species of plants and animals that are listed as threatened or endangered. Federal agencies study the population numbers and trends for a species (or distinct geographic group of a species) and determine if it is threatened or endangered. The ESA offers unique protections because it requires protection of the plants or animals and their habitats.

How does the ESA affect boat owners?

There are probably regulations in your area that are derived from the ESA. These regulations may take the form of a fishing restriction to protect an endangered fish species or a restricted, or limited, access area to protect critical habitat. Most likely you will not be aware of the specific reason for a particular restriction. However, they are usually well posted and publicized. If there is an endangered species in your area, such as an endangered fish population, you may be restricted from access to certain rivers, lakes, or bays during certain times of the year.

What are some examples of endangered species that may affect boaters?

Many species of marine animals are considered threatened or endangered. Other laws, such as the MMPA, may also protect some of these species. Examples include: various sea turtles; certain salmon and sturgeon species; various abalone and corals; many whale species (such as blue, humpback, beluga, sperm, and bowhead); various seals and otters, and polar bears.

The Appendix has directions on how to obtain a list of marine plants and animals that are considered threatened or endangered.

Wild Atlantic Salmon were designated as endangered in some Northeast U.S. rivers in 1980. Some species of wild Pacific Salmon are considered threatened in certain Pacific Northwest Rivers.

What are marine habitats, bird and animal reserves?

In some areas there are specific islands, portions of islands, coastline areas, and underwater areas, that have been designated as critical habitats for plants or animals that are protected under the MMPA, the ESA, and other environmental protection laws. These areas are clearly designated in guidebooks and by signs. Some may have restrictions such as speed limits and limited or prohibited access. It is your responsibility as a boat owner to know and recognize these areas and restrictions and abide by them.

What are the penalties for violating these laws?

A violation of the MMPA can incur a fine of up to $10,000. Knowing violations can be fined up to $20,000, with one year in jail. Fines for violations of the ESA range from $500 to $25,000. Prices are per violation. The fines for one act of carelessness could be substantial. The fines could certainly be enough to ruin your day.

Provisions regarding MMPA and ESA violations are reprinted in the Appendix.

Marine Law Enforcement

There are a variety of law enforcement agencies, depending upon how and where a vessel is operated. These agencies include the U.S. Coast Guard, U.S. Customs and Border Protection, the Drug Enforcement Agency, National Marine Fisheries Service, State Fish and Wildlife agencies, and local marine patrols. Interaction between boaters and law enforcement officers is expected to increase in the future.

What is the enforcement role of the U.S. Coast Guard?

Besides local marine patrols, the U.S. Coast Guard is the most frequently encountered enforcement agency. The U.S. Coast Guard has authority to stop any vessel and to *go aboard any vessel and examine, inspect, and search the vessel and examine every part thereof and any person.* When

The U.S. Coast Guard is playing an increasing role in protecting against terrorism. Checks of recreational boats are increasing. This large cutter is an example of an offshore patrol ship.

Our First Boarding

We experienced our first U.S. Coast Guard boarding in our twenty-first year of cruising. I was at the helm of a friend's boat while we motored on a warm, sunny afternoon. A U.S. Coast Guard patrol boat passed by, made an abrupt stop, turned, then came alongside our boat. We were verbally hailed and asked if the boat had been previously boarded. We were asked if we had any firearms and then informed that they wished to do a boarding inspection. They came up to our stern and boarded via the swim step. One seaman remained in the cockpit while two others conducted the inspection. I stayed at the helm and the vessel owner accompanied the two below. We were allowed to continue on our course at normal speed.

I had an amicable conversation with the seaman in the cockpit (about sailing, cruising, etc.) while the inspec-

tion took place. There was a bit of confusion trying to find the air-horn and the officer in charge noted that we did not have a waste management plan. He explained how we could write up and post the waste management plan and asked that we buy a new air-horn at our next stop.

They also asked about our cruising plans and our proposed destinations. Before they left the officer reminded me that it is illegal to operate a boat while under the influence. This was prompted by the fact that I was casually drinking a beer. However, I was obviously not intoxicated, and it was just a friendly reminder.

The officer and seamen were courteous and professional. The entire event lasted about 30 minutes and we proceeded to our destination.

recreational boating accidents occur the U.S. Coast Guard may conduct drug and alcohol tests.

What happens during a U.S. Coast Guard boarding?

A U.S. Coast Guard boarding is relatively simple, but somewhat intimidating. The U.S. Coast Guard will hail the vessel, request identification, ask if the vessel has been boarded before, and also ask if there are any firearms are aboard. The boarding officers will be armed. They will inspect registration and documentation papers and check for compliance with equipment and safety requirements. The owner or operator will receive a written report that specifies compliance or violation of such requirements. Summaries of various laws enforced by the U.S. Coast Guard are reprinted in the Appendix.

Can the U.S. Coast Guard terminate a trip?

Yes, the U.S. Coast Guard is empowered to seize the vessel or order it into port for immediate compliance.

Small rigid hull inflatable boats can be deployed from the larger U.S. Coast Guard cutters and used for local patrols. These boats are useful for making contact with recreational boaters and conducting on-the-water inspections. If you are asked to heave to and allow a boarding, you must comply.

Boarding Procedures

U.S. Coast Guard Boarding Policy

The U.S. Coast Guard is the primary maritime law enforcement agency of the United States.

Authority

Section 89 of Title 14 of the United States Code authorizes the U.S. Coast Guard to board vessels subject to the jurisdiction of the U.S. anytime upon the high seas and upon waters over which the United States has jurisdiction. The U.S. Coast Guard may board vessels to make inquiries, examinations, inspections, searches, seizures and arrests.

What to Expect

A uniformed U.S. Coast Guard boarding team will notify you that they are coming aboard to conduct a boarding. Like other law enforcement officers, they will be armed. Once aboard they will conduct an initial safety inspection to identify any obvious safety hazards and to ensure the sea worthiness of your vessel. The boarding officer will then ask to see the vessel registration or documentation and pro-

ceed to inspect your vessel. The scope of the vessel inspection, during most boardings, is limited to determining the vessel's regulatory status (e.g. commercial, recreational, passenger, cargo, and/or fishing vessel) and checking for compliance with U.S. civil law applicable to vessels of that status. The U.S. Coast Guard may also enforce U.S. criminal law. The boarding officer will complete a U.S. Coast Guard boarding form and note any discrepancies. You will get a signed copy before they depart.

Report of Boarding

When a U.S. Coast Guard officer issues you a boarding report, he will either issue a yellow copy, if no discrepancies were noted, or a white copy if there were. A white copy will indicate a warning or a notice of violation. The boarding officer should explain the procedures to follow in each case. In any event, those procedures are written on the reverse of the form. If you have any questions, ask the boarding officer or call the U.S. Coast Guard Infoline at 800-368-5647.

This is not a common event but will almost certainly occur if an operator is intoxicated, or if the vessel is being operated in an unsafe manner creating an especially hazardous condition. The following are some U.S. Coast Guard examples of situations that may result in trip termination:

- Insufficient number of approved Personal Flotation Devices.
- Insufficient fire extinguishers.
- Overloading beyond manufacturer's recommended safe loading capacity.
- Improper navigation lights.
- Improper ventilation requirements for fuel tank and engine spaces.
- Fuel leakage or fuel in bilges.
- Improper backfire flame control.
- Manifestly unsafe voyage.
- Intoxication.

An operator who refuses to terminate the unsafe use of a vessel may be cited for failure to comply with the directions of a U.S. Coast Guard boarding officer, as well as for the specific violations that were the basis for the termination order.

The Basics of Chartering

For purposes of clarity and simplicity, the discussion below will refer to the owner of a charter boat as *owner* and the user of a charter boat as *charterer*. Usually there is a third party that manages the charter boat and acts as a middleman between the owner and charterer. We call this the *charter company*.

Interaction between the boat owner, charter company, and a charterer creates legal issues that are not present when you only use a boat for personal recreational purposes. Our discussion is focused on chartering from the perspective of the owner, and we will address some of the most common and important issues. The following discussion does not address the far more complex issues involving commercial charters.

What is a charter company and are there different types of charter companies?

As used in this discussion, the term charter company refers to a business that manages a fleet of recreational boats that is available for charter for a defined period of time. The charter company may itself own the boats, though in most cases someone else owns the boats. The industry generally recognizes two classes of charter companies. First Tier charter companies have boats that are usually not more than four or five years old. A First Tier company may have more than one boat of a particular make or model and operate from more than one location. A boat in a First Tier company's inventory will usually come into the program when it is new. A boat is generally retired after four or five years. The owner either chooses to use the boat personally, to sell the boat, or to place it with a Second Tier company. A Second Tier charter company is one that has a fleet composed of older boats. If you decide to rent a boat from a charter company, it is important to decide whether you want to deal with a First or Second Tier company. The costs will differ, but so will the boat's level of quality. Both tiers include large and small companies.

What are the different types of charters?

The technical terminology for types of vessel charters is: voyage, time, and demise charters. However, within the three general types there are many variations, depending upon the type of vessel and the services in which the vessel is engaged. Each type is explained below:

- **Voyage charter.** The vessel is rented to complete a specific voyage. The owner is responsible for the actual operation of the vessel. A voyage charter is used for a specific destination(s) and where the time period is unknown.
- **Time charter.** A vessel is rented for a specified time. Again, the owner supplies the crew and operates the vessel. A time charter is commonly used when someone wants the use of a boat for a specific time period, and wants it operated by the owner or owner's crew.
- **Demise charter.** A charterer takes full use of the vessel, provides the master and crew, and pays the expenses of running the vessel. Demise charters are usually referred to as a *bareboat* charter (especially in the context of recreational vessels). Hereafter, we will use the term bareboat charter instead of demise charter, since it is more common.

What are the important characteristics of a recreational bareboat charter?

A bareboat charter is pretty much what it sounds like. The charterer takes possession of a bare boat for a specific a period of time. The charterer is usually the skipper of the boat and solely responsible for its operation during the charter period. The charterer is responsible for provisioning the boat (although most charter companies will do this for a fee) and sets the itinerary, courses, and destinations. The charterer is responsible for any harm or damage to the boat, its passengers, and crew.

What is a skippered charter?

Some bareboat charters also have a paid skipper to operate the boat and assist with the cruise. Some boats (usually the larger ones) may only be chartered if the charterer also hires a skipper for the trip. Most charter companies (if requested) will supply a list of experienced skippers for hire. The charterer makes the arrangements and pays the skipper. The skipper can be hired for a day or more, or for the entire cruise. The skipper should be familiar with the boat or other similar vessels, have local knowledge of the cruising area, and able to help find fun and interesting places to go. Be sure to check references, background, and experience. Not all skippers are equal. Some owners require a skipper in an effort to limit the chances of accidents and equipment breakdown due to misuse. If the charter vessel is large or has complicated equipment and systems, it may be a good idea to require skippered charters.

What is a flotilla charter?

Flotilla charters are popular in Mediterranean countries and the Caribbean. A flotilla charter is a bareboat charter where the vessel is part of a group. Each charterer is responsible for a boat, but within the group there will be a lead boat with a skipper and other crew members such as a hostess and mechanic. The lead boat may also carry spare parts, extra gear, and perhaps a few extra toys. The lead boat skipper will have local knowledge of the area, and the crew will assist him or her with such tasks as docking, navigating, planning, etc. There may also be planned group activities like morning briefings on weather, courses, and destinations. There may be planned events like parties, group meals, etc. A flotilla charter usually involves a pre-planned itinerary with some flexibility to accommodate changes in weather and other contingencies. It offers a compromise between a bareboat charter and a skippered charter. The use of a vessel in a flotilla charter program may help limit problems and

Choose Your Skipper With Care

Several years ago I took some friends cruising on our sailboat. We began provisioning the boat and putting away our gear, and then relaxed in the cockpit at the dock as we were not planning to leave that day.

Later that afternoon a 34-foot powerboat came slowly down the fairway and started turning into the vacant slip next to us. I hopped onto the dock to assist with the landing. The helmsman was taking directions from someone else on the fly bridge and the crew had their boat hook and lines ready. As they approached, I offered to take the bow line and fend the boat off the dock while someone came off with the stern line. The other person on the bridge yelled at me to not help.

They did not tie up to the dock but immediately reversed, went back out the fairway, then reappeared for another landing. This time they told us they were practicing and did not need any assistance on the dock. We watched as they crashed time and again, with the instructor yelling instructions and verbally abusing the helmsman and the crew. It was pretty bad and this went on for about two hours. However, they got much better as time

went by and we clapped and congratulated the helmsman and crew as they improved.

Finally, they left and did not return. Later in the trip, we crossed paths again and learned they were on a bareboat charter with a skipper for the first two days. His job was to teach them basic piloting and boat-handling skills. However, they had few good things to say about the fellow. In fact, they got very tired of his lack of diplomacy and heavy-handed teaching techniques. They told me they had dumped him off soon after that last encounter. They referred to the guy as *Captain Ron* in a manner that did not give the connotation of a favorite friend. I believe they got the name from a popular movie about sailing, even though in the movie, *Captain Ron* was an amiable oafish fellow.

I respected the group for taking the time and trouble to learn proper boating skills, but pitied them for the poor choice of a skipper. Fortunately they went on to have a very enjoyable cruise. I think the experience with *Captain Ron* is the exception, but it illustrates the need to be careful when selecting a skipper to assist with your cruise.

damage due to misuse, inexperience, local hazards, or bad judgment.

What does a charter company do?

Most owners place their boat with a charter company to book charters, collect deposits and fees, pay expenses, evaluate a charterer's expertise and experience, check the boat in and out, and do routine maintenance and cleaning. If there is no charter company, the owner has to do these things. Agreements vary, but typically the charter company deals directly with the charterer and the owner has no contact. Some agreements state that the owner leases the vessel to the charter company for a specified period of time (usually annually), and the charter company then charters the boat to charterers. The owner will have specific obligations vis-à-vis the charter company and vice versa. The written contract between the owner and charter company should clearly state the mutual obligations and responsibilities.

What should an owner consider before contracting with a charter company?

An owner needs to carefully choose the charter company with proper consideration for reputation, reliability, location, type of boat, income expectations, etc. There must be a written agreement between the owner and the charter company. Some specific contractual considerations follow:

- **The length of the agreement**. Most agreements run from year to year and must be renewed annually. Some renew automatically unless one party gives notice of termination. This allows either party to end the relationship if things are not going as expected. If the agreement automatically renews, it will have a period of time during which notice of non-renewal must be given. If a notice of non-renewal is not given during the required time period, the contract will automatically renew.

- **The charter fee**. The owner and charter company must together establish the charter price and set various discounts based upon the time of year, length of the charter, and special rates for return customers. These are important decisions and the owner should be fully aware of all discounts and specials that the charter company may offer. The charter fee will be divided between the charter company and the owner, based upon a fixed percentage specified in the contract.

- **Specific services the charter company provides**. Most handle all reservations, collection of fees, and inspection of the vessel for damages. Some contracts allow the owner to perform certain services (such as check-out or check-in and cleaning) and take some deductions from the charter fee. Charter companies do not provide services to the owner without charge. In most situations the various fees and costs charged by the charter company will be deducted from the gross amount received from the charterer. Some contracts also provide that if an owner finds a charterer through the owner's own efforts, the charter company's percentage of the charter fee will be lower. It is important that the owner understand all the fees and charges and when they will be incurred.

- **Policies and procedures to pre-qualify charterers**. Before a boat leaves the dock, a charterer must provide proof of basic skills and knowledge. The contract should spell out in detail the policies and procedures for checking out charterers and establishing that they are qualified. Every charterer should submit a resume and be personally checked out on use and operation of the boat before leaving. The Appendix has additional information on specific items that should be covered in the charterer's resume.

- **Owner's personal use of the boat**. Most agreements have provisions for the owner's use of the vessel. Some do not allow the owner to make the vessel available to any other person. This is important. If not prohibited, the owner might be able to charter the vessel during the owner's time, and collect a fee independent of the charter company. Such arrangements are a way for charterers to get a cheaper rate on a vessel since an owner is dealing directly with them, rather than paying a portion to a charter company.

- **Replacement/repair of lost or damaged equipment**. Some charter companies collect a daily insurance fee from charterers. These fees are pooled into a fund that is used to pay for damages or losses up to the owner's insurance deductible amount. The idea behind such charges is to provide a means by which repairs can be paid for without the owner incurring any cost. The contractual provisions regarding the collection of such daily fees, and the specific ways that fund will be spent, should be carefully reviewed and completely understood by the owner.

- **General or specific advertising**. An owner has a right to expect that a charter company will advertise its services. Most do not advertise specific boats. Most charter companies print brochures and flyers that list the boats, the seasonal rates, trip itineraries, etc. An owner should check to see what kind of advertising a charter company does and how it will market your boat.

- **Authority to make repairs**. Agreements often give the charter company authority to make repairs at the owner's expense up to a specified dollar amount. This allows for quick repairs and maintenance, but the owner must also have some protection from extravagant costs or unnecessary items. Big-ticket items should be subject to the owner's prior approval. Even small items may be charged to the owner at a rate substantially higher than expected. The contractual language regarding repairs should be carefully scrutinized. Try to avoid using terms such as "reasonable efforts to contact the owner," or "qualified boatyard." Also, the dollar limitation will be waived in some situations, such as an emergency or if the owner cannot be contacted. The times when the dollar limitation does not apply should be clearly stated and fully understood.

- **Payments to the charter company**. The charter company keeps a percentage of the fee paid by charterers. Usually there is also a fixed fee for cleaning the vessel and making it ready for each charter. This may be referred to as a turn-around fee. In some cases an owner is permitted to take care of the turn-around, thereby reducing the fee. In addition to turn-around fees, there may be charges for an annual inspection of the boat, preparation of an operations manual, underwater inspections (after every charter and personal use), use of a chase boat in the event of breakdowns, etc. The contract should specifically list all charges that may be deducted before the owner gets paid.

- **Inventory and equipment.** The contract should have a specific list of items that must be on the boat and all other items that the owner has provided. Items such as electronics should state more than just the generic name and include the age, manufacturer, model, etc. If a hand-held GPS has to be replaced it will be very important to know exactly what it was. The inventory list should be carefully prepared by the owner.

What are the responsibilities of the owner in a bareboat charter?

The owner is responsible for the physical condition of the boat and its equipment when the charter begins. The boat must be clean, fully commissioned, seaworthy, reasonably equipped, and ready for operation. The law implies a warranty of seaworthiness. It means that the vessel is reasonable for the purpose of the charter. The owner must provide the required documents (such as registration, title, and U.S. Coast Guard documentation). Other specific obligations of the owner (such as time and place of delivery, equipment, fuel, provisions, etc.) will be stated in the agreement between the owner and the charterer.

Does an owner need any special insurance?

A standard yacht policy does not provide coverage for commercial use of the vessel, including charters. Therefore, the owner must purchase additional coverage for damages that occur while the vessel is in charter. Some charter companies negotiate a group rate with an insurance company to try to save owners money. Some charter companies also collect a daily fee from charterers to cover the deductible portion of claims or to pay for small repairs or replacements without making a claim.

Regular Maintenance Can Get Expensive

During ownership of our second boat, we had it in charter for a few years. I was always amazed at the cost of replacing ordinary items. One month we got our statement and I noted a deduction of about $130 for a new battery. I called the manager at the charter company and learned that the house battery (only two years old) had died.

I learned that the new battery cost $89 at the marine store. Then the charter company added 10 percent for overhead and charged for two hours of labor to install. In addition, the new battery did not have the same quality or capacity as the original. Given the location of the battery, and the ease of detaching and attaching cables for the terminals, I could not determine how it took two hours to accomplish.

It is important to be clear as to who will make decisions regarding equipment replacement and repair, and what charges may be added to the normal costs.

What are the responsibilities of the charterer?

These responsibilities should be addressed in detail in the charter contract. The following discussion addresses bareboat situations. Under the general principles of admiralty law the owner gives the charterer full use of the vessel and the charterer obtains exclusive possession. In fact, the charterer is sometimes referred to as the *owner pro hac vice*, that is, an owner for one particular occasion. The charterer is responsible for damage (or loss) to the boat or any equipment during the time period of the charter. The charterer must report accidents pursuant to state and federal laws. The charterer must comply with all customs and immigration laws and notify the charter company of problems or breakdowns.

What are some important provisions in a charter contract?

The charter contract is the agreement between the charter company (or the owner if no company is involved) and the charterer. The contract is extremely important. It should always be in writing. Charter contracts vary substantially; some are simple, one-page forms, while others are multiple pages of small print. Before chartering, the contract should be reviewed carefully and any questions answered. Many charter companies have copies of their contracts

The Daily Insurance Fund

The administration and distribution of a daily insurance fund collected from charterers can substantially benefit the owner or the charter company.

- The fund is collected by the charter company directly from the charterer and is not divided with the owner, as is the charter fee. The owner gets no portion of the daily insurance fund. The charter company advertises and provides the boat at a lower charter rate and collects the insurance fee on top of the charter rate.

- The charter company decides which damages are going to be covered by the fund and which ones are not. If the charter company decides that an item is normal wear and tear and not damage then the owner will end up paying for the repair without reimbursement. In some cases the difference between damage and normal wear and tear may be fairly faint. In others, there may be distinct clarity, but a stubborn owner or stubborn charter company may take an unreasonable position. In one such instance an owner friend of mine noted gel coat damage to his boat after a charter but was told by the company that the charterers claimed no responsibility and that the gel coat must have just chipped off.

- The charter company may decide to use the fund to pay for a repair and then direct its own employees to do the work and pay itself. Although this may be an efficient means of completing a repair, in effect, the charter company is using the insurance fund to help pay a portion of its operating overhead.

Avoiding disputes over the distribution of the daily insurance fund is a multi-faceted process.

- Read the contract language carefully. If possible, make sure it is very specific about when and how money from the fund will be paid to the owner.

- Try to avoid discretionary language or undefined terms such as "use our best efforts" or "normal charter usage."

- Talk to a manager at the charter company and get specific examples when funds have been used to repair damages. It may be helpful to talk to some other owners who deal with the company and get the benefit of their experiences.

- Ask the charter company who, specifically, will be making the repair.

- Ask the charter company who will actually purchase replacement equipment or inventory. For example, if binoculars disappear, will they be replaced with a new and comparable set? If a cushion is torn will it be replaced with something new and comparable or a cheap substitute from a second hand store?

- Discuss and specify who gets to choose the boatyard or repair person for damaged items. For example, if the dodger or bimini frame is bent, will someone from the charter company just bend it back good enough to work, or will a skilled technician replace the bent piece?

available online at their web sites. The following are some important clauses.

- **Charter fee, departure and return.** Most contracts recite at the beginning the charter fee, the deposit, and the dates and time for departure and return.

- **Delivery, substitution, cancellation, and acceptance.** The contract should specify that the vessel will be delivered to the charterer in full working order, fully equipped, and ready for use. Most contracts give the charter company the right to substitute a similar vessel due to circumstances beyond its control and a grace period (usually 24 hours) for late delivery. If delivery is not completed during the grace period then the charterer may cancel the contract. The charterer must inspect the vessel and make sure it is acceptable.

- **Insurance.** The contract should recite that the owner has insurance on the vessel, the amount of insurance on the vessel, and the amount of the deductible. Some contracts specifically state that the charterer is responsible for damages up to the deductible amount and for any damages in excess of the insurance amount.

- **Restrictions of use and navigation limits.** Most contracts will state specific restrictions on use of the vessel. Some examples are operator restrictions (persons named on the boating resume), pleasure use only (no transportation of merchandise or passengers), no nighttime motoring or sailing, no smoking below decks, no pets, and no illegal activities. The contract will also specify navigation limits and may either restrict use to specific areas (named bays, channels, and distances offshore) or name specific areas that may not be visited. The navigation limits might coincide with the owner's insurance or be more restrictive. Violation of the navigation limits will constitute a default under the contract. If damage occurs while in default, the charterer may be held solely responsible for all costs.

- **Breakdowns and accidents.** The charterer is responsible to report all breakdowns and accidents. Except for emergencies, charterers are usually specifically prohibited from making repairs or authorizing repairs. Most contracts give the charter company time (usually 24 hours or 48 hours) to make repairs, with a pro-rata return of the charter fee if the breakdown exceeds the specified time. Some contracts allow the charterer to cancel for breakdowns not caused by the charterer that exceed the specified repair time.

- **Trip expenses.** The charterer is solely responsible for all running expenses, such as fuel, water, food, port charges, etc.

- **Crew and skipper competence and experience.** The contract will usually contain a specific provision that the charterer certifies experience, seamanship, and competence necessary to operate the vessel and engage in the proposed voyage. The contract might also refer to the resume submitted prior to the charter. This means that the specific representations and statements in the resume are part of the contract.

- **Redelivery.** The contract will require the charterer to bring the vessel back to a specific place at a specific time in as good condition as at the beginning of the charter except for normal wear and tear. Most contracts require a fee if the charterer has not pumped the holding tank and filled the fuel tank and water tanks. There may also be a charge if the vessel requires excess cleaning. The charterer is responsible to pay for replacement or repair of any lost or damaged equipment or furnishings.

- **Governing law and attorneys fees.** The contract will specify what law applies in the event of a dispute and the state or country where the vessel is located. This means that the charterer may have to appear in court far from home if there is a dispute. Additionally, the losing party may have to pay attorneys fees to the winner.

Who has responsibility if a vessel breaks down or equipment fails?

These issues will be addressed in the charter contract. However, there must be careful attention paid to this question. If a bareboat charter contract does not specifically state that the charter company or owner has responsibility for a problem, the responsibility remains with the charterer. Additionally, the contract will usually allow a designated time limit for repairs during a trip, after which the charterer may be entitled to a pro-rata refund or a cancellation of the charter. There will not be a refund or cancellation if the charterer causes the breakdown or damage. However, the cause of a breakdown can be a topic of dispute. For example, if a charterer runs out of diesel fuel and needs mechanical assistance to restart the engine, the time lost is the charterer's problem. However, if the fuel gauge is defective or inaccurate, the charterer might contend the problem arose from that defect and not the charterer's conduct.

Who has responsibility if a charterer violates the law?

If a charterer breaks the law, he or she will be responsible for fines or criminal penalties due to the charterer's personal conduct. However, there are situations where a vessel can be seized or forfeited. If a charterer uses a boat for some prohibited activities (illegal drugs, illegal immigration, etc.) local, state, or federal law enforcement authorities may seize it and ownership of the vessel might be forfeited. In other words, the government might take the boat and keep it. It may be sold and the agency that took it gets to keep the money. To get the boat back the owner will have to prove that he had no knowledge of, or participation in, the illegal activity. Although such situations are rare, the legal fees alone in such a case can amount to tens of thousands of dollars. This is another very good reason why charterers must be carefully screened before the boat leaves the dock. Additionally, there should be a very clear statement in the front of the boat's operation manual, and in the charter contract, that illegal activities are strictly prohibited and that they will result in immediate termination of the charter and criminal charges. An owner who can show clear and reasonable efforts to prevent any illegal activity can more readily establish total lack of participation and knowledge of an illegal act and reverse a forfeiture of the vessel.

What is the best way for an owner to avoid problems arising from charters?

Most owners do not have the time or experience to charter a boat to someone else without assistance. Therefore, most owners use the services of a charter company. That is the first, and probably foremost, method to avoid or limit the many possible problems. However, just having a charter company manage the boat is not enough. Choose the charter company very carefully. Here are a few suggestions.

- Talk to local boat brokers about their favorite charter companies and find out why they prefer one to another.

- Visit the charter company office and ask about chartering one of the boats. If possible, take a look at the boats in the fleet and pay particular attention to the condition of each vessel.

- Get copies of the contract between the company and owners, as well as the charterer contract. Read them carefully. Then go online and visit other charter company web sites. Compare the contracts and see how the one you are considering measures up.

- Ask the charter company for references from other owners and charterers. *Check the references.*

- Ask the charter company whom it uses for repairs. If possible, get the names of local companies and technicians who do work on the yachts. Call those persons and find out what they think about the charter company. Does it pay its bills on time? Does it get boats fixed right the first time, or does it try and do things quick and cheap?

Putting a yacht in charter is a method to help pay the costs of ownership, but the wear and tear on the boat will be significantly greater than simple personal use. With that in mind, be careful choosing the charter company, and make sure it is well organized, respected in the area, and professional.

Boating Etiquette, Towing, and Salvage

A. Boating Etiquette

There are many unwritten rules of etiquette which make boating more enjoyable and relaxing, especially in crowded or busy areas. For most people, the purpose of owning a boat is to relax and enjoy some time away from daily routines and stresses. Following some simple rules of etiquette will contribute to that goal. Furthermore, some irritating conduct may not be illegal, but it could cause damage and resulting liability. The last thing you need is a lawsuit because you were rude, inconsiderate or negligent.

- **Do not always insist on the right of way.** When you are under way, adhere to the rules of the road but also be reasonable. Just because you have the right of way does not mean you must always force another vessel to yield or change course. Take a moment to consider the other skipper's intent and make adjustments accordingly. Remember also, when a large vessel's course or movement is restricted by location or conditions, it has the right of way.

- **Watch your wake.** Be aware of the effect your wake will have on other vessels particularly those that are smaller or not under power (such as kayaks). Modern power cruisers can generate large wakes, especially at slower speeds. *Skippers are legally responsible for any damage that their wake might cause.* Additionally, it is very rude to power by a smaller boat while trailing a large wake that will rock and roll the other craft abruptly and dangerously. When passing a smaller or slower boat, consider the possibility that your wake could cause someone to fall overboard or fall down inside the cabin. It never ceases to amaze how some large boat cruisers seem oblivious to the effect their wakes have on other boats or on the shoreline. Slow down or alter your course slightly to minimize the effect of your wake. Be particularly aware of the fact that a large wake in a constricted channel or harbor may cause damage to shorelines, docks, bulkheads, and boats.

- **Be cautious and predictable.** When you alter your course to avoid another vessel, do so carefully and predictably. Make your course change significant enough that the other skipper can easily determine your intent. Accident avoidance should always be the first consideration.

- **Never leave the helm unattended.** When you are on autopilot, do not leave the helm or lose your attention. An autopilot will not change course to avoid another vessel (or a log or a buoy). If you enter a waypoint that exactly corresponds to a buoy or marker and then let your autopilot steer to that point, it may very well run you into the buoy. Correspondingly, it is never safe to assume an approaching vessel will change course to prevent a collision. It is increasingly common to see cruising boats holding to a straight, unaltered course because the autopilot is engaged and no one is watching.

- **Never motor quickly through an anchorage.** Noise and wakes are unnecessary in an anchorage. Watch carefully for anchor lines and small craft such as kayaks and dinghies.

- **Never run your engine or genset after dark or before sunrise.** If you have noisy equipment (including wind generators) that must operate, find a spot to anchor away from other vessels.

- **When anchoring do not infringe on someone else's space.** Anchor next to vessels similar to yours with similar ground tackle. If you are a large powerboat with all chain tackle, move away from smaller boats that do not have chain and that will swing differently. If after anchoring you find that you are too close to another boat that was there first, it is your obligation to move to a safer spot.

- **Never leave halyards or lines loose to flap noisily in the wind.** Powerboats are not the only noisy vessels on the water. When the wind comes up, a slapping halyard can be a real irritation to other boaters. Use a line or elastic cord to secure those halyards.
- **Do not allow your dog to sit and bark.** If you cruise with a dog, do not leave him/her alone on the boat frightened and barking. It is not fair to your pet and it is not fair to other cruisers. Remember that your pet may be uncomfortable on the water and scared to be left alone. Constant barking out of fear is not uncommon. Additionally, in many enclosed anchorages an echo effect is common. Some dogs will sit and bark at their own echo for hours.

There are many other informal rules and procedures that do not need to be reiterated here. Suffice to say, boating etiquette is mostly common sense and common courtesy. Cruising is about relaxing, not competing.

This small towboat stands ready to assist recreational boaters with routine breakdowns. Such services are increasingly common in popular cruising areas.

B. Towing and Salvage

Hopefully, you will never be in a crisis situation and you will never need to know the difference between salvage and towing. However, here is a brief summary just in case you ever have an accident or go aground.

What is salvage?

Salvage involves saving a vessel or property from a serious peril. The vessel or property must be in a situation where it could not have been saved without assistance. All or part of the vessel or property must be saved and the act of salvage must be voluntary (no official duty or legal duty involved). A person who renders assistance in a salvage situation is called a salvor. A crewmember cannot qualify as a salvor, nor can passengers.

What is a salvage award?

A person who saves property at sea is entitled to a generous reward. The whole point is to provide compensation to encourage prompt assistance in emergencies. The amount of a salvage award may be much greater than the value of the labor involved. The compensation will be a percentage of the value of the ship, cargo, and freight. The following circumstances will be considered:

- The labor expended by the salvors in rendering the salvage service.
- The value of the property employed by the person rendering the service and the risks and dangers to that property.
- The risk incurred by the persons who render assistance.
- The value of the property saved.
- The degree of danger from which the property was rescued.

What is towing and how does it differ from salvage?

Towing is different from salvage in that a towing situation does not involve imminent hazard to the vessel or the environment. In other words, a vessel may be disabled due to engine trouble but not in danger of sinking. A vessel may be soft aground, but not in danger of serious damage. Towing services are often provided by commercial towboats available at most busy harbors.

What should you do prior to accepting assistance?

Prior to accepting assistance, a vessel owner or operator must clearly determine whether it is salvage or a tow. When dealing with a commercial operator offering assistance there should be a written contract that must be read carefully prior to signing. The point here is to try and avoid a salvage situation if it is not necessary. In most cases involving a tow, the towboat will charge an hourly fee for the services provided. The amount of the charge and any extra fees or costs should be specified in writing prior to accepting assistance.

Should you sign a salvage contract?

The answer is definitely *Yes!* However, the form of the contract is very important. Since you will be under a lot of stress at the time, you probably will not be emotionally ready to sit back and calmly read a contract offered to you, but it is very important that you try and understand the terms and conditions. One way to solve the problem is to keep a copy of a salvage contract on your boat, just in case. The Boat Owners Association of the United States (703-823-9550) has a simple contract form it recommends to its members, and you should consider keeping that form, or some other similar form in your *Keeping Your Boat Legal* binder. Chances are you will never need this form, but, like your lifejackets, you will want it if the time comes. The sample contract is reprinted in the Appendix.

SECTION 14

State Laws and Regulations

States have many different laws and regulations affecting boats and owners. Some states require registration and numbering in addition to federal documentation. Some states issue a title certificate similar to an automobile, with registration and/or licensing fees. Most states have some method of taxing vessels and will limit the amount of time a visiting vessel may be in the state without paying a fee. Other common subject areas of state regulation include operator age and education, water skiing, boat noise, overboard discharge, safety equipment, alcohol consumption, and personal flotation devices.

Every vessel owner and operator must know the applicable state laws. Contact your relevant state agencies for information. Additionally, the National Association of State Boating Law Administrators (NASBLA) publishes an overview of state laws. It can be downloaded free from the NASBLA web site.

Most states have handbooks that explain boating laws and requirements. These are usually available for free either by contacting the applicable state agency or by downloading the handbook from the Internet.

The following table lists the names of state agencies and their Internet addresses.

State Name	State Agency	Internet Address
Alabama	Conservation & Natural Resources	www.dcnr.state.al.us/boating
Alaska	Department of Natural Resources	www.alaskaboatingsafety.org
Arizona	Game & Fish Department	www.azgfd.com
Arkansas	Arkansas Game and Fish Commission	www.agfc.state.ar.us
California	California Resources Agency	www.dbw.ca.gov
Colorado	Department of Natural Resources	www.parks.state.co.us
Connecticut	Department of Environ. Protection	www.dep.state.ct.us/rec/boating/index.htm
Delaware	Division of Fish & Wildlife Enforcement	www.dnrec.state.de.us/dnrec2000/
Dist. Columbia	Harbor Patrol	www.mpdc.org
Florida	Fish & Wildlife Conservation Commission	www.myfwc.com/boating/
Georgia	Department of Natural Resources	www.georgiawildlife.dnr.state.ga.us/
Hawaii	Division of Boating and Ocean Recreation	www.hawaii.gov/dlnr/dbor/dbor.htm
Idaho	Department of Parks & Recreation	www.idahoparks.org/rec/boating.html
Illinois	Department of Natural Resources	www.dnr.state.il.us/admin/systems/boats.htm
Indiana	Department of Natural Resources	www.in.gov/dnr/boating/
Iowa	Department of Natural Resources	www.iowadnr.com/
Kansas	Department of Wildlife & Parks	www.kdwp.state.ks.us/boating/boating.html

State Name	State Agency	Internet Address
Kentucky	Department of Fish & Wildlife	www.fw.ky.gov/
Louisiana	Department of Wildlife & Fisheries	www.wlf.state.la.us
Maine	Department of Inland Fisheries & Wildlife	www.state.me.us/ifw/
Maryland	Department of Natural Resources	www.dnr.state.md.us/boating/
Massachusetts	Massachusetts Environmental Police	www.mass.gov/dfwele/dle/dle_toc.htm
Michigan	Department of Natural Resources	www.dnr.state.mi.us
Minnesota	Department of Natural Resources	www.dnr.state.mn.us/boating/index.html
Mississippi	Department of Wildlife, Fisheries & Parks	www.mdwfp.com
Missouri	Department of Public Safety	www.mswp.state.mo.us
Montana	Department of Fish, Wildlife & Parks	www.fwp.state.mt.us
Nebraska	Game & Parks Commission	www.ngpc.state.ne.us/boating
Nevada	Dept. of Conservation & Natural Resources	www.boatnevada.org/
New Hampshire	Department of Safety	www.nh.gov/safety/
New Jersey	Department of Law & Public Safety	www.nj.gov/lps/
New Mexico	New Mexico State Parks	www.emnrd.state.nm.us/nmparks/
New York	NY State Parks & Recreation	www.nysparks.com/boats
North Carolina	Environmental & Natural Resources	www.state.nc.us/wildlife
North Dakota	Game and Fish Department	www.state.nd.us/gnf/boating/
Ohio	Department of Natural Resources	www.dnr.state.oh.us/watercraft/
Oklahoma	Highway Patrol, Lake Patrol Section	www.dps.state.ok.us
Oregon	State Marine Board	www.boatoregon.com
Pennsylvania	Fish & Boat Commission	www.fish.state.pa.us
Rhode Island	Department Environmental Management	www.state.ri.us/dem
South Carolina	Department of Natural Resources	www.dnr.state.sc.us/etc/boating.html
South Dakota	Department of Game, Fish & Parks	www.sdgfp.info/Wildlife/Boating/
Tennessee	Parks & Wildlife Department	www.state.tn.us/twra/boatmain.html
Texas	Parks & Wildlife Department	www.tpwd.state.tx.us/boat/
Utah	Division of Parks & Recreation	www.parks.state.ut.us/boating/default.htm
Vermont	Vermont State Police, Marine Division	www.dps.state.vt.us/vtsp/
Virginia	Department of Game & Inland Fisheries	www.dgif.state.va.us/boating/
West Virginia	Division of Natural Resources, L.E. Section	www.wvdnr.gov/lenforce/boating.shtm
Washington	Parks & Recreation Commission	www.parks.wa.gov/boating.asp
Wisconsin	Department of Natural Resources	www.dnr.state.wi.us/OutdoorActivities.html
Wyoming	Game & Fish Department	www.gf.state.wy.us/fish/boating/index.asp

The following table is a summary of state law requirements.

	Min. Age Boat or PWC	Educ. Req'd?	Lic. Reg'd?	MSD Req'd	Y-Valve Lock?	Boat Title?	Alcohol (BUI) Law?
Alabama	12	no	yes	no	no	no	yes
Alaska	none	no	no	no	no	no	yes
Arizona	12	no	no	no	no	no	yes
Arkansas	12	yes	no	no	yes	no	yes
California	16	no	no	no	yes	yes	yes
Colorado	16	yes	no	no	yes	no	yes
Connecticut	12	yes	yes	yes	no	no	yes
Delaware	none	yes	no	no	yes	no	yes
Dist. Columbia	13	yes	no	yes	yes	yes	yes
Florida	14	yes	no	yes	yes	yes	yes
Georgia	12	yes	no	no	yes	no	yes
Hawaii	none	no	no	yes	yes	no	yes
Idaho	none	yes	no	no	yes	yes	yes
Illinois	10	yes	no	no	yes	yes	yes
Indiana	15	yes	yes	no	yes	yes	yes
Iowa	12	yes	yes	no	no	yes	yes
Kansas	12	yes	no	yes	yes	no	yes
Kentucky	12	yes	no	yes	yes	yes	yes
Louisiana	13	yes	no	yes	yes	no	yes
Maine	12	no	no	yes	no	no	yes
Maryland	none	yes	no	yes	yes	yes	yes
Massachusetts	12	yes	no	no	no	yes	yes
Michigan	12	yes	no	no	yes	yes	yes
Minnesota	12	yes	no	no	yes	yes	yes
Mississippi	12	yes	no	yes	no	no	yes
Missouri	14	yes	no	yes	n/a	yes	yes
Montana	13	no	no	yes	no	yes	yes
Nebraska	14	yes	no	yes	yes	yes	yes
Nevada	none	yes	no	yes	yes	yes	yes
New Hampshire	16	yes	no	yes	n/a	no	yes
New Jersey	16	yes	yes	no	yes	yes	yes
New Mexico	13	no	no	yes	yes	yes	yes
New York	10	yes	no	yes	yes	yes	yes
North Carolina	12	no	no	no	no	yes	yes
North Dakota	12	no	no	yes	yes	no	yes
Ohio	12	yes	no	no	no	yes	yes
Oklahoma	none	no	no	yes	yes	yes	yes

	Min. Age Boat or PWC	Educ. Req'd?	Lic. Reg'd?	MSD Req'd	Y-Valve Lock?	Boat Title?	Alcohol (BUI) Law?
Rhode Island	none	yes	no	yes	yes	yes	yes
South Carolina	none	yes	no	no	no	yes	yes
South Dakota	12	no	no	no	no	yes	yes
Tennessee	12	no	no	yes	yes	no	yes
Texas	13	yes	no	yes	yes	yes	yes
Utah	16	no	no	no	no	yes	yes
Vermont	12	yes	no	no	no	yes	yes
Virginia	14	no	no	no	no	yes	yes
West Virginia	15	yes	no	no	no	yes	yes
Washington	14	no	no	yes	yes	yes	yes
Wisconsin	10	yes	no	yes	yes	yes	yes
Wyoming	16	no	no	no	no	no	yes

The Appendix has instructions how to obtain specific information for your state.

REFERENCE GUIDE TO STATE BOATING LAWS

sixth edition

Ed Carter, Chairman
Law Enforcement Committee

Chris Moore and Ron Sarver, Editors

Produced under a grant from the Aquatic Resources (Wallop-Breaux) Trust Fund administered by the U.S. Coast Guard

The National Association of State Boating Law Administrators publishes an excellent guide to state boating laws.

SECTION 15

Equipment Information And Specifications To Keep Aboard

Although your vessel is a substantial investment, the equipment aboard also has significant value. This is particularly true for larger sailboats and powerboats that have modern electronic equipment such as radar, GPS, various radios, etc.

Why should I keep information equipment aboard my boat?

When you cross various borders, as well as when you re-enter the U.S., you may be asked to prove prior ownership of certain items that may have been purchased in another country. Additionally, if something breaks or if you want to buy a spare part you will need basic information regarding the item. Finally, if something is stolen it will help if you can specifically identify each thing that is missing.

The Appendix has a sample form you can use to record information regarding equipment on your boat.

The *Keeping Your Boat Legal* binder has space for you to store this information.

SECTION 16

Free Booklets, Pamphlets, and Information

The following publications are available free. Call or write the number or address. Most of the various state boating guides are also available online as PDF files. To get the PDF version just visit the web site and download the publication.

Alaska Boaters Handbook
Dept. of Natural Resources Public Information Center
550 W 7th Avenue, Suite 1260
Anchorage, AK 99501
www.alaskaboatingsafety.org

Arizona Boaters Guide
Arizona Game and Fish Department
2221 W Greenway Road
Phoenix, AZ 85023
www.azgfd.com

Boating Safely in Colorado
Colorado State Parks Department
Denver Administrative Office
1313 Sherman Street #618
Denver, CO 80203
www.parks.state.co.us

California Boating Law
Department of Boating and Waterways
2000 Evergreen Street, Suite 100
Sacramento, CA 95815-3888
www.dbw.ca.gov

Canada Safe Boating Guide: Fisheries and Oceans
Canadian Coast Guard
Ottawa, Ontario, K1A 0E6
Canada

Connecticut Boaters Guide: State of Connecticut
Department of Environmental Protection
79 Elm Street
Hartford, CT 06106-5127
www.dep.state.ct.us/rec/boating/index.htm

Fast Facts About Sewage Pollution.
Fast Facts About Oil and Fuel Pollution.
The Ocean Conservancy
1725 NW DeSales Street, Suite 600
Washington, DC 20036
www.oceanconservancy.org

Federal Requirements and Safety Tips
United States Coast Guard
Office of Boating Safety
202-267-1060
www.uscgboating.org

Guide For A Cleaner Boating Environment
Marine Environmental Education Foundation
1819 L Street, NW
Washington, DC 20003
www.meef.org

Handbook of Idaho Boating Laws
Idaho Parks and Recreation, Boating Program
P.O. Box 83720
Boise, ID 83720-0065
www.idahoparks.org/rec/boating.html

Handbook of Indiana Boating Laws
Indiana Department of Natural Resources
402 W Washington Street
Indianapolis, IN 46204
www.in.gov/dnr/boating/

Handbook of Iowa Boating Laws
Iowa Department of Natural Resources
502 E 9th Street
Des Moines, IA 50319-0034
www.iowadnr.com

Kentucky Sport Fishing and Boating Guide
Kentucky Department Of Fish and Wildlife Resources
1 Game Farm Road
Frankfort, KY 40601
www.fw.ky.gov

Know Before You Go
U.S. Customs Online Brochure
www.customs.gov

Maine Boating Laws
Department of Inland Fisheries & Wildlife
41 State House Station
284 State Street
Augusta, ME 04333-0041
www.state.me.us/ifw/

Michigan Boating Laws
Department of Natural Resources
Mason Building, Sixth Floor
P.O. Box 30028
Lansing, MI 48909
www.dnr.state.mi.us

Minnesota Boating Guide
DNR Information Center
500 Lafayette Road
St. Paul, MN 55155-4040
www.dnr.state.mn.us/boating/index.html

Nevada Boating Laws
Nevada Department of Wildlife
1100 Valley Road
Reno, NV 89512
www.boatnevada.org

New Hampshire Boating Guide
Division of Safety Services, Marine Patrol Bureau
31 Dock Road
Gilford, NH 03249-7627
www.nh.gov/safety/

New York State Boaters Guide
Office of Parks, Recreation and Historic Preservation
Bureau of Marine & Recreational Vehicles
Gov. Nelson A. Rockefeller Empire State Plaza
Agency Building 1, 11th Floor
Albany, NY 12238
www.nysparks.com/boats

North Carolina Vessel Operator's Guide
NC Wildlife Resources Commission, Division of
Engineering Services
1720 Mail Service Center
Raleigh, NC 27699-1720
www.state.nc.us/wildlife

Ohio Boat Operator's Guide: A Summary of Laws and
Rules
Send postal mailing address to: watercraft@dnr.state.
oh.us
1-877-4BOATER (Ohio only)
www.dnr.state.oh.us/watercraft/

Oklahoma Boating Laws
Oklahoma Highway Patrol Lake Patrol Section,
Department of Public Safety
P.O. Box 11415
Oklahoma City, OK 73136-0415
www.dps.state.ok.us

Pennsylvania Boating Handbook
Pennsylvania Fish and Boat Commission
P.O. Box 67000
Harrisburg, PA 17106-7000
www.fish.state.pa.us

Rhode Island Boating Guide
Department of Environmental Management
235 Promenade Street
Providence, RI 02908-5767
www.state.ri.us/dem

Reference Guide to State Boating Laws
National Association of State Boating Law
Administrators
1500 W Main Street, Suite 210
Lexington, KY 40511
859-225-9487
www.nasbla.org

Tennessee Boating
Tennessee Wildlife Resources Agency, Ellington
Agricultural Center
P.O. Box 41489
Nashville, TN 37204
www.state.tn.us/twra/boatmain.html

Texas Boating Guide
Texas Parks and Wildlife
4200 Smith School Road
Austin, TX 78744
www.tpwd.state.tx.us/boat/

Utah's Boating Laws and Rules
State of Utah Natural Resources
P.O. Box 145610
Salt Lake City, UT 84114
www.parks.state.ut.us/boating/default.htm

Vermont Boating Guide
Vermont State Police Marine Division
103 S Main Street
Waterbury, VT 05671-2101
www.dps.state.vt.us/vtsp/

Washington Boating Handbook
Washington State Parks and Recreation Commission
Boating Programs
P.O. Box 42650
Olympia, WA 98504-2650
www.parks.wa.gov/boating.asp

Water Watch
National Marine Manufacturers Association
200 E. Randolph Drive, #5100
Chicago, IL 60601-6528

Wisconsin Boating Regulations
Department of Natural Resources
P.O. Box 7921
Madison, WI 53707-7921
www.dnr.state.wi.us/OutdoorActivities.html

Appendix

This appendix includes additional information, sample forms, and reference material for your convenience. The appendix is organized and arranged with sections that correlate to the main body of the book for ease of use.

Section 1: Important Basic Vessel Information

Sample Form

Background Information

The sample form that follows is for recording important basic information about your boat. This form is included in the *Keeping Your Boat Legal* binder.

Vessel Information

Name: _____

Date of Purchase: _____

Vessel Home Port: _____

Documentation number: _____

State Registration number: _____

Owner Information

Name: _____

Mailing Address: _____

Street or P.O Box: _____

City: _____

State: _____ Zip: _____

Vessel Manufacture Information

Make: _____

Model: _____

Year Built: _____ Hull # _____

LOA: _____

Displacement: _____

Engine: _____

Tender/Dinghy Information

Make: _____ Model:_____

Engine make/model: _____

Horsepower: _____

Serial #: _____

State Registration #: _____

Section 2: Vessel, Ownership, Income Taxes, U.S. Coast Guard Documentation, and State Registration

A. Ownership

Every state has different laws and regulations governing the formation and operation of corporations and LLCs. However, many states have simplified the process of forming a corporation of LLC.

B. Income Tax Considerations

It is not necessary to read or memorize the tax code or all the IRS regulations. However, if you use your boat for business purposes, or if you have it in charter or other form of rental, it may help to be familiar with some of the regulations. Reprinted below are portions of IRS publications that deal with business expense deductions, rental properties (and the vacation home rules) and activities that are not for profit. We have only reprinted portions of the IRS Publications, available in 2004. Complete, updated IRS Publications can be downloaded for free from the IRS web site at www.irs.ustreas.gov.

IRS Publication 463 (Selected sections dealing with business expenses)

What Entertainment Expenses Are Deductible?

This section explains different types of entertainment expenses that you may be able to deduct. It also explains the directly-related test and the associated test.

Entertainment. Entertainment includes any activity generally considered to provide entertainment, amusement, or recreation. Examples include entertaining guests at nightclubs; at social, athletic, and sporting clubs; at theaters; at sporting events; on yachts; or on hunting, fishing, vacation, and similar trips.

Entertainment also may include meeting personal, living, or family needs of individuals, such as providing meals, a hotel suite, or a car to customers or their families.

A meal as a form of entertainment. Entertainment includes the cost of a meal you provide to a customer or client, whether the meal is a part of other entertainment or by itself. A meal expense includes the cost of food, beverages, taxes, and tips for the meal. To deduct an entertainment-related meal, you or your employee must be present when the food or beverages are provided.

 You cannot claim the cost of your meal both as an entertainment expense and as a travel expense.

 Meals sold in the normal course of your business are not considered entertainment.

Deduction may depend on your type of business. Your kind of business may determine if a particular activity is considered entertainment. For example, if you are a dress designer and have a fashion show to introduce your new designs to store buyers, the show generally is not considered entertainment. This is because fashion shows are typical in your business. But, if you are an appliance distributor and hold a fashion show for the spouses of your retailers, the show generally is considered entertainment.

Separating costs. If you have one expense that includes the costs of entertainment, and other services (such as lodging or transportation), you must allocate that expense between the cost of entertainment and the cost of other services. You must have a reasonable basis for making this allocation. For example, you must allocate your expenses if a hotel includes entertainment in its lounge on the same bill with your room charge.

Taking turns paying for meals or entertainment. If a group of business acquaintances take turns picking up each others' meal or entertainment checks without regard to whether any business purposes are served, no member of the group can deduct any part of the expense.

Lavish or extravagant expenses. You cannot deduct expenses for entertainment that are lavish or extravagant. An expense is not considered lavish or extravagant if it is reasonable considering the facts and circumstances. Expenses will not be disallowed just because they are more than a fixed dollar amount or take place at deluxe restaurants, hotels, nightclubs, or resorts.

Allocating between business and nonbusiness. If you entertain business and nonbusiness individuals at the same event, you must divide your entertainment expenses between business and nonbusiness. You can deduct only the business part. If you cannot establish the part of the expense for each person participating, allocate the expense to each participant on a pro rata basis.

Example. You entertain a group of individuals that includes yourself, three business prospects, and seven social guests. Only 4/11 of the expense qualifies as a business entertainment expense. You cannot deduct the expenses for the seven social guests because those costs are nonbusiness expenses.

Trade association meetings. You can deduct entertainment expenses that are directly related to and necessary for attending business meetings or conventions of certain exempt organizations if the expenses of your attendance are related to your active trade or business. These organizations include business leagues, chambers of commerce, real estate boards, trade associations, and professional associations.

Entertainment tickets. Generally, you cannot deduct more than the face value of an entertainment ticket, even if you paid a higher price. For example, you cannot deduct service fees you pay to ticket agencies or brokers or any amount over the face value of the tickets you pay to scalpers.

Exception for events that benefit charitable organizations. Different rules apply when the cost of a ticket to a sports event benefits a charitable organization. You can take into account the full cost you pay for the ticket, even if it is more than the face value, if all of the following conditions apply.

1. The event's main purpose is to benefit a qualified charitable organization.

2. The entire net proceeds go to the charity.

3. The event uses volunteers to perform substantially all the event's work.

 The 50% limit on entertainment does not apply to any expense for a package deal that includes a ticket to such a charitable sports event.

Example 1. You purchase tickets to a golf tournament organized by the local volunteer fire company. All net proceeds will be used to buy new fire equipment. The volunteers will run the tournament. You can deduct the entire cost of the tickets as a business expense if they otherwise qualify as an entertainment expense.

Example 2. You purchase tickets to a college football game through a ticket broker. After having a business discussion, you take a client to the game. Net proceeds from the game go to colleges that qualify as charitable organizations. However, since the colleges also pay individuals to perform services, such as coaching and recruiting, you can only use the face value of the tickets in determining your business deduction.

Skyboxes and other private luxury boxes. If you rent a skybox or other private luxury box for more than one event at the same sports arena, you generally cannot deduct more than the price of a nonluxury box seat ticket.

To determine whether a skybox has been rented for more than one event, count each game or other performance as one event. For example, renting a skybox for a series of playoff games is considered renting it for more than one event. All skyboxes you rent in the same arena, along with any rentals by related parties, are considered in making this determination.

Related parties include:

1. Family members (spouses, ancestors, and lineal descendants),

2. Parties who have made a reciprocal arrangement involving the sharing of skyboxes,

3. Related corporations,

4. A partnership and its principal partners, and

5. A corporation and a partnership with common ownership.

Example. You pay $3,000 to rent a 10-seat skybox at Team Stadium for three baseball games. The cost of regular nonluxury box seats at each event is $20 a seat. You can deduct (subject to the 50% limit) $600 ((10 seats × $20 each) × 3 events).

Table 2-1. **When Are Entertainment Expenses Deductible?**

General rule	You can deduct ordinary and necessary expenses to entertain a client, customer, or employee if the expenses meet the directly-related test or the associated test.
Definitions	• <u>Entertainment</u> includes any activity generally considered to provide entertainment, amusement, or recreation, and includes meals provided to a customer or client. • An <u>ordinary</u> expense is one that is common and accepted in your field of business, trade, or profession. • A <u>necessary</u> expense is one that is helpful and appropriate, although not necessarily required, for your business.
Tests to be met	Directly-related test • Entertainment took place in a clear business setting, or • Main purpose of entertainment was the active conduct of business, and You did engage in business with the person during the entertainment period, and You had more than a general expectation of getting income or some other specific business benefit. Associated test • Entertainment is associated with your trade or business, *and* • Entertainment directly precedes or follows a substantial business discussion.
Other rules	• You cannot deduct the cost of your meal as an entertainment expense if you are claiming the meal as a travel expense. • You cannot deduct expenses that are lavish or extravagant under the circumstances. • You generally can deduct only 50% of your unreimbursed entertainment expenses (see *50% Limit*).

Food and beverages in skybox seats. If expenses for food and beverages are separately stated, you can deduct these expenses in addition to the amounts allowable for the skybox, subject to the requirements and limits that apply. The amounts separately stated for food and beverages must be reasonable. You cannot inflate the charges for food and beverages to avoid the limited deduction for skybox rentals.

Directly-Related Test

To meet the directly-related test for entertainment expenses (including entertainment-related meals), you must show that:

1. The main purpose of the combined business and entertainment was the active conduct of business,

2. You did engage in business with the person during the entertainment period, and

3. You had more than a general expectation of getting income or some other specific business benefit at some future time.

Business is generally not considered to be the main purpose when business and entertainment are combined on hunting or fishing trips, or on yachts or other pleasure boats. Even if you show that business was the main purpose, you generally cannot deduct the expenses for the use of an entertainment facility. See *Entertainment facilities* earlier in this chapter.

You must consider all the facts, including the nature of the business transacted and the reasons for conducting business during the entertainment. It is not necessary to devote more time to business than to entertainment. However, if the business discussion is only incidental to the entertainment, the entertainment expenses do not meet the directly-related test.

 You do not have to show that business income or other business benefit actually resulted from each entertainment expense.

Clear business setting. If the entertainment takes place in a clear business setting and is for your business or work, the expenses are considered directly related to your business or work. The following situations are examples of entertainment in a clear business setting.

1. Entertainment in a hospitality room at a convention where business goodwill is created through the display or discussion of business products.

2. Entertainment that is mainly a price rebate on the sale of your products (such as a restaurant owner providing an occasional free meal to a loyal customer).

3. Entertainment of a clear business nature occurring under circumstances where there is no meaningful personal or social relationship between you and the persons entertained. An example is entertainment of business and civic leaders at the open-

ing of a new hotel or play when the purpose is to get business publicity rather than to create or maintain the goodwill of the persons entertained.

Expenses not considered directly related. Entertainment expenses generally are not considered directly related if you are not there or in situations where there are substantial distractions that generally prevent you from actively conducting business. The following are examples of situations where there are substantial distractions.

1. A meeting or discussion at a nightclub, theater, or sporting event.

2. A meeting or discussion during what is essentially a social gathering, such as a cocktail party.

3. A meeting with a group that includes persons who are not business associates at places such as cocktail lounges, country clubs, golf clubs, athletic clubs, or vacation resorts.

Associated Test

Even if your expenses do not meet the directly-related test, they may meet the associated test.

To meet the associated test for entertainment expenses (including entertainment-related meals), you must show that the entertainment is:

1. Associated with the active conduct of your trade or business, and

2. Directly before or after a substantial business discussion (defined later).

Associated with trade or business. Generally, an expense is associated with the active conduct of your trade or business if you can show that you had a clear business purpose for having the expense. The purpose may be to get new business or to encourage the continuation of an existing business relationship.

Substantial business discussion. Whether a business discussion is substantial depends on the facts of each case. A business discussion will not be considered substantial unless you can show that you actively engaged in the discussion, meeting, negotiation, or other business transaction to get income or some other specific business benefit.

The meeting does not have to be for any specified length of time, but you must show that the business discussion was substantial in relation to the meal or entertainment. It is not necessary that you devote more time to business than to entertainment. You do not have to discuss business during the meal or entertainment.

Meetings at conventions. You are considered to have a substantial business discussion if you attend meetings at a convention or similar event, or at a trade or business meeting sponsored and conducted by a business or professional organization. However, your reason for attending the convention or meeting must be to further your trade or business. The organization that sponsors the convention or meeting must schedule a program of business activities that is the main activity of the convention or meeting.

Figure A. Does the 50% Limit Apply to Your Expenses?
There are exceptions to these rules. See *Exceptions to the 50% Limit.*

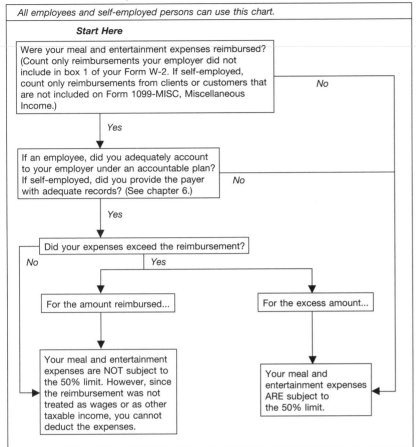

All employees and self-employed persons can use this chart.

Start Here

Were your meal and entertainment expenses reimbursed? (Count only reimbursements your employer did not include in box 1 of your Form W-2. If self-employed, count only reimbursements from clients or customers that are not included on Form 1099-MISC, Miscellaneous Income.)

No

Yes

If an employee, did you adequately account to your employer under an accountable plan? If self-employed, did you provide the payer with adequate records? (See chapter 6.)

No

Yes

Did your expenses exceed the reimbursement?

No   *Yes*

For the amount reimbursed...

For the excess amount...

Your meal and entertainment expenses are NOT subject to the 50% limit. However, since the reimbursement was not treated as wages or as other taxable income, you cannot deduct the expenses.

Your meal and entertainment expenses ARE subject to the 50% limit.

Directly before or after business discussion. If the entertainment is held on the same day as the business discussion, it is considered to be held directly before or after the business discussion.

If the entertainment and the business discussion are not held on the same day, you must consider the facts of each case to see if the associated test is met. Among the facts to consider are the place, date, and duration of the business discussion. If you or your business associates are from out of town, you must also consider the dates of arrival and departure, and the reasons the entertainment and the discussion did not take place on the same day.

Example. A group of business associates comes from out of town to your place of business to hold a substantial business discussion. If you entertain those business guests on the evening before the business discussion, or on the evening of the day following the business discussion, the entertainment generally is considered to be held directly before or after the discussion. The expense meets the associated test.

Expenses for spouses. You generally cannot deduct the cost of entertainment for your spouse or for the spouse of a customer. However, you can deduct these costs if you can show that you had a clear business purpose, rather than a personal or social purpose, for providing the entertainment.

Example. You entertain a customer. The cost is an ordinary and necessary business expense and is allowed under the entertainment rules. The customer's spouse joins you because it is impractical to entertain the customer without the spouse. You can deduct the cost of entertaining the customer's spouse. If your spouse joins the party because the customer's spouse is present, the cost of the entertainment for your spouse is also deductible.

50% Limit

In general, you can deduct only 50% of your business-related meal and entertainment expenses. (If you are subject to the Department of Transportation's "hours of service" limits, you can deduct a higher percentage. See *Individuals subject to "hours of service" limits,* later.)

The 50% limit applies to employees or their employers, and to self-employed persons (including independent contractors) or their clients, depending on whether the expenses are reimbursed.

Figure A summarizes the general rules explained in this section.

The 50% limit applies to business meals or entertainment expenses you have while:

1. Traveling away from home (whether eating alone or with others) on business,

2. Entertaining customers at your place of business, a restaurant, or other location, or

3. Attending a business convention or reception, business meeting, or business luncheon at a club.

Included expenses. Expenses subject to the 50% limit include:

1. Taxes and tips relating to a business meal or entertainment activity,

2. Cover charges for admission to a nightclub,

3. Rent paid for a room in which you hold a dinner or cocktail party, and

4. Amounts paid for parking at a sports arena.

However, the cost of transportation to and from a business meal or a business-related entertainment activity is not subject to the 50% limit.

Application of 50% limit. The 50% limit on meal and entertainment expenses applies if the expense is otherwise deductible and is not covered by one of the exceptions discussed later.

The 50% limit also applies to certain meal and entertainment expenses that are not business related. It applies to meal and entertainment expenses you have for the production of income, including rental or royalty income. It also applies to the cost of meals included in deductible educational expenses.

When to apply the 50% limit. You apply the 50% limit after determining the amount that would otherwise qualify for a deduction. You first have to determine the amount of meal and entertainment expenses that would be deductible under the other rules discussed in this publication.

Example 1. You spend $100 for a business-related meal. If $40 of that amount is not allowable because it is lavish and extravagant, the remaining $60 is subject to the 50% limit. Your deduction cannot be more than $30 (50% × $60).

Example 2. You purchase two tickets to a concert and give them to a client. You purchased the tickets through a ticket agent. You paid $150 for the two tickets, which had a face value of $60 each ($120 total). Your deduction cannot be more than $60 (50% × $120).

Exceptions to the 50% Limit

Generally, business-related meal and entertainment expenses are subject to the 50% limit. *Figure A* can help you determine if the 50% limit applies to you.

Expenses not subject to 50% limit. Your meal or entertainment expense is not subject to the 50% limit if the expense meets one of the following exceptions.

1 - Employee's reimbursed expenses. If you are an employee, you are not subject to the 50% limit on expenses for which your employer reimburses you under an accountable plan. Accountable plans are discussed in chapter 6.

2 - Self-employed. If you are self-employed, your deductible meal and entertainment expenses are not subject to the 50% limit if all three of the following requirements are met.

1. You have these expenses as an independent contractor.

2. Your customer or client reimburses you or gives you an allowance for these expenses in connection with services you perform.

3. You provide adequate records of these expenses to your customer or client. (See chapter 5.)

In this case, your client or customer is subject to the 50% limit on the expenses.

Example. You are a self-employed attorney who adequately accounts for meal and entertainment expenses to a client who reimburses you for these expenses. You are not subject to the directly-related or associated test, nor are you subject to the 50% limit. If the client can deduct the expenses, the client is subject to the 50% limit.

If you (the contractor) have expenses for meals and entertainment related to providing services for a client but do not adequately account for and seek reimbursement from the client for those expenses, you are subject to the directly-related or associated test and to the 50% limit.

3 - Advertising expenses. You are not subject to the 50% limit if you provide meals, entertainment, or recreational facilities to the general public as a means of advertising or promoting goodwill in the community. For example, neither the expense of sponsoring a television or radio show nor the expense of distributing free food and beverages to the general public is subject to the 50% limit.

4 - Sale of meals or entertainment. You are not subject to the 50% limit if you actually sell meals, entertainment, goods and services, or use of facilities to the public. For example, if you run a nightclub, your expense for the entertainment you furnish to your customers, such as a floor show, is not subject to the 50% limit.

5 - Charitable sports event. You are not subject to the 50% limit if you pay for a package deal that includes a ticket to a qualified charitable sports event. For the conditions the sports event must meet, see *Exception for events that benefit charitable organizations* under *Entertainment tickets,* earlier.

Individuals subject to "hours of service" limits. You can deduct a higher percentage of your meal expenses while traveling away from your tax home if the meals take place during or incident to any period subject to the Department of Transportation's "hours of service" limits. The percentage is 70% for 2004, and it gradually increases to 80% by the year 2008.

Individuals subject to the Department of Transportation's "hours of service" limits include the following persons.

1. Certain air transportation workers (such as pilots, crew, dispatchers, mechanics, and control tower operators) who are under Federal Aviation Administration regulations.

2. Interstate truck operators and bus drivers who are under Department of Transportation regulations.

3. Certain railroad employees (such as engineers, conductors, train crews, dispatchers, and control operations personnel) who are under Federal Railroad Administration regulations.

4. Certain merchant mariners who are under Coast Guard regulations.

IRS Publication 527 (Selected sections dealing with personal use of rental property)

Not Rented for Profit

If you do not rent your property to make a profit, you can deduct your rental expenses only up to the amount of your rental income. You cannot carry forward to the next year any rental expenses that are more than your rental income for the year. For more information about the rules for an activity not engaged in for profit, see chapter 1 of Publication 535.

Where to report. Report your not-for-profit rental income on Form 1040, line 21. You can include your mortgage interest (if you use the property as your main home or second home), real estate taxes, and casualty losses on the appropriate lines of Schedule A (Form 1040) if you itemize your deductions.

Claim your other rental expenses, subject to the rules explained in chapter 1 of Publication 535, as miscellaneous itemized deductions on line 22 of Schedule A (Form 1040). You can deduct these expenses only if they, together with certain other miscellaneous itemized deductions, total more than 2% of your adjusted gross income.

Postponing decision. If your rental income is more than your rental expenses for at least 3 years out of a period of 5 consecutive years, you are presumed to be renting your property to make a profit. You may choose to postpone the decision of whether the rental is for profit by filing Form 5213.

See Publication 535 for more information.

Renting Part of Property

If you rent part of your property, you must divide certain expenses between the part of the property used for rental purposes and the part of the property used for personal purposes, as though you actually had two separate pieces of property.

You can deduct the expenses related to the part of the property used for rental purposes, such as home mortgage interest and real estate taxes, as rental expenses on Schedule E (Form 1040). You can also deduct as a rental expense a part of other expenses that normally are non-deductible personal expenses, such as expenses for electricity, or painting the outside of your house.

You can deduct the expenses for the part of the property used for personal purposes, subject to certain limitations, only if you itemize your deductions on Schedule A (Form 1040).

You cannot deduct any part of the cost of the first phone line even if your tenants have unlimited use of it.

You do not have to divide the expenses that belong only to the rental part of your property. For example, if you paint a room that you rent, or if you pay premiums for liability insurance in connection with renting a room in your home, your entire cost is a rental expense. If you install a second phone line strictly for your tenant's use, all of the cost of the second line is deductible as a rental expense. You can deduct depreciation, discussed later, on the part of the property used for rental purposes as well as on the furniture and equipment you use for rental purposes.

How to divide expenses. If an expense is for both rental use and personal use, such as mortgage interest or heat for the entire house, you must divide the expense between rental use and personal use. You can use any reasonable method for dividing the expense. It may be reasonable to divide the cost of some items (for example, water) based on the number of people using them. However, the two most common methods for dividing an expense are one based on the number of rooms in your home and one based on the square footage of your home.

Example. You rent a room in your house. The room is 12 × 15 feet, or 180 square feet. Your entire house has 1,800 square feet of floor space. You can deduct as a rental expense 10% of any expense that must be divided between rental use and personal use. If your heating bill for the year for the entire house was $600, $60 ($600 × 10%) is a rental expense. The balance,

If a dwelling unit is used for personal purposes on a day it is rented at a fair rental price, do not count that day as a day of rental use in applying (2) above. Instead, count it as a day of personal use in applying both (1) and (2) above. This rule does not apply when dividing expenses between rental and personal use.

Fair rental price. A fair rental price for your property generally is the amount of rent that a person who is not related to you would be willing to pay. The rent you charge is not a fair rental price if it is substantially less than the rents charged for other properties that are similar to your property.

Ask yourself the following questions when comparing another property with yours.

- Is it used for the same purpose?
- Is it approximately the same size?
- Is it in approximately the same condition?
- Does it have similar furnishings?
- Is it in a similar location?

If any of the answers are no, the properties probably are not similar.

Examples

The following examples show how to determine whether you used your rental property as a home.

Example 1. You converted the basement of your home into an apartment with a bedroom, a bathroom, and a small kitchen. You rented the basement apartment at a fair rental price to college students during the regular school year. You rented to them on a 9-month lease (273 days). You figured 10% of the total days rented to others at a fair rental price is 27 days.

During June (30 days), your brothers stayed with you and lived in the basement apartment rent free.

Your basement apartment was used as a home because you used it for personal purposes for 30 days. Rent-free use by your brothers is considered personal use. Your personal use (30 days) is more than the greater of 14 days or 10% of the total days it was rented (27 days).

Example 2. You rented the guest bedroom in your home at a fair rental price during the local college's homecoming, commencement, and football weekends (a total of 27 days). Your sister-in-law stayed in the room, rent free, for the last 3 weeks (21 days) in July. You figured 10% of the total days rented to others at a fair rental price is 3 days.

The room was used as a home because you used it for personal purposes for 21 days. That is more than the greater of 14 days or 10% of the 27 days it was rented (3 days).

Example 3. You own a condominium apartment in a resort area. You rented it at a fair rental price for a total of 170 days during the year. For 12 of these days, the tenant was not able to use the apartment and allowed you to use it even though you did not refund any of the rent. Your family actually used the apartment for 10 of those days. Therefore, the apartment is treated as having been rented for 160 (170 − 10) days.

You figure 10% of the total days rented to others at a fair rental price is 16 days. Your family also used the apartment for 7 other days during the year.

You used the apartment as a home because you used it for personal purposes for 17 days. That is more than the greater of 14 days or 10% of the 160 days it was rented (16 days).

Use as Main Home Before or After Renting

For purposes of determining whether a dwelling unit was used as a home, you may not have to count days you used the property as your main home before or after renting it or offering it for rent as days of personal use. Do not count them as days of personal use if:

- You rented or tried to rent the property for 12 or more consecutive months.
- You rented or tried to rent the property for a period of less than 12 consecutive months and the period ended because you sold or exchanged the property.

This special rule does not apply when dividing expenses between rental and personal use.

Example 1. On February 28, you moved out of the house you had lived in for 6 years because you accepted a job in another town. You rent your house at a fair rental price from March 15 of that year to May 14 of the next year (14 months). On the following June 1, you move back into your old house.

The days you used the house as your main home from January 1 to February 28 and from June 1 to December 31 of the next year are not counted as days of personal use.

Example 2. On January 31, you moved out of the condominium where you had lived for 3 years. You offered it for rent at a fair rental price beginning on February 1. You were unable to rent it until April. On September 15, you sold the condominium.

The days you used the condominium as your main home from January 1 to January 31 are not counted as days of personal use when determining whether you used it as a home.

Figuring Days of Personal Use

A day of personal use of a dwelling unit is any day that the unit is used by any of the following persons.

1. You or any other person who has an interest in it, unless you rent it to another owner as his or her main home under a shared equity financing agreement (defined later). However, see *Use as Main Home Before or After Renting* under *Dwelling Unit Used As Home,* earlier.

2. A member of your family or a member of the family of any other person who has an interest in it, unless the family member uses the dwelling unit as his or her main home and pays a fair rental price. Family includes only brothers and sisters, half-brothers and half-sisters, spouses, an-

cestors (parents, grandparents, etc.) and lineal descendants (children, grandchildren, etc.).

3. Anyone under an arrangement that lets you use some other dwelling unit.

4. Anyone at less than a fair rental price.

Main home. If the other person or member of the family in (1) or (2) above has more than one home, his or her main home is ordinarily the one he or she lived in most of the time.

Shared equity financing agreement. This is an agreement under which two or more persons acquire undivided interests for more than 50 years in an entire dwelling unit, including the land, and one or more of the co-owners is entitled to occupy the unit as his or her main home upon payment of rent to the other co-owner or owners.

Donation of use of property. You use a dwelling unit for personal purposes if:

- You donate the use of the unit to a charitable organization,
- The organization sells the use of the unit at a fund-raising event, and
- The "purchaser" uses the unit.

Examples

The following examples show how to determine days of personal use.

Example 1. You and your neighbor are co-owners of a condominium at the beach. You rent the unit to vacationers whenever possible. The unit is not used as a main home by anyone. Your neighbor uses the unit for 2 weeks every year.

Because your neighbor has an interest in the unit, both of you are considered to have used the unit for personal purposes during those 2 weeks.

Example 2. You and your neighbors are co-owners of a house under a shared equity financing agreement. Your neighbors live in the house and pay you a fair rental price.

Even though your neighbors have an interest in the house, the days your neighbors live there are not counted as days of personal use by you. This is because your neighbors rent the house as their main home under a shared equity financing agreement.

Example 3. You own a rental property that you rent to your son. Your son has no interest in this property. He uses it as his main home. He pays you a fair rental price for the property.

Your son's use of the property is not personal use by you because your son is using it as his main home, he has no interest in the property, and he is paying you a fair rental price.

Example 4. You rent your beach house to Rosa. Rosa rents her house in the mountains to you. You each pay a fair rental price.

You are using your house for personal purposes on the days that Rosa uses it because your house is used by Rosa under an arrangement that allows you to use her house.

Example 5. You rent an apartment to your mother at less than a fair rental price. You are using the apartment for personal purposes on the days that your mother rents it because you rent it for less than a fair rental price.

Days Used for Repairs and Maintenance

Any day that you spend working substantially full time repairing and maintaining your property is not counted as a day of personal use. Do not count such a day as a day of personal use even if family members use the property for recreational purposes on the same day.

Example. You own a cabin in the mountains that you rent during the summer. You spend 3 days at the cabin each May, working full time to repair anything that was damaged over the winter and get the cabin ready for the summer. You also spend 3 days each September, working full time to repair any damage done by renters and getting the cabin ready for the winter.

These 6 days do not count as days of personal use even if your family uses the cabin while you are repairing it.

How To Divide Expenses

If you use a dwelling unit for both rental and personal purposes, divide your expenses between the rental use and the personal use based on the number of days used for each purpose. You can deduct expenses for the rental use of the unit under the rules explained in *How To Figure Rental Income and Deductions*, later.

When dividing your expenses, follow these rules.

1. Any day that the unit is rented at a fair rental price is a day of rental use even if you used the unit for personal purposes that day. This rule does not apply when determining whether you used the unit as a home.

2. Any day that the unit is available for rent but not actually rented is not a day of rental use.

Example. Your beach cottage was available for rent from June 1 through August 31 (92 days). Your family uses the cottage during the last 2 weeks in May (14 days). You were unable to find a renter for the first week in August (7 days). The person who rented the cottage for July allowed you to use it over a weekend (2 days) without any reduction in or refund of rent. The cottage was not used at all before May 17 or after August 31.

You figure the part of the cottage expenses to treat as rental expenses by using the following steps.

1. The cottage was used for rental a total of 85 days (92 − 7). The days it was available for rent but not rented (7 days) are not days of rental use. The July weekend (2 days) you used it is rental use because you received a fair rental price for the weekend.

2. You used the cottage for personal purposes for 14 days (the last 2 weeks in May).

3. The total use of the cottage was 99 days (14 days personal use + 85 days rental use).

4. Your rental expenses are 85/99 (86%) of the cottage expenses.

When determining whether you used the cottage as a home, the July weekend (2 days) you used it is personal use even though you received a fair rental price for the weekend. Therefore, you had 16 days of personal use and 83 days of rental use for this purpose. Because you used the cottage for personal purposes more than 14 days and more than 10% of the days of rental use (8 days), you used it as a home. If you have a net loss, you may not be able to deduct all of the rental expenses. See *Property Used as a Home* in the following discussion.

How To Figure Rental Income and Deductions

How you figure your rental income and deductions depends on whether you used the dwelling unit as a home (see *Dwelling Unit Used as Home,* earlier) and, if you used it as a home, how many days the property was rented at a fair rental price.

Property Not Used as a Home

If you do not use a dwelling unit as a home, report all the rental income and deduct all the rental expenses. See *How To Report Rental Income and Expenses*, later.

Your deductible rental expenses can be more than your gross rental income. However, see *Limits on Rental Losses*, later.

Property Used as a Home

If you use a dwelling unit as a home during the year, how you figure your rental income and deductions depends on how many days the unit was rented at a fair rental price.

Rented fewer than 15 days. If you use a dwelling unit as a home and you rent it fewer than 15 days during the year, do not include any rental income in your income. Also, you cannot deduct any expenses as rental expenses.

Rented 15 days or more. If you use a dwelling unit as a home and rent it 15 days or more during the year, you include all your rental income in your income. See *How To Report Rental Income and Expenses*, later. If you had a net profit from the rental property for the year (that is, if your rental income is more than the total of your rental expenses, including depreciation), deduct all of your rental expenses. However, if you had a net loss, your deduction for certain rental expenses is limited.

Limit on deductions. If your rental expenses are more than your rental income, you cannot use the excess expenses to offset income from other sources. The excess can be carried forward to the next year and treated as rental expenses for the same property. Any expenses carried forward to next year will be subject to any limits that apply next year. You can deduct the expenses carried over to a year only up to the amount of your rental income for that year, even if you do not use the property as your home for that year.

IRS Publication 535 (Selected sections)

Not-for-Profit Activities

If you do not carry on your business or investment activity to make a profit, you cannot use a loss from the activity to offset other income. Activities you do as a hobby, or mainly for sport or recreation, are often not entered into for profit.

The limit on not-for-profit losses applies to individuals, partnerships, estates, trusts, and S corporations. It does not apply to corporations other than S corporations.

In determining whether you are carrying on an activity for profit, several factors are taken into account. No one factor alone is decisive. Among the factors to consider are whether:

1. You carry on the activity in a businesslike manner,

2. The time and effort you put into the activity indicate you intend to make it profitable,

3. You depend on the income for your livelihood,

4. Your losses are due to circumstances beyond your control (or are normal in the start-up phase of your type of business),

5. You change your methods of operation in an attempt to improve profitability,

6. You, or your advisors, have the knowledge needed to carry on the activity as a successful business,

7. You were successful in making a profit in similar activities in the past,

8. The activity makes a profit in some years, and

9. You can expect to make a future profit from the appreciation of the assets used in the activity.

Presumption of profit. An activity is presumed carried on for profit if it produced a profit in at least 3 of the last 5 tax years, including the current year. Activities that consist primarily of breeding, training, showing, or racing horses are presumed carried on for profit if they produced a profit in at least 2 of the last 7 tax years, including the current year. The activity must be substantially the same for each year within this period. You have a profit when the gross income from an activity exceeds the deductions.

If a taxpayer dies before the end of the 5-year (or 7-year) period, the "test" period ends on the date of the taxpayer's death.

If your business or investment activity passes this 3- (or 2-) years-of-profit test, IRS will presume it is carried on for profit. This means the limits discussed here will not apply. You can take all your business deductions from the activity, even for the years that you have a loss. You can rely on this presumption unless the IRS later shows it to be invalid.

Using the presumption later. If you are starting an activity and do not have 3 (or 2) years showing a profit, you may want to elect to have the presumption made after you have the 5 (or 7) years of experience allowed by the test.

You can choose to do this by filing Form 5213. Filing this form postpones any determination that your activity is not carried on for profit until 5 (or 7) years have passed since you started the activity.

The benefit gained by making this choice is that the IRS will not immediately question whether your activity is engaged in for profit. Accordingly, it will not restrict your deductions. Rather, you will gain time to earn a profit in the required number of years. If you show 3 (or 2) years of profit at the end of this period, your deductions are not limited under these rules. If you do not have 3 (or 2) years of profit, the limit can be applied retroactively to any year with a loss in the 5-year (or 7-year) period.

Filing Form 5213 automatically extends the period of limitations on any year in the 5-year (or 7-year) period to 2 years after the due date of the return for the last year of the period. The period is extended only for deductions of the activity and any related deductions that might be affected.

 You must file Form 5213 within 3 years after the due date of your return for the year in which you first carried on the activity, or, if earlier, within 60 days after receiving written notice from the Internal Revenue Service proposing to disallow deductions attributable to the activity.

Limit on Deductions

If your activity is not carried on for profit, take deductions in the following order and only to the extent stated in the three categories. If you are an individual, these deductions may be taken only if you itemize. These deductions may be taken on Schedule A (Form 1040).

Category 1. Deductions you can take for personal as well as for business activities are allowed in full. For individuals, all nonbusiness deductions, such as those for home mortgage interest, taxes, and casualty losses, belong in this category. Deduct them on the appropriate lines of Schedule A (Form 1040). You can deduct a casualty loss on property you own for personal use only to the extent it is more than $100 and exceeds 10% of your adjusted gross income. See Publication 547 for more information on casualty losses. For the limits that apply to mortgage interest, see Publication 936.

Category 2. Deductions that do not result in an adjustment to the basis of property are allowed next, but only to the extent your gross income from the activity is more than your deductions under the first category. Most business deductions, such as those for advertising, insurance premiums, interest, utilities, and wages, belong in this category.

Category 3. Business deductions that decrease the basis of property are allowed last, but only to the extent the gross income from the activity exceeds the deductions you take under the first two categories. Deductions for depreciation, amortization, and the part of a casualty loss an individual could not deduct in category (1) belong in this category. Where more than one asset is involved, allocate depreciation and these other deductions proportionally.

 Individuals must claim the amounts in categories (2) and (3) as miscellaneous deductions on Schedule A (Form 1040). They are subject to the 2%-of-adjusted-gross-income limit. See Publication 529 for information on this limit.

Example. Ida is engaged in a not-for-profit activity. The income and expenses of the activity are as follows.

Gross income		$3,200
Subtract:		
Real estate taxes	$700	
Home mortgage interest	900	
Insurance	400	
Utilities	700	
Maintenance	200	
Depreciation on an automobile	600	
Depreciation on a machine . .	200	3,700
Loss		**$(500)**

Ida must limit her deductions to $3,200, the gross income she earned from the activity. The limit is reached in category (3), as follows.

Limit on deduction		$3,200
Category 1: Taxes and interest	$1,600	
Category 2: Insurance, utilities, and maintenance . . .	1,300	2,900
Available for Category 3		**$ 300**

The $800 of depreciation is allocated between the automobile and machine as follows.

$$\frac{\$600}{\$800} \times \$300 = \$225 \quad \text{depreciation for the automobile}$$

$$\frac{\$200}{\$800} \times \$300 = \$75 \quad \text{depreciation for the machine}$$

The basis of each asset is reduced accordingly.

The $1,600 for category (1) is deductible in full on the appropriate lines for taxes and interest on Schedule A (Form 1040). Ida deducts the remaining $1,600 ($1,300 for category (2) and $300 for category (3)) as other miscellaneous deductions on Schedule A (Form 1040) subject to the 2%-of-adjusted-gross-income limit.

Partnerships and S corporations. If a partnership or S corporation carries on a not-for-profit activity, these limits apply at the partnership or S corporation level. They are reflected in the individual shareholder's or partner's distributive shares.

More than one activity. If you have several undertakings, each may be a separate activity or several undertakings may be combined. The following are the most significant facts and circumstances in making this determination.

- The degree of organizational and economic interrelationship of various undertakings.

- The business purpose that is (or might be) served by carrying on the various undertakings separately or together in a business or investment setting.

- The similarity of the undertakings.

The IRS will generally accept your characterization if it is supported by facts and circumstances.

 If you are carrying on two or more different activities, keep the deductions and income from each one separate. Figure separately whether each is a

C. Vessel Documentation

The U.S. Coast Guard has regulations that implement the U.S. statutes for vessel documentation. Some of those regulations are reprinted below. Printed copies of all the Documentation Regulations can be obtained by contacting:

Superintendent of Documents

P.O. Box 371954
Pittsburgh, PA 15250-7954
202-512-1800
www.bookstore.gpo.gov/index.html

More information and free forms are available at the National Vessel Documentation (www.uscg.mil/hq/g-m/vdoc/nvdc.htm).

All of Title 46 CFR, part 67, Vessel Documentation Regulations are in text and PDF formats on the Internet at www.access.gpo.gov/nara/cfr/waisidx_01/46cfr67_01.html.

TITLE 46–SHIPPING CHAPTER I

COAST GUARD, DEPARTMENT OF TRANSPORTATION

PART 67: DOCUMENTATION OF VESSELS

Sec. 67.5 Vessels eligible for documentation.

Any vessel of at least five net tons wholly owned by a citizen or citizens of the United States is eligible for documentation under this part. This includes, but is not limited to, vessels used exclusively for recreational purposes and vessels used in foreign trade.

Sec. 67.7 Vessels requiring documentation.

Any vessel of at least five net tons which engages in the fisheries on the navigable waters of the United States or in the Exclusive Economic Zone, Great Lakes trade, or coastwise trade, unless exempt under Sec. 67.9(c), must have a Certificate of documentation bearing a valid endorsement appropriate for the activity in which engaged.

Sec. 67.9 Vessels excluded from or exempt from documentation.

(a) A vessel of less than five net tons is excluded from documentation.

(b) A vessel which does not operate on the navigable waters of the United States or in the fisheries in the Exclusive Economic Zone is exempt from the requirement to have a Certificate of Documentation.

(c) A non-self-propelled vessel, qualified to engage in the coastwise trade is exempt from the requirement to be documented with a coastwise endorsement when engaged in coastwise trade:

(1) Within a harbor;

(2) On the rivers or lakes (except the Great Lakes) of the United States; or

(3) On the internal waters or canals of any State.

(d) A vessel exempt from the requirement to be documented by paragraph (b) or (c) of this section may be documented at the option of the owner, provided it meets the other requirements of this part.

Sec. 67.11 Restriction on transfer of an interest in documented vessels to foreign persons; foreign registry or operation.

(a) Unless approved by the Maritime Administration--

(1) A documented vessel or a vessel last documented under the laws of the United States may not be placed under foreign registry or operated under the authority of a foreign country.

(2) A documented vessel or a vessel last documented under the laws of the United States owned by a citizen of the United States as defined in section 2 of the Shipping Act, 1916 (46 U.S.C. app. 802), may not be sold, mortgaged, leased, chartered, delivered, or otherwise transferred to any person who is not a citizen of the United States as defined in section 2 of the Shipping Act, 1916 (46 U.S.C. app. 802).

(b) The restrictions in paragraph (a)(2) of this section do not apply to a vessel that has been operated only as:

(1) A fishing vessel, fish processing vessel, or fish tender vessel as defined in 46 U.S.C. 2101;

(2) A recreational vessel; or

(3) Both.

Note: For purposes of carrying out its responsibilities under the provisions of this part only, the Coast Guard will deem a vessel which has been documented exclusively with a fishery or recreational endorsement or both from the time it was first documented, or for a period of not less than one year prior to foreign transfer or registry, to qualify for the exemption granted in paragraph (b) of this section.

(c) The exemption in paragraph (b) of this section does not relieve all vessels from meeting the fishery endorsement requirements of this part. If your vessel is less than 100 feet in length and is a fishing vessel, fish processing vessel, or fish tender vessel as defined in 46 U.S.C. 2101, you must meet the fishery endorsement requirements set out in this part. Each vessel 100 feet and greater in length applying for a fishery endorsement is regulated by the Maritime Administration requirements found in 46 CFR part 356.

Sec. 67.15 Form of document--all endorsements.

(a) The form of document is a Certificate of Documentation, form CG-1270.

(b) Upon application in accordance with subpart K of this part and determination of qualification by the Director, National Vessel Documentation Center, a Certificate of Documentation may be issued with a registry, coastwise, Great Lakes, fishery, or recreational endorsement.

(c) A Certificate of Documentation may bear simultaneous endorsements for recreation and more than one trade, including operation under 46 CFR part 68.

Note: Where a vessel possesses a Certificate of Documentation bearing more than one endorsement, the actual use of the vessel determines the endorsement under which it is operating.

Sec. 67.23 Recreational endorsement.

(a) A recreational endorsement entitles a vessel to pleasure use only.

(b) Any vessel eligible for documentation under Sec. 67.5 is eligible for a recreational endorsement.

Note: A vessel having a Certificate of Documentation endorsed only for recreation may be bareboat chartered only for recreational use. Guidance on the elements of a valid bareboat charter should be obtained through private legal counsel.

Sec. 67.30 Requirement for citizen owner.

Certificates of Documentation may be issued under this part only to vessels which are wholly owned by United States citizens. Pursuant to extraordinary legislation at 46 U.S.C. app. 883-1 (Bowater Amendment) and 46 U.S.C. 12106(d) (Oil Pollution Act of 1990), Certificates of Documentation with limited endorsements may be issued in accordance with part 68 of this chapter to vessels owned by certain persons who are not citizens as defined in this part.

Sec. 67.43 Evidence of citizenship.

When received by the Coast Guard, a properly completed original Application for Initial Issue, Exchange, or Replacement of Certificate of Documentation; or redocumentation (form CG-1258) establishes a rebuttable presumption that the applicant is a United States citizen.

Sec. 67.117 Vessel name designation.

(a) The owner of a vessel must designate a name for the vessel on the Application for Initial Issue, Exchange, or Replacement of Certificate of Documentation; or Re-documentation (form CG-1258) submitted to the Director, National Vessel Documentation Center:

(1) Upon application for initial documentation of the vessel; or

(2) When the owner elects to change the name of the vessel.

(b) The name designated:

(1) Must be composed of letters of the Latin alphabet or Arabic or Roman numerals;

(2) May not be identical, actually or phonetically, to any word or words used to solicit assistance at sea; and

(3) May not contain nor be phonetically identical to obscene, indecent, or profane language, or to racial or ethnic epithets.

(c) The name of a documented vessel may not be changed without the prior approval of the Director, National Vessel Documentation Center.

(d) Until such time as the owner of a vessel elects to change the name of a vessel, the provisions of paragraph (b) of this section do not apply to vessels validly documented before January 1, 1994.

Sec. 67.119 Hailing port designation.

(a) Upon application for any Certificate of Documentation in accordance with subpart K of this part, the owner of a vessel must designate a hailing port to be marked upon the vessel.

(b) The hailing port must be a place in the United States included in the U.S. Department of Commerce's Federal Information Processing Standards Publication 55DC.

(c) The hailing port must include the State, territory, or possession in which it is located.

(d) The Director, National Vessel Documentation Center has final authority to settle disputes as to the propriety of the hailing port designated.

(e) Until such time as the vessel owner elects to designate a new hailing port, the provisions of paragraph (c) of this section do not apply to vessels which were issued a Certificate of Documentation before July 1, 1982.

Sec. 67.120 General requirement.

No Certificate of Documentation issued under this part will be deemed valid for operation of the vessel until the vessel is marked in accordance with this subpart.

Sec. 67.121 Official number marking requirement.

The official number of the vessel, preceded by the abbreviation ``NO.'' must be marked in block-type Arabic numerals not less than three inches in height on some clearly visible interior structural part of the hull. The number must be permanently affixed to the vessel so that alteration, removal, or replacement would be obvious. If the official number is on a separate plate, the plate must be fastened in such a manner that its removal would normally cause some scarring of or damage to the surrounding hull area.

Sec. 67.123 Name and hailing port marking requirements.

(a) For vessels other than those covered in paragraphs (b) and (c) of this section, the name of the vessel must be marked on some clearly visible exterior part of the port and starboard bow and the stern of the vessel. The hailing port of the vessel must be marked on some clearly visible exterior part of the stern of the vessel.

(b) Vessels with square bow. For vessels having a square bow, the name of the vessel must be marked on some clearly visible exterior part of the bow in a manner to avoid obliteration. The name and hailing port must be marked on some clearly visible exterior part of the stern.

(c) Recreational vessels. For vessels documented exclusively for recreation, the name and hailing port must be marked together on some clearly visible exterior part of the hull.

(d) The markings required by paragraphs (a), (b), and (c) of this section, which may be made by the use of any means and materials which result in durable markings, must be made in clearly legible letters of the Latin alphabet or Arabic or Roman numerals not less than four inches in height.

D. State Registration

The registration rules for boats vary from state to state. Below are two organizations that are excellent resources for this subject. The National Association of State Boating Law Administrators publishes an excellent guide that discusses state requirements and has tables and charts as guides to information for all 50 states. The BoatU.S. Foundation for Boating Safety and Clean Water also publishes a guide that contains directions for finding your state regulations. To obtain more information, contact:

National Association of State Boating Law Administrators
1500 Leestown Road, Suite 330
Lexington, KY 40505
www.nasbla.org

BoatU.S. Foundation for Boating Safety and Clean Water
880 South Pickett Street
Alexandria, VA 22304
703-823-9550
www.boatus.com

Section 3: Recreational Boat Insurance

It is also very important that you understand your insurance obligations in the event of an accident. Policies vary and the language is not always the same. However, it is not enough to simply have insurance, you must have a way to contact your insurer in the event of an accident. That is why it is so important to keep the contact information on your boat. The following form is an example of the information you need. This form is also included in the *Keeping Your Boat Legal* binder.

Sample Form

Insurance Contact Information

Insurance Agency Name: _____

Address: _____

Phone: _____ Fax: _____

Agent Name: _____

Insurance Company Name: (from Policy Declarations Page). _____

Policy Number: _____

Information phone number for company: _____

Claims Department phone number: _____

IN THE EVENT OF A LOSS

A. Immediately upon a loss, you must:

1. Take all necessary steps to protect the boat and its equipment from further loss. We will pay the reasonable costs you incur in preventing further damage ("Sue and Labor Expense") if the loss is covered under Coverage A of this policy. This Sue and Labor Coverage is in addition to those coverages noted under Coverage A. We do not cover your labor or personal expense nor any amount in excess of the agreed value.

2. Give us immediate notification of the loss and its circumstances.

B. Following a loss you must:

1. Give us the opportunity to inspect the damaged boat or equipment before it is repaired or discarded.

2. Submit a statement describing the loss and any records needed to verify the loss, its amount, and you interest in any property damaged or lost.

3. Assume no obligation, admit no liability and incur no expense for which you or the Company may be liable without our written permission, other than reasonable expenses incurred to protect the property from further damage.

4. Immediately notify us about and forward to us any legal papers or notices received in connection with the loss.

5. Co-operate with us in the investigation, defense, or settlement of any loss, and agree to be examined under oath if we so request.

6. Allow examination by physicians of our choice, when pertinent to the loss.

7. Help us to obtain copies of medical reports and records.

8. Give us a final notarized statement (Proof of Loss), if requested.

In the text we mentioned that various organizations may offer insurance as a benefit of membership. Not all organizations do so and policies of insurance vary as do the costs. Nevertheless, it is worthwhile to look into the opportunities. Even though many organizations do not offer any insurance opportunities they may be able to assist you with finding a company or policy that suits your needs. The end of this Appendix has a list of some of the many boating organizations and agencies.

Bluewater Cruising Association
8886 Hudson Street
Vancouver, BC V6P 4N2
www.bluewatercruising.org

BoatU.S.
880 S Pickett Street
Alexandria, VA 22304
800-395-2628
www.boatus.com

National Boat Owners Association
4404 N Tamiami Trail
Sarasota, FL 34234-3864
800-248-3512
www.nboat.com

National Safe Boating Council
P.O. Box 509
Bristow, VA 20136
703-361-4294
www.safeboatingcouncil.org

Seven Seas Cruising Association
2501 E Commercial Boulevard, Suite 201
Fort Lauderdale, FL 33308
www.ssca.org

United States Power Squadrons
1504 Blue Ridge Road
P.O. Box 30423
Raleigh, NC 27622
www.usps.org

Canadian Yachting Association
Portsmouth Olympic Harbour
53 Yonge Street
Kingston, ON K7M 6G4
www.bcsailing.bc.ca

World Cruising Club
120 High Street
Cowes, UK PO31 7AX
www.worldcruising.com

Section 4: Personal Information to Keep on Your Boat

The following form can be used to record the personal information you should keep aboard while you are cruising.

You should have aboard the following minimum information, especially if you will be cruising in the vicinity of an international border or will cross an international border. When you re-enter the United States you will be asked for this information.

Sample Form

Personal Information

Vessel owner/operator full name: _____

Owner/Operator birth date: _____

Street address: _____

City _____ State _____ Zip _____

Home phone number: _____

Spouse's full name and birth date: _____

Children(s)' full names and birth dates:

_____

_____

_____

_____

_____

Guests full names, ages, places of birth, nationality and address:

_____

_____

_____

_____

_____

_____

_____

Section 5: Vessel Survey and Repair Information

There are several Surveyor organizations.

The National Association of Marine Surveyors
P.O. Box 9306
Chesapeake, VA 23321-9306
800-822-6267
www.nams-cms.org

The Society of Accredited Marine Surveyors
4605 Cardinal Boulevard
Jacksonville, FL 32210
800-344-9077
www.marinesurvey.org

The Association of Certified Marine Surveyors
209/241 Nooseneck Hill Road
West Greenwich, RI 02817
www.acms-usa.com

The following is a summary of information contained in a typical Condition and Value Survey for a sailboat.

Vessel Name, Type & Model, HIN/Official Number, Year Built.

Hailing Port, Particulars (LOA, LWL, Beam, Draft, Displacement), Hull Colors, Designer, Builder, Approximate values ((Fair Market & Replacement Cost).

Particular information regarding the construction, materials, deck layout, hatches, etc.

Power or Auxiliary Power. (Engine type, size, make & model, drivetrain, etc.)

Mast and Rigging. (Mast type, Standing rigging, halyards, blocks & tackle, etc.)

Sails & Canvas. (mainsail, genoa, spinnaker, etc.) Winches. Steering gear. Compass.

Tankage. Fuel, Water, Waste.

Bilge pumps and water pumps. (number and types of each pump).

Navigation lighting, interior lighting, safety equipment, fire extinguishers, ground tackle, navigation electronics, batteries and electrical service, galley equipment and layout, dinghy or tender.

Additional gear and equipments such as ship's papers, toilet type, vents and ventilation, cushions, spare parts, docklines and fenders, charts and navigation tools, etc.

The survey may also have recommendations for navigational limits. (inshore, coastal cruising, offshore, etc.)

The survey will then recite the surveyor's comments. Such things as the method of inspection, condition of the bottom, the topsides, the gelcoat or paint, winches, rigging, sails, interior fit and finish, etc.

The final section will recite the Surveyor's Remarks and Recommendations. In this section you will find specific comments for items that need maintenance, repair, or replacement.

The survey will conclude with the seal and signature of the Surveyor.

Sample Form
Survey Information:

Date	Name	Address	Phone #

Sample Form

Service and Repair Information:

Date of haul out: _____ Boat Yard: _____

Address: _____ Phone # _____

Manager's name: _____

Summary of work: _____

_____

_____

_____

Date of haul out: _____ Boat Yard: _____

Address: _____ Phone # _____

Manager's name: _____

Summary of work: _____

_____

_____

_____

Date of haul out: _____ Boat Yard: _____

Address: _____ Phone # _____

Manager's name: _____

Summary of work: _____

_____

_____

_____

Date of haul out: _____ Boat Yard: _____

Address: _____ Phone # _____

Manager's name: _____

Summary of work: _____

Sample Form

Service and Repair Technician Information:

Engine mechanic's name, address, & phone #: _____
_____
_____
_____

Rigger's name, address, & phone #: _____
_____
_____
_____

Marine electrician's name, address, & phone #: _____
_____
_____
_____

Sanitation repair name, address, & phone #: _____
_____
_____
_____

Canvas Repair name, address, & phone #: _____
_____
_____

Other: _____
_____
_____
_____
_____
_____
_____

Section 6: Vessel Navigation Rules and Requirements

Rules of the Road

The following index of the Navigation Rules and Regulations is reprinted to show the scope of subjects covered by the Rules. The navigation rules can be downloaded from the internet (www.navcen.uscg.gov/mwv/navrules/download.htm).

NAVIGATION RULES AND REGULATIONS – International and Inland

The International Rules and the Inland Rules are divided by lines of demarcation called the COLREGS Demarcation Lines. These lines are shown on nautical charts and are published in 33 CFR 80 and in the Navigation Rules manual (pp 176 – 198).

Notice to Mariners. Local Notices to Mariners can be viewed on the Internet at www.navcen.uscg.gov/lnm/default.htm.

Vessel Traffic Separation. Detailed information about Vessel Traffic Separation areas is available on the internet at www.navcen.uscg.gov/mwv/vts/vts_home.htm.Navigation Rules 9 & 10 apply in narrow channels and in VTS areas.

INLAND: Steering and Sailing Rules.

RULE 9, Narrow Channels

(a) (i) A vessel proceeding along the course of a narrow channel or fairway shall keep as near to the outer limit of the channel or fairway which lies on her starboard side as is safe and practicable.

(ii) Notwithstanding paragraph (a)(i) and Rule 14(a), a power-driven vessel operating in narrow channels or fairways on the Great Lakes, Western Rivers, or waters specified by the Secretary, and proceeding downbound with a following current shall have the right-of-way over an upbound vessel, shall propose the manner and place of passage, and shall initiate the maneuvering signals prescribed by Rule 34(a)(i), as appropriate. The vessel proceeding upbound against the current shall hold as necessary to permit safe passing.

(b) A vessel of less than 20 meters in length or a sailing vessel shall not impede the passage of a vessel that can safely navigate only within a narrow channel or fairway.

(c) A vessel engaged in fishing shall not impede the passage of any other vessel navigating within a narrow channel or fairway.

(d) A vessel shall not cross a narrow channel or fairway if such crossing impedes the passage of a vessel which can safely navigate only within that channel or fairway. The latter vessel shall use the danger signal prescribed in Rule 34(d) if in doubt as to the intention of the crossing vessel.

(e) (i) In a narrow channel or fairway when overtaking, the power-driven vessel intending to overtake another power-driven vessel shall indicate her intention by sounding the appropriate signal prescribed in Rule 34(c) and take steps to permit safe passing. The power-driven vessel being overtaken, if in agreement, shall sound the same signal and may, if specifically agreed to take steps to permit safe passing. If in doubt she shall sound the danger signal prescribed in Rule 34(d).

(ii) This Rule does not relieve the overtaking vessel of her obligation under Rule 13.

(f) A vessel nearing a bend or an area of a narrow channel or fairway where other vessels may be obscured by an intervening obstruction shall navigate with particular alertness and caution and shall sound the appropriate signal prescribed in Rule 34(e).

(g) Every vessel shall, if the circumstances of the case admit, avoid anchoring in a narrow channel.

RULE 10 Traffic Separation Schemes

(a) This Rule applies to traffic separation schemes and does not relieve any vessel of her obligation under any other Rule.

(b) A vessel using a traffic separation scheme shall:

(i) proceed in the appropriate traffic lane in the general direction of traffic flow for that lane;

(ii) so far as practicable keep clear of a traffic separation line or separation zone;

(iii) normally join or leave a traffic lane at the termination of the lane, but when joining or leaving from either side shall do so at as small an angle to the general direction of traffic flow as practicable.

(c) A vessel shall, so far as practicable, avoid crossing traffic lanes but if obliged to do so shall cross on a heading as nearly as practicable at right angles to the general direction of traffic flow.

(d) (i) A vessel shall not use an inshore traffic zone when she can safely use the appropriate traffic lane within the adjacent traffic separation scheme. However, vessels of less than 20 meters in length, sailing vessels, and vessels engaged in fishing may use the inshore traffic zone.

(ii) Notwithstanding subparagraph (d) (i), a vessel may use an inshore traffic zone when en route to or from a port, offshore installation or structure, pilot station, or any other place situated within the inshore traffic zone, or to avoid immediate danger.

(e) A vessel other than a crossing vessel or a vessel joining or leaving a lane shall not normally enter a separation zone or cross a separation line except:

(i) in cases of emergency to avoid immediate danger; or

(ii) to engage in fishing within a separation zone.

(f) A vessel navigating in areas near the terminations of traffic separation schemes shall do so with particular caution.

(g) A vessel shall so far as practicable avoid anchoring in a traffic separation scheme or in areas near its terminations.

(h) A vessel not using a traffic separation scheme shall avoid it by as wide a margin as is practicable.

(i) A vessel engaged in fishing shall not impede the passage of any vessel following a traffic lane.

(j) A vessel of less than 20 meters in length or a sailing vessel shall not impede the safe passage of a power-driven vessel following a traffic lane.

A simple instruction manual for small vessels in VTS areas can be downloaded for free from www.uscg.mil/d13/units/vts/boaters.html. The following is re-printed from that manual.

Advice from the Captains

Know and follow the "Rules of the Road." Be aware that specific rules apply in the vicinity of large ships when operating in narrow channels (Rule 9) and traffic separation schemes (Rule 10). Stay clear of tankers and freighters. They have limited ability to maneuver and risk grounding or colliding with other boats if forced to take evasive action.

Take early positive action to avoid close quarters situations. Avoid crossing ahead of, or operating close to a deep draft ship. Never cross between a tug and their tow, be wary of submerged apparatus trailing barges.

Develop a situational awareness of all the vessels in your vicinity. Be aware that strict adherence to the Rules of the Road may not be practical in crowded situations (Rule 2).

Maintain a proper lookout. Autopilot does not relieve you of the responsibility of keeping a good lookout. Take early and substantial action to indicate your intention to change course and speed. Show a side.

Use your navigation lights between sunset and sunrise, and in restricted visibility.

A list of VHF channels for VTS areas is published on the internet at www.navcen.uscg.gov/mwv/vts/vts_table.htm. The regulations are also published on the internet. The current regulations (taken from the Coast Guard VTS web site) are as follows:

New York[3]: *"New York Traffic"*[4]
Channel Designation: Ch 11 (156.550 MHz) Ch 14 (156.700 MHz)
Monitoring Area: The navigable waters of the Lower New York Harbor bounded on the east by a line drawn from Norton Point to Breezy Point; on the south by a line connecting the entrance buoys at the Ambrose Channel, Swash Channel and Sandy Hook Channel to Sandy Hook Point; and on the southeast including the waters of the Sandy Hook Bay south to a line drawn at latitude 40° 25' N.; then west into waters of the Raritan Bay to the Raritan River Rail Road Bridge; and then north including the waters of the Arthur Kill and Newark Bay to the Lehigh Valley Draw Bridge at latitude 40° 41.95' N.; and then east including the waters of the Kill Van Kull and Upper New York Bay north to a line drawn east-west from the Holland Tunnel Ventilator Shaft at latitude 40° 43.7' N.; longitude 74° 01.6' W. in the Hudson River; and continuing east including the waters of the East River to the Throgs Neck Bridge, excluding the Harlem River.

Channel Designation: Ch 12 (156.600 MHz)
Monitoring Area: Each vessel at anchor within the above areas.

Houston[3]: *"Houston Traffic"*
(The navigable waters north of 29° N., west of 94° 20'W., south of 29° 49' N., and east of 95° 20' W.:)
Channel Designation: Ch 11 (156.550 MHz)
Monitoring Area: The navigable waters north of a line extending due west from the southern most end of Exxon Dock #1 (29° 43.37' N., 95° 01.27' W.).
Channel Designation: Ch 12 (156.600 MHz)
Monitoring Area: The navigable waters north of a line extending due west from the southern most end of Exxon Dock #1 (29° 43.37' N., 95° 01.27' W.).

Berwick Bay: *"Berwick Traffic"*
Channel Designation: Ch 11 (156.550 MHz)
Monitoring Area: The navigable waters south of 29° 45' N., west of 91° 10' W., north of 29° 37' N., and east of 91° 18' W.

St. Mary's River: *"Soo Control"*
Channel Designation: Ch 11 (156.550 MHz) Ch 12 (156.600 MHz)
Monitoring Area: The navigable waters of the St. Marys River between 45° 57' N. (De Tour Reef Light) and 46° 38.7' N. (Ile Parisienne Light), except the St. Marys Falls Canal and those navigable waters east of a line from 46° 04.16'N. and 46° 01.57' N. (La Pointe to Sims Point in Patagannissing Bay and Worsley Bay).

San Francisco[3]:
"San Francisco Offshore Vessel Movement Reporting Service"
Channel Designation: Ch 12 (156.600 MHz)
Monitoring Area: The waters within a 38 nautical mile radius of Mount Tamalpais (37° 55.8' N., 122° 34.6' W.) excluding the San Francisco Offshore Precautionary Area.
"San Francisco Traffic"
Channel Designation: Ch 14 (156.700 MHz)
Monitoring Area: The waters of the San Francisco Offshore Precautionary Area eastward to San Francisco Bay including its tributaries extending to the ports of Stockton, Sacramento and Redwood Clty.

Puget Sound[5]:
"Seattle Traffic"[6]
Channel Designation: Ch 14 (156.700 MHz)
Monitoring Area: The navigable waters of Puget Sound, Hood Canal and adjacent waters south of a line connecting Marrowstone Point and Lagoon Point in

Admiralty inlet and south of a line drawn due east from the southernmost tip of Possession Point on Whidbey Island to the shoreline.

Channel Designation: Ch 5A (156.250 MHz)

Monitoring Area: The navigable waters of the Strait of Juan de Fuca east of 124° 40' W. excluding the waters in the central portion of the Strait of Juan de Fuca north and east of Race Rocks; the navigable waters of the Strait of Georgia east of 122° 52' W.; the San Juan Island Archipelago, Rosario Strait, Bellingham Bay; Admiralty Inlet north of a line connecting Marrowstone Point and Lagoon Point and all waters east of Whidbey Island north of a line drawn due east from the southernmost tip of Possession Point on Whidbey Island to the shoreline.

"Tofino Traffic"[7]
Channel Designation: Ch 74 (156.725 MHz)
Monitoring Area: The waters west of 124° 40' W. within 50 nautical miles of the coast of Vancouver Island including the waters north of 48° N., and east of 127° W.

"Vancouver Traffic"
Channel Designation: Ch 11 (156.550 MHz)
Monitoring Area: The navigable waters of the Strait of Georgia west of 122° 52' W., the navigable waters of the central Strait of Juan de Fuca north and east of Race Rocks, Including the Gulf Island Archipelago, Boundary Pass and Haro Strait.

Prince William Sound: *"Valdez Traffic"*
Channel Designation: Ch 13 (156.650 MHz)
Monitoring Area: The navigable waters south of 61° 05' N., east of 147° 20' W., north of 60° N., and west of 146° 30' W.; and, all navigable waters in Port Valdez.

Louisville: *"Louisville Traffic"*
Channel Designation: Ch 13 (156.650 MHz)
Monitoring Area: The navigable waters of the Ohio River between McAlpine Locks (Mile 606) and Twelve Mile Island (Mile 593), only when the McAlpine upper pool gauge is at approximately 13.0 feet or above.

Notes:
VTS regulations are denoted in 33 CFR Part 161. All geographic coordinates (latitude and longitude) are expressed in North American Datum of 1983 (NAD 83).

In the event of a communication failure either by the vessel traffic center or the vessel or radio congestion on a designated VTS frequency, communications may be established on an alternate VTS frequency. The bridge-to-bridge navigational frequency 156.650 MHz (Channel 13), is monitored in each VTS area; and it may be used as an alternate frequency, however, only to the extent that doing so provides a level of safety beyond that provided by other means.

Designated frequency monitoring is required within U.S. navigable waters. In areas which are outside the U.S. navigable waters, designated frequency monitoring is voluntary. However, prospective VTS Users are encouraged to monitor the designated frequency.

VMRS participants shall make their initial report (Sail Plan) to New York Traffic on Channel 11 (156.550 MHz). All other reports, including the Final Report, shall be made on Channel 14 (156.700 MHz.). VMRS and other VTS Users shall monitor Channel 14 (156.700 MHz) while transiting the VTS area. New York Traffic may direct a vessel to monitor and report on either primary frequency depending on traffic density, weather conditions, or other safety factors. This does not require a vessel to monitor both primary frequencies.

A Cooperative Vessel Traffic Service was established by the United States and Canada within adjoining waters. The appropriate vessel traffic center administers the rules issued by both nations; however, it will enforce only its own set of rules within its jurisdiction.

Seattle Traffic may direct a vessel to monitor the other primary VTS frequency 156.250 MHz or 156.700 MHz (Channel 5A or 14) depending on traffic density, weather conditions, or other safety factors, rather than strictly adhering to the designated frequency required for each monitoring area as defined above. This does not require a vessel to monitor both primary frequencies.

A portion of Tofino Sector's monitoring area extends beyond the defined CVTS area. Designated frequency monitoring is voluntary in these portions outside of VTS jurisdiction, however, prospective VTS Users are encouraged to monitor the designated frequency.

The bridge-to-bridge navigational frequency, 156.650 MHz (Channel 13), is used in these VTSs because the level of radiotelephone transmissions does not warrant a designated VTS frequency. The listening watch required by 26.05 of this chapter is not limited to the monitoring area.

Penalties and Fines. Violations of the Navigation Rules are serious. The following are reprints of penalty and enforcement provisions from the United States Code.

PENALTY PROVISIONS

VIOLATIONS OF INTERNATIONAL NAVIGATION RULES AND REGULATIONS (33 U.S.C. 1608)

(a) Whoever operates a vessel, subject to the provisions of this Chapter, in violation of this chapter or of any regulation promulgated pursuant to section 1607 of this title, shall be liable to a civil penalty of not more than $5,000 for each such violation.

(b) Every vessel subject to the provisions of this Chapter, other than a public vessel being used for noncommercial purposes, which is operated in violation of this Chapter or of any regulation promulgated pursuant to section 1607 of this title, shall be liable to a civil penalty of not more than $5,000 for each such violation, for which penalty the vessel may be seized and proceeded against in the district court of the United States of any district within which such vessel may be found.

(c) The Secretary of the department in which the Coast Guard is operating may assess any civil penalty authorized by this section. No such penalty may be assessed until the person charged, or the owner of the vessel charged, as appropriate, shall have been given notice of the violation involved and an opportunity for a hearing. For good cause shown, the Secretary may remit, mitigate, or compromise any penalty assessed. Upon the failure of the person charged, or the owner of the vessel charged, to pay an assessed penalty, as it may have been mitigated or compromised, the Secretary may request the Attorney General to commence an action in the appropriate district court of the United States for collection of the penalty as assessed, without regard to the amount involved, together with such other relief as may be appropriate.

VIOLATIONS OF INLAND NAVIGATION RULES AND REGULATIONS (33 U.S.C. 2072)

(a) Whoever operates a vessel in violation of this Chapter, or of any regulation issued thereunder, or in violation of a certificate of alternative compliance issued under Rule 1 is liable to a civil penalty of not more than $5,000 for each violation.

(b) Every vessel subject to this Chapter, other than a public vessel being used for noncommercial pur-

poses, that is operated in violation of this Chapter, or of any regulation issued thereunder, or in violation of a certificate of alternative compliance issued under Rule 1 is liable to a civil penalty of not more than $5,000 for each violation, for which penalty the vessel may be seized and proceeded against in the district court of the United States of any district within which the vessel may be found.

(c) The Secretary may assess any civil penalty authorized by this section. No such penalty may be assessed until the person charged, or the owner of the vessel charged, as appropriate, shall have been given notice of the violation involved and an opportunity for a hearing. For good cause shown, the Secretary may remit, mitigate, or compromise any penalty assessed. Upon the failure of the person charged, or the owner of the vessel charged, to pay an assessed penalty, as it may have been mitigated or compromised, the Secretary may request the Attorney General to commence an action in the appropriate district court of the United States for collection of the penalty as assessed, without regard to the amount involved, together with such other relief as may be appropriate.

(d) (1) If any owner, operator, or individual in charge of a vessel is liable for a penalty under this section, or if reasonable cause exists to believe that the owner, operator, or individual in charge may be subject to a penalty under this section, the Secretary of the Treasury, upon the request of the Secretary, shall with respect to such vessel refuse or revoke any clearance required by section 4197 of the Revised Statutes of the United States (46 App. U.S.C. 91).

(2) Clearance or a permit refused or revoked under this subsection may be granted upon filing of a bond or other surety satisfactory to the Secretary.

CHAPTER 23—OPERATIONS OF VESSELS GENERALLY

[Enacted on August 26,1983]

Sec.

§2301 Application

This chapter applies to a vessel operated on waters subject to the jurisdiction of the United States and, for a vessel owned in the United States, on the high seas.

§ 2302 Penalties for negligent operations

(a) A person operating a vessel in a negligent manner that endangers the life, limb, or property of a person is liable to the United States Government for a civil penalty of not more than $1,000.

(b) A person operating a vessel in a grossly negligent manner that endangers the life, limb, or property of a person shall be fined not more than $5,000, imprisoned for not more than one year, or both.

(c) An individual who is under the influence of alcohol, or a dangerous drug in violation of a law of the United States when operating a vessel, as determined under standards prescribed by the Secretary by regulation—

(1) is liable to the United States Government for a civil penalty of not more than $1,000 for a first violation and not more than $5,000 for a subsequent violation; or

(2) commits a class A misdemeanor.

(d) For a penalty imposed under this section, the vessel also is liable in rem unless the vessel is—

(1) owned by a State or a political subdivision of a State;

(2) operated principally for governmental purposes; and

(3) identified clearly as a vessel of that State or subdivision.

§ 2303 Duties related to marine casualty assistance and information

(a) The master or individual in charge of a vessel involved in a marine casualty shall—

(1) render necessary assistance to each individual affected to save that affected individual from danger caused by the marine casualty, so far as the master or individual in charge can do so without serious danger to the master's or individual's vessel or to individuals aboard; and

(2) give the master's or individual's name and address and identification of the vessel to the master or individual in charge of any other vessel involved in the casualty, to any individual injured, and to the owner of any property damaged.

(b) An individual violating this section or a regulation prescribed under this section shall be fined not more than $1,000 or imprisoned for not more than 2 years. The vessel also is liable in rem to the United States Government for the fine.

(c) An individual complying with subsection (a) of this section or gratuitously and in good faith rendering assistance at the scene of a marine casualty without objection by an individual assisted, is not liable for damages as a result of rendering assistance or for an act or omission in providing or arranging salvage, towage, medical treatment, or other assistance when the individual acts as an ordinary, reasonable, and prudent individual would have acted under the circumstances.

§2304 Duty to provide assistance at sea

(a) A master or individual in charge of a vessel shall render assistance to any individual found at sea in danger of being lost, so far as the master or individual in charge can do so without serious danger to the master's or individual's vessel or individuals aboard.

(b) A master or individual violating this section shall be fined not more than $1,000, imprisoned for not more than 2 years, or both.

§ 2305 Injunctions

(a) The district courts of the United States have jurisdiction to enjoin the negligent operation of vessels prohibited by this chapter on the petition of the Attorney General for the United States Government.

(b) When practicable, the Secretary shall—

(1) give notice to any person against whom an action for injunctive relief is considered under this section an opportunity to present that person's views; and

(2) except for a knowing and willful violation, give the person a reasonable opportunity to achieve compliance.

(c) The failure to give notice and opportunity to present views under subsection (b) of this section does not preclude the court from granting appropriate relief.

§ 2306 Vessel Reporting Requirements

(a) (1) An owner, charterer, managing operator, or agent of a vessel of the United States, having reason to believe (because of lack of communication with or nonappearance of a vessel or any other incident) that the vessel may have been lost or imperiled, immediately shall—

(A) notify the Coast Guard; and

(B) use all available means to determine the status of the vessel.

(2) When more than 48 hours have passed since the owner, charterer, managing operator, or agent of a vessel required to report to the United States Flag Merchant Vessel Location Filing System under authority of section 212 (A) of the Merchant Marine Act, 1936 (46 App. U.S.C. 1122a), has received a communication from the vessel, the owner, charterer, managing operator, or agent immediately shall—

(A) notify the Coast Guard; and

(B) use all available means to determine the status of the vessel.

(3) A person notifying the Coast Guard under paragraph (1) or (2) of this subsection shall provide the name and identification number of the vessel, the names of individuals aboard, and other information that may be requested by the Coast Guard. The owner, charterer, managing operator, or agent also shall submit written confirmation to the Coast Guard 24 hours after nonwritten notification to the Coast Guard under those paragraphs.

(4) An owner, charterer, managing operator, or agent violating this subsection is liable to the United States Government for a civil penalty of not more than $5,000 for each day during which the violation occurs.

(b) (1) The master of a vessel of the United States required to report to the System shall report to the

owner, charterer, managing operator, or agent at least once every 48 hours.

(2) A master violating this subsection is liable to the Government for a civil penalty of not more than $1,000 for each day during which the violation occurs.

(c) The Secretary may prescribe regulations to carry out this section.

Security Zones

Every boat owner and operator should memorize the following poster.

WARNING!

Do not approach within 100 yards of any U.S. naval vessel. If you need to pass within 100 yards of a U.S. naval vessel in order to ensure a safe passage in accordance with the Navigation Rules, you must contact the U.S. naval vessel or the Coast Guard escort vessel on VHF-FM channel 16.

OPERATE AT MINIMUM SPEED

You must operate at minimum speed within 500 yards of any U.S. naval vessel and proceed as directed by the Commanding Officer or the official patrol.

Violations of the Naval Vessel Protection Zone are a felony offense, punishable by up to 6 years in prison and/or up to $250,000 in fines

Section 7: Operation and Safety Requirements

A. Safety Equipment

The following chart shows the minimum U.S. safety equipment requirements.

You can perform a safety check on your own using a form available for free from the U.S. Coast Guard Auxiliary web site at www.cgaux.org. The U.S. Coast Guard Auxiliary provides voluntary Vessel Safety Checks. A copy of a safety check form is reproduced and follows.

U. S. COAST GUARD MINIMUM REQUIREMENTS FOR RECREATIONAL VESSELS				
EQUIPMENT	Less than 16ft/ 4.9m	16 to less than 26 ft/7.9m	26 to less than 40 ft/12.2m	40 to not more than 65 ft/19.8m
Personal Flotation Devices (PFDs)	One approved Type I, II, III or V(must be worn) PFD for each person aboard or being towed on water skis, tubes, etc.	One approved Type I, II or III PFD for each person aboard or being towed on water skis, etc.; and one throwable Type IV device. (A type V PFD may be used in lieu of any wearable PFD, if approved for the activity in which the boat is being used. **A TYPE V HYBRID MUST be worn to be legal.**)		
Check state laws for PFD wearing requirements for children and for certain water craft and sports.				
Visual Distress Signals (Coastal Waters, the Great Lakes & US owned boats on the high seas)	Required to carry approved visual distress signals for night-time use.	Must carry approved visual distress signals for both daytime and night-time use.		
Fire Extinguisher (Must be Coast Guard approved)	One B-I type approved hand portable fire extinguisher. (Not required on outboard motorboats less than 26 ft in length if the construction of the motorboat is such that it does not permit the entrapment of explosive or flammable gases or vapors and if fuel tanks are not permanently installed.)	Two B-I type **OR** one B-II type approved portable fire extinguishers.		Three B-I type **OR** one B-I type **PLUS** one B-II type approved portable fire extinguishers.
When a fixed fire extinguishing system is installed in machinery spaces it will replace one B-I portable fire extinguisher.				
Ventilation (Boats built on or after 8/1/80)	At least two ventilation ducts capable of efficiently ventilating every closed compartment that contains a gasoline engine and/or tank, except those having permanently installed tanks which vent outside of the boat and which contain no unprotected electrical devices. Engine compartments containing a gasoline engine with a cranking motor are additionally required to contain power operated exhaust blowers which can be controlled from the instrument panel.			
Ventilation (Boats built before 8/1/80)	At least two ventilation ducts fitted with cowls (or their equivalent) for the purpose of efficiently and properly ventilating the bilges of every closed engine and fuel tank compartment using gasoline as fuel or other fuels having a flashpoint of 110 degrees or less. Applies to boats constructed or decked over after April 25, 1940.			
Back-fire Flame Arrestor	One approved device on each carburetor of all gasoline engines installed after April 25, 1940, except outboard motors.			
Note: Some states have requirements in addition to the federal requirements. Check your state's boating laws for additional requirements.				

VESSEL SAFETY CHECK (VSC)

To be completed by a U. S. Coast Guard approved Vessel Examiner.
See the back of this form for a brief explanation of required items.
A federal Requirements Pamphlet is also available.

Owner / Operator has attended a CGAUX, USPS, State or [ ] Boating Safety Class: Yes [ ] No [ ]	**VSC Decal:** Awarded [ ] not Awarded [ ] **Number:**
Replaced decal was: Last Year [ ] Outdated [ ] First time [ ]	**Date of VSC:** [ ]
Owner/Operator Name:	Registration or Doc. No.

VESSEL INFORMATION:

Location of VSC - County: State:	HIN:
Length <16 [ ] 16-25 [ ] 26-39 [ ] 40-65 [ ] > 65 [ ]	Area of Operations: Inland [ ] Coastal [ ]
Powered by: Gas [ ] Diesel [ ] Sail [ ] Other [ ]	Type: PWC [ ] Open [ ] Cabin [ ] Other [ ]

VESSEL SAFETY CHECK DECAL REQUIREMENTS | RECOMMENDED AND DISCUSSION ITEMS

Item	Yes	No	NA	Item	Yes	No	NA
1. Display of Numbers				**(While encouraged, items below are not VSC requirements)**			
2. Registration / Documentation				**I.** Marine Radio			
3. Personal Flotation Devices (PFD)				**II.** Dewatering Device & Backup			
4. Visual Distress Signals (VDS)				**III.** Mounted Fire Extinguishers			
5. Fire Extinguishers				**IV.** Anchor & Line for Area			
6. Ventilation				**V.** First Aid and PIW Kits (**over)			
7. Backfire Flame Control				**VI.** Inland Visual Distress Signals			
8. Sound Producing Devices / Bell				**VII.** Capacity / Cert. of Compliance			
9. Navigation Lights				**VIII.** Discussion Items: **as applies**			
10. Pollution Placard				a. Accident Reporting / Owner Responsibility			
11. MARPOL Trash Placard				b. Offshore Operations			
12. Marine Sanitation Devices				c. Nautical Charts / Navigation Aids			
13. Navigation Rules				d. Survival Tips / First Aid			
14. State and/ or Local Requirements				e. Fueling / Fuel Management			
15. Overall Vessel Condition: **as applies**				f. Float Plan / Weather & Sea Conditions			
a. Deck free of hazards / clean Bilge				g. Insurance Considerations			
b. Safe Electrical / Fuel Systems				h. Boating Check List			
c. Safe Galley / Heating Systems				i. Safe Boating Classes			

I certify that I have personally examined this vessel and find it meets the above requirements at the time of this Vessel Safety Check. I am a qualified Vessel Examiner of the: CGAUX [ ], USPS [ ], State of _____ [ ], or _____ [ ]

Printed Name of the Examiner _____ **Examiner Number** _____

Examiner Signature: _____ **Telephone Number** _____

Additional Comments: *This is not an official boarding for law enforcement purposes. It is recommended that you correct any deficiencies noted. This checklist is furnished for your information. There is no assumption of liability of any kind for advice given or opinions expressed in connection to this examination. By accepting the Vessel Safety Check decal you are pledging to maintain your boat and equipment to the standard of safety exhibited during this examination.* **Please remove the Vessel Safety Check decal if the boat is sold or no longer meets these requirements.** **SAFE BOATING.**

Brief Explanation of VSC Required Items:

❑ **1. NUMBERING:** The boat's registration number must be permanently attached to each side of the forward half of the boat They must be plain, vertical, block characters, not less than three (3) inches high, and in a color contrasting with the background. A space or hyphen must separate the letters from the numbers. Place State tax sticker according to State policy.
(e.g. **FL 1234 AB** or **FL-1234-AB**)

❑ **2. REGISTRATION / DOCUMENTATION:** Registration or Documentation papers must be on board and available. Documentation numbers must be permanently marked on a visible part of the interior structure. The documented boat's name and hailing port must be displayed on the exterior hull in letters not less than 4 inches in height. To be documented a boat must be 5 net tons or greater.

❑ **3. PERSONAL FLOTATION DEVICES (PFDs):** Acceptable PFDs (also known as Life Jackets) must be U.S. Coast Guard approved, in good serviceable condition, and of suitable size for the each person on the boat. Children must have properly fitted PFDs designed for children. Wearable PFDs shall be *"readily accessible."* Throwable devices shall be *"immediately available."* PFDs shall NOT be stored in unopened plastic packaging. For Personal Watercraft riders, the PFD must be worn and indicate an impact rating. Boats 16 Feet or longer, must also have one Type IV.

❑ **4. VISUAL DISTRESS SIGNALS:** All recreational boats used on coastal waters or the Great Lakes are required to carry a minimum of three Coast Guard approved (current dated) day and night visual distress signals. Some signals (e.g. red flares) can serve for both day and night.

Boats operating on inland waters should have some means of making a suitable day and night distress signal. The number and type of Visual Distress Signals is best judged by considering conditions under which the boat will be operating. Alternatives to pyrotechnic devices (flares) include:

Night	*Day*
Strobe light	**Signal mirror**
Flashlight	**Red or orange flags**
Lantern	**Hand signals**

❑ **5. FIRE EXTINGUISHERS:** Every power boat requires a minimum of one Coast Guard approved "B-1" extinguisher. Only row boats and sailboats less than 16 feet with no mechanical propulsion are exempt. *NOTE: Fire extinguishers must be readily accessible and verified as serviceable.*

Minimum number of extinguishers required

Boat Length	No Fixed System	With Fixed System
Less than 26'	one B-1	one B-1
26' to less than 40'	two B-1 or one B-2	one B-1
40' to 65'	three B-1 or one B-1 & one B-2	two B-1 or one B-2

❑ **6. VENTILATION:** Boats with gasoline engines in closed compartments, built after 1 August 1980 must have a powered ventilation system. Those built prior to that date must have natural or powered ventilation.

Boats with closed fuel tank compartments built after 1 August 1978 must meet requirements by displaying a "certificate of compliance." Boats built before that date must have either natural or powered ventilation in the fuel tank compartment.

❑ **7. BACKFIRE FLAME ARRESTER:** All gasoline powered inboard/outboard or inboard motor boats must be equipped with an approved backfire flame control device.

❑ **8. SOUND PRODUCING DEVICES:** To comply with Navigation Rules and for distress signaling purposes all boats must carry a sound producing device (whistle, horn, siren, etc.) capable of a 4-second blast audible for ½ mile. Boats larger than 39.4 ft. are also required to have a bell (see Navigation Rules.)

❑ **9. NAVIGATION LIGHTS:** All boats must be able to display navigation lights between sunset and sunrise and in conditions of reduced visibility. Boats 16 feet or more in length must have properly installed, working navigation lights and an all-around anchor light capable of being lit independently from the red/green/white "running" lights.

❑ **10. POLLUTION PLACARD:** Boats 26 feet and over with a machinery compartment must display an oily waste "pollution" placard.

❑ **11. MARPOL TRASH PLACARD:** Boats 26 feet and over in length must display a "MARPOL" trash placard. Boats 40 feet and over must also display a written trash disposal plan.

❑ **12. MARINE SANITATION DEVICE:** Any installed toilet must be a Coast Guard approved device. Overboard discharge outlets must be capable of being sealed.

❑ **13. NAVIGATION RULES:** Boats 39.4 feet and over must have on board a current copy of the Navigation Rules.

❑ **14. STATE AND LOCAL REQUIREMENTS:** These requirements must be met before the *"Vessel Safety Check"* decal can be awarded. A boat must meet the requirements of the state in which it is being examined.

❑ **15. OVERALL BOAT CONDITION:** As it **applies to this Vessel. Including, but not limited to:**

a. Deck free of hazards and clean bilge - The boat must be free from fire hazards, in good overall condition, with bilges reasonably clean and visible hull structure generally sound. The use of automobile parts on boat engines is not acceptable. The engine horsepower must not exceed that shown on the capacity plate.

b. Safe Electrical and Fuel Systems:
The **electrical system** must be protected by fuses or manual reset circuit breakers. Switches and fuse panels must be protected from rain or water spray. Wiring must be in good condition, properly installed and with no exposed areas or deteriorated insulation. Batteries must be secured and terminals covered to prevent accidental arcing.. **If installed,** self-circling or kill switch mechanism must be in proper working order. All *PWCs* **require** an operating self circling or kill switch mechanism.

Fuel Systems - Portable fuel tanks (normally 7 gallon capacity or less) must be constructed of non-breakable material and free of corrosion and leaks. All vents must be capable of being closed. The tank must be secured and have a vapor-tight, leak-proof cap. Each **permanent fuel tank** must be properly ventilated.

c. Safe Galley and Heating Systems - System and fuel tanks must be properly secured with no flammable materials nearby.

I. - VIII. RECOMMENDED AND DISCUSSION ITEMS: (Not required for the award of the *"Vessel Safety Check"* decal.) For the very best boaters, we recommend these additional items. Meeting these requirements reflects your concern for Boating Safety.

Discussion Items are educational in nature and add value to the Vessel Safety Check program.

** **Person in the Water (PIW) kit** consists of one extra **wearable PFD and a throwable type IV PFD w/line.**

For more information: Ask your Vessel Examiner,
Visit **http://SafetySeal.net** or
Call the Boating Safety Hotline – **800-368-5647**

The following U.S. Coast Guard chart shows the various equipment requirements for U.S. recreational vessels.

Vessel Length (in feet)				Equipment	Requirement
<16	16<26	26<40	40<65		
X	X	X	X	Certificate of Number (State Registration)	All undocumented vessels equipped with propulsion machinery must be State registered. Certificate of Number must be aboard when vessel is in use. Note: some States require all vessels to be registered.
X	X	X	X	State Numbering	(a) Plain Block letters/numbers not less than 3 inches in height must be affixed on each side of the forward half of the vessel (Contrasting color to boat exterior). (b) State validation sticker must be affixed within six inches of the registration number
	X	X	X	Certificate of Documentation	Applies only to "Documented" vessels: (a) Original and current certificate must be aboard (b) Vessel name/hailing port marked on exterior part of hull — letters not less than 4 inches in height. (c) Official Number permanently affixed on interior structure — numbers not less than 3 inches in height.
X	X	X	X	Life Jackets (PFDs)	(a) One Type I, II, III, or V wearable PFD for each person aboard. (must be USCG approved)
	X	X	X		(b) In addition to paragraph (a), must carry One Type IV (throwable) PFD.
X				Visual Distress Signal (VDS)	(a) One electric distress light or Three combination (day/night) red flares. Note: only required to be carried aboard when operating between sunset and sunrise. (b) One orange distress flag and One electric distress light - or -Three hand-held or floating orange smoke signals and One electric distress light - or - Three combination (day/night) red flares: hand-held, meteor or parachute type.
	X	X	X		
X	X			Fire Extinguishers	(a) One B-I (when enclosed compartment)
		X			(b) One B-II or Two B-I. Note: fixed system equals One B-I
			X		(c) One B-II and One B-I or Three B-I. Note: fixed system equals One B-I or Two B-II
X	X	X	X	Ventilation	(a) All vessels built after 25 April 1940 that use gasoline as their fuel with enclosed engine and /or fuel tank compartments must have natural ventilation (at least two ducts fitted with cowls). (b) In addition to paragraph (a), a vessel built after 31 July 1980 must have rated power exhaust blower.
X	X	X		Sound Producing Devices	(a) A vessel 39.4 ft must, at a minimum, have some means of making an "efficient" sound signal - (i.e. handheld air horn, athletic whistle - Human voice/ sound not acceptable).
		X	X		(b) A vessel 39.4 ft (12 meters) or greater, must have a sound signaling appliance capable of producing an efficient sound signal, audible for 1/2 mile with a 4 to 6 seconds duration. In addition, must carry aboard a bell with a clapper (bell size not less than 7.9 inches - based on the diameter of the mouth)

Vessel Length (in feet)				Equipment	Requirement
<16	16<26	26<40	40<65		
X	X	X	X	Backfire Flame Arrestor	Required on gasoline engines installed after 25 April 1940, except outboard motors
X	X	X	X	Navigational Lights	Required to be displayed from sunset to sunrise and in or near areas of reduced visibility.
		X	X	Oil Pollution Placard	(a) Placard must be at least 5 by 8 inches, made of durable material. (b) Placard must be posted in the machinery space or at the bilge station.
		X	X	Garbage Placard	(a) Placard must be at least 4 by 9 inches, made of durable material. (b) Displayed in a conspicuous place notifying all aboard the discharge restrictions.
X	X	X	X	Marine Sanitation Device	If installed toilet: Vessel must have an operable MSD TypeI, II, or III.
		X	X	Navigation Rules (Inland Only)	The operator of a vessel 39.4 ft (12 meters) or greater must have aboard a copy of these rules.

Equipment Checklist:

Canadian Federal Regulations

Canadian federal requirements for small vessels are different in many respects from U.S. requirements. U.S. vessels are not required to comply with the Canadian requirements for trips that are less than 45 days duration. Nevertheless, some knowledge of the different requirements may be helpful. If you are interested in reviewing the Canadian small vessel equipment requirements they are re-printed in full on the Internet at www.laws.justice.gc.ca/en/S-9/C.R.C.-c.1487/index.html. The Canadian Sewage Pollution requirements are re-printed at www.laws.justice.gc.ca/en/S-9/SOR-91-661/52864.html.

Canadian Provincial Regulations

Just as the united States have different laws and regulations to govern boating so do the provinces in Canada. For further information, visit the following Internet web sites.

British Columbia: www.qp.gov.bc.ca/statreg/

Ontario: www.e-laws.gov.on.ca/home_E.asp?lang=en

Quebec: www.canlii.org/qc/laws/index.html

New Brunswick: www.gnb.ca/0062/acts/acts-f.asp

Nova Scotia: www.gov.ns.ca/legi/legc/index.htm

Prince Edward Island: www.gov.pe.ca/law/statutes/index.php3

Newfoundland: www.gov.nf.ca/hoa/sr/

A great deal more helpful information about boating regulations in Canada can be obtained on the Internet at Pat's Boating In Canada, boating.ncf.ca/index.html#reg.

B. Equipment Checklist

Sample Form

Personal Flotation Devices (PFDs)
- ☐ One Coast Guard approved device per passenger. A minimum of two aboard.
- ☐ Throw able device (boats over 16')

Sound Producing Devices (Whistle)
- ☐ Horn for boats over 39.4'. (blast audible for 4 seconds for at least ½ mile). Have a spare can of gas or air or an alternate devise as well.

Lights and Shapes
- ☐ All required navigation lights Flashlight on-board.

Distress Signals
- ☐ Easily accessible flares, day signals, etc.

Tools and Spares
- ☐ Basic tool box.
- ☐ Box of misc. spare parts. (fuel filter, light bulbs, head parts, through hull plugs, belts, hoses, etc.

Ventilation
- ☐ Check for any gas or fuel leaks. Ventilate all interior spaces. before departure.

Fire Extinguishers
- ☐ Accessible fire extinguisher(s) as required by the U.S.C.G.? Show locations to crew. Discuss procedures.

Fuel and Oil
- ☐ Sufficient fuel for destination and return.
- ☐ Check engine oil and coolant.

Bilges
- ☐ Bilges dry. Pumps ok.
- ☐ Remove & clean any spilled oil or waste in bilge.

Battery Care
- ☐ Batteries sufficiently charged. Set battery switch to correct position.
- ☐ Spare batteries for items like handheld radio, flashlight, portable navigational aid, etc.

Weather Forecast & VHF.
- ☐ Check weather forecast.
- ☐ Check operation of VHF radio.

Docking and Anchoring
- ☐ Ground tackle sufficient for destination.
- ☐ Docklines and extras. Inspect all lines.
- ☐ Fenders sufficient for trip.
- ☐ Line sufficient for towing if necessary.

Documentation
- ☐ Documentation or Registration papers, radio license, fishing permit, etc. aboard.
- ☐ Current Charts for intended area and destination.

VHF Channels

The chart below summarizes a portion of the FCC rules for VHF radios. Note: Under recent changes channel 9 is now designated as a recreational calling channel for non-commercial vessels.

TYPE OF MESSAGE	APPROPRIATE CHANNEL(S)
DISTRESS SAFETY AND CALLING - Use this channel to get the attention of another station (calling) or in emergencies (distress and safety).	16
INTERSHIP SAFETY - Use this channel for ship-to-ship safety messages and for search and rescue messages and ships and aircraft of the Coast Guard.	6
COAST GUARD LIAISON - Use this channel to talk to the Coast Guard (but first make contact on Channel 16).	22
NONCOMMERCIAL - Working channels for voluntary boats. Messages must be about the needs of the ship. Typical uses include fishing reports, rendezvous,scheduling repairs and berthing information. Use Channels 67 and 72 only for ship-to-ship messages.	96, 68, 69, 71, 72, 78, 794, 804, 677.
COMMERCIAL - Working channels for working ships only. Messages must be about business or the needs of the ship. Use channels 8, 67, 72 and 88 only for ship-to-ship messages.	15, 7, 8, 9, 10, 11, 18, 19, 635, 677, 79, 80, 881
PUBLIC CORRESPONDENCE (MARINE OPERATOR) - Use these channels to call the marine operator at a public coast station. By contacting a public coast station, you can make and receive calls from telephones on shore. Except for distress calls, public coast stations usually charge for this service.	24, 25, 26, 27, 28, 84, 85, 86, 87, 882
PORT OPERATIONS - These channels are used in directing the movement of ships in or near ports, locks or waterways. Messages must be about the operational handling movement and safety of ships. In certain major ports, Channels 11,12 and are not available for general port operations messages. Use channel 20 only for ship-to-coast messages. Channel 77 is limited to intership communications to and from pilots	15, 53, 12, 14, 20, 635, 65, 66, 73, 74, 77
NAVIGATIONAL - (Also known as the bridge-to-bridge channel.) This channel is available to all ships. Messages must be about ship navigation, for example, passing or meeting other ships. You must keep your messages short. Your power output must not be more than one watt. This is also the main working channel at most locks and drawbridges.	13, 67
MARITIME CONTROL - This channel may be used to talk to ships and coast stations operated by state or local governments. Messages must pertain to regulation and control, boating activities, or assistance to ships.	17
DIGITAL SELECTIVE CALLING - Use this channel for distress and safety calling and for general purpose calling using only digital selective calling techniques.	70
WEATHER - On these channels you may receive weather broadcasts of the National Oceanic and Atmospheric Administration. These channels are only for receiving. You cannot transmit on them.	Wx-1 162.55 Wx-2 162.4 Wx-3 162.475

Channel Superscript Translation

1. Not available in the Great Lakes, St. Lawrence Seaway, or the Puget Sound and the Strait of Juan de Fuca and its approaches.

2. Only for use In the Great Lakes, St Lawrence Seaway, and Puget Sound and the Strait of Juan de Fuca and its approaches.

3. Available only In the Houston and New Orleans areas.

4. Available only in the Great Lakes.

5. Available only In the New Orleans area.

6. Available for Intership, ship, and coast general purpose calling by noncommercial ships.

7. Available only In the Puget Sound and the Strait of Juan de Fuca.

The letter "A" on a VHF Channel indicates simplex use of the ship station transmit side of an international duplex channel. The operations are different than international operations on that channel. Some VHF transceivers are equipped with an "International - U.S." switch for that purpose. "A" channels are generally only used in the United States, and use is normally not recognized or allowed outside the U.S. The letter "B" indicates simplex use of the coast station transmit side of an international duplex channel. The U.S. does not currently use "B" channels for simplex communications in this band.

Boaters should normally use channels listed as Non-Commercial. Channel 16 is used for calling other stations or for distress alerting. Channel 13 should be used to contact a ship when there is danger of collision. All ships of length 20m or greater are required to guard VHF channel 13, in addition to VHF channel 16, when operating within U.S. territorial waters. Users may be fined by the FCC for improper use of these channels.

If you are boating in the Pacific Northwest area of the United States there is a free publication available that is useful. It is titled, "VHF Frequencies for Pleasure Vessels in the Pacific Northwest – 14h Edition. It includes information regarding use of your VHF radio in British Colombia, Canada. The Recreational Boating Association of Washington (www.RBAW.org) and the North Pacific Marine Radio Council publish the guide. A free copy is available from the RBAW and can be downloaded by visiting the RBAW web site.

Boating accidents

Reporting accidents is required by both Federal and State Laws. A copy of an accident reporting form used in the State of Tennessee is reproduced below. The following form is just a sample, your state requirements may be different.

Sample Form.

A two-page Boating Accident Report form is on the next page.

Tennessee Wildlife Resources Agency
P.O. Box 40747
Nashville, TN 37204
615-781-6682

BOATING ACCIDENT REPORT

ACCIDENT REPORT NUMBER

DATE OF REPORT

Whenever an accident involves any vessel and results in the death, disappearance, or injury of any person, or in property damage in excess of $500, the operators of all vessels involved must file a written report with the Wildlife Resources Agency. Death or disappearance must be reported within 48 hours; personal injury or property damage within 10 days.

COMPLETE ALL BLOCKS. (incidate those not applicable by "NA")

NAME AND ADDRESS OF OPERATOR

AGE OF OPERATOR

DATE OF BIRTH

OPERATOR'S EXPERIENCE

This type of boat
[ ] Under 20 hours
[ ] 20 to 100 hours
[ ] 100 to 500 hours
[ ] Over 500 hours

Other Boat Operating Exp.
[ ] Under 20 hours
[ ] 20 to 100 hours
[ ] 100 to 500 hours
[ ] Over 500 hours

OPERATOR TELEPHONE NUMBER

OWNER TELEPHONE NUMBER

NAME AND ADDRESS OF OWNER

RENTED BOAT
[ ] Yes
[ ] No

NUMBER OF PERSONS ON BOARD

FORMAL INSTRUCTION IN BOATING SAFETY
[ ] None
[ ] USCG Auxiliary
[ ] U.S. Power Squadrons
[ ] American Red Cross
[ ] State
[ ] Other (Indicate)

VESSEL NO. 1 (this vessel)

BOAT REGISTRATION	BOAT NAME	BOAT MAKE	BOAT MODEL	MFR HULL IDENTIFICATION NO.

TYPE OF BOAT
[ ] Open Motorboat
[ ] Cabin Motorboat
[ ] Auxiliary Sail
[ ] Sail (only)
[ ] Rowboat
[ ] Canoe
[ ] Other (Specify)

HULL MATERIAL
[ ] Wood
[ ] Aluminum
[ ] Steel
[ ] Fiberglass
[ ] Rubber/vinyl /canvas
[ ] Other (Spec.)

ENGINE
[ ] Outboard
[ ] Inboard Gasoline
[ ] Inboard Diesel
[ ] Inboard-Outdrive
[ ] Jet
[ ] Other (Specify)

BOAT DATA (propulsion)
No. of Engines _____
Horsepower (total) _____
Type of Fuel _____

BOAT DATA (construction)
Length _____
Year Built (Boat) _____

Has boat had a Safety Examination [ ] Yes [ ] No
For Current Year [ ] Yes [ ] No   Year_____
Indicate whether [ ] USCG Auxiliary Courtesy Marine Exam.
[ ] State/local examination, [ ] other

ACCIDENT DATA

DATE OF ACCIDENT	TIME ___AM ___PM	NAME OF BODY OF WATER	LOCATION (Give location precisely)
STATE	NEAREST CITY OR TOWN		COUNTY

WEATHER
[ ] Clear   [ ] Rain
[ ] Cloudy   [ ] Snow
[ ] Fog   [ ] Hazy

WATER CONDITIONS
[ ] Calm (waves less than 6")
[ ] Choppy (waves 6"–2')
[ ] Rough (waves over 2'–6')
[ ] Very Rough (greater than 6')
[ ] Strong Current

TEMPERATURE (Estimate)
Air _____F
Water _____F

WIND
[ ] None
[ ] Light (0–6 MPH)
[ ] Moderate (7–14 MPH)
[ ] Strong (15-25 MPH)
[ ] Storm (Over 25 MPH)

VISIBILITY
Day   Night
[ ] Good [ ]
[ ] Fair [ ]
[ ] Poor [ ]

OPERATION AT TIME OF ACCIDENT
(Check all applicable)
[ ] Commercial Activity
[ ] Cruising
[ ] Maneuvering
[ ] Approaching Dock
[ ] Leaving Dock
[ ] Water Skiing
[ ] Racing
[ ] Towing
[ ] Being Towed
[ ] Drifting
[ ] At Anchor
[ ] Tied to Dock
[ ] Fueling
[ ] Fishing
[ ] Hunting
[ ] Skin Diving/ Swimming
[ ] Other (Specify)

TYPE OF ACCIDENT
[ ] Grounding
[ ] Capsizing
[ ] Flooding
[ ] Sinking
[ ] Fire or Explosion (Fuel)
[ ] Fire or Explosion (Other than fuel)
[ ] Burns
[ ] Collision with Vessel
[ ] Collision with Fixed Object
[ ] Collision with Floating Object
[ ] Falls Overboard
[ ] Falls in Boat
[ ] Hit by Boat or Propeller
[ ] Fallen Skier
[ ] Other (Specify)

WHAT IN YOUR OPINION CONTRIBUTED TO THE ACCIDENT (Check all applicable)
[ ] Weather
[ ] Excessive Speed
[ ] No Proper Lookout
[ ] Overloading
[ ] Improper Loading
[ ] Restricted Vision
[ ] Hazardous Waters
[ ] Operator Inexperience
[ ] Operator Inattention
[ ] Alcohol use
[ ] Drug use
[ ] Fault of Machinery
[ ] Fault of Equipment
[ ] Other (Specify)

PERSONAL FLOATATION DEVICES (PFD'S)

PROPERTY DAMAGE

Was the boat adequately equipped with **CG APPROVED FLOATATION DEVICES?**
[ ] Yes [ ] No
Were they accessible   [ ] Yes [ ] No
Were they serviceable [ ] Yes [ ] No
Were they used by   [ ] Yes [ ] No
  survivors

What type
[ ] I   [ ] II
[ ] III [ ] IV
[ ] V (specify)_____

Were PFD's properly:
used   [ ] yes [ ] no
adjusted [ ] yes [ ] no
sized   [ ] yes [ ] no

Was the vessel carrying NON approved floatation devices
Were they accessible [ ] yes [ ] no
Were they used   [ ] yes [ ] no
If Yes, indicate kind _____

DESCRIBE PROPERTY DAMAGE

FIRE EXTINGUISHERS
Were they used—(If yes, list Type(s) and number used.)
[ ] Yes [ ] No [ ] Not Applicable
Type(s)

Estimated amount
This Boat $ _____
Other Boat $ _____
Other Property $ _____

NAME AND ADDRESS OF OWNER OF DAMAGED PROPERTY

WR0306 (Rev 7/93)   Previous editions are obsolete   Complete Both Sides

(If more than 3 fatalities and/or injuries, attach additional form(s).)

	NAME	ADDRESS	BIRTH DATE	WAS VICTIM	DEATH CAUSED BY	WAS PFD WORN
DECEASED				[ ] Swimmer [ ] Non Swimmer	[ ] Drowning [ ] Other DISAPPEARANCE ( )	[ ] Yes [ ] No What Type
				[ ] Swimmer [ ] Non Swimmer	[ ] Drowning [ ] Other DISAPPEARANCE ( )	[ ] Yes [ ] No What Type
				[ ] Swimmer [ ] Non Swimmer	[ ] Drowning [ ] Other DISAPPEARANCE ( )	[ ] Yes [ ] No What Type
INJURED				NATURE OF INJURY		MEDICAL TREATMENT [ ] Yes [ ] No
						[ ] Yes [ ] No
						[ ] Yes [ ] No

ACCIDENT DESCRIPTION

DESCRIBE WHAT HAPPENED (Sequence of events. Include Failure of Equipment. If diagram is needed attach separately. Continue on additional sheets if necessary. Include any information regarding the involvement of alcohol and/or drugs in causing or contributing to the accident. If a test for alcohol or drugs was given, indicate the type of test, results and blood alcohol content if possible. Include any descriptive information about the use of PFD's.)

VESSEL NO. 2 (If more than 2 vessels, attach additional form(s).)

Name of Operator	Address	Boat Number
Telephone Number		Boat Name
Name of Owner	Address	

WITNESSES

Name	Address	Telephone Number

PERSON COMPLETING REPORT

SIGNATURE	Address	DATE SUBMITTED
QUALIFICATION (Check One) [ ] Operator [ ] Owner [ ] Investigator [ ] Other		TELEPHONE

(do not use)—FOR REPORTING AUTHORITY REVIEW (use agency date stamp)

Causes based on (check one) [ ] This report [ ] Investigation and this report [ ] Investigation [ ] Could not be determined	Name of Reviewing Office	Date Received
Primary Cause of Accident		
Secondary Cause of Accident	Reviewed by	

Section 8: Crossing the Border

The following information about bringing valuable goods back into the United State is reprinted from the U.S. Customs and Border Protection.

What You Must Declare

- Items you purchased and are carrying with you upon return to the United States.

- Items you received as gifts, such as wedding or birthday presents.

- Items you inherited.

- Items you bought in duty-free shops, on the ship, or on the plane.

- Repairs or alterations to any items you took abroad and then brought back, even if the repairs/alterations were performed free of charge.

- Items you brought home for someone else.

- Items you intend to sell or use in your business.

- Items you acquired (whether purchased or received as gifts) in the U.S. Virgin Islands, American Samoa, Guam, or in a Caribbean Basin Economic Recovery Act country (please see section on $600 exemption for a list of these countries) that are not in your possession when you return. In other words, if you acquired things in any of these island nations and asked the merchant to send them to you, you must still declare them when you go through CBP. This differs from the usual procedure for mailed items, which is discussed in the section on Sending Goods to the United States.

You must state on the declaration, in United States currency, what you actually paid for each item. The price must include all taxes. If you did not buy the item yourself — for example, if it is a gift - get an estimate of its fair retail value in the country where you received it. If you bought something on your trip and wore or used it on the trip, it is still dutiable. You must declare the item at the price you paid or, if it was a gift, at its fair market value.

Family members who live in the same home and return together to the United States may combine their personal exemptions. This is called a joint declaration. For example, if Mr. and Mrs. Smith travel overseas and Mrs. Smith brings home a $1,000 piece of glassware, and Mr. Smith buys $600 worth of clothing, they can combine their $800 exemptions on a joint declaration and not have to pay duty.

Children and infants are allowed the same exemption as adults, except for alcoholic beverages.

One liter (33.8 fluid ounces) of alcoholic beverages may be included in your exemption if:

- You are 21 years old.

- It is for your own use or as a gift.

- It does not violate the laws of the state in which you arrive.

Federal regulations allow you to bring back more than one liter of alcoholic beverage for personal use, but, as with extra tobacco, you will have to pay duty and Internal Revenue Service tax.

If you cannot claim other exemptions because you have been out of the country more than once in a 30-day period or because you have not been out of the country for at least 48 hours, you may still bring back $200 worth of items free of duty and tax. As with the exemptions discussed earlier, these items must be for your personal or household use.

Each traveler is allowed this $200 exemption, but, unlike the other exemptions, family members may not group their exemptions. Thus, if Mr. and Mrs. Smith spend a night in Canada, each may bring back up to $200 worth of goods, but they would not be allowed a collective family exemption of $400.

If you are returning directly from any one of the following 24 Caribbean Basin countries, your exemption is $600:

Antigua and Barbuda	Haiti
Aruba	Honduras
Bahamas	Jamaica
Barbados	Montserrat
Belize	Netherlands Antilles
British Virgin Islands	Nicaragua
Costa Rica	Panama
Dominica	Saint Kitts and Nevis
Dominican Republic	Saint Lucia
El Salvador	Saint Vincent and the
Grenada	Grenadines
Guatemala	Trinidad and Tobago
Guyana	

If you are returning from anywhere other than a Caribbean Basin country or a U.S. insular possession (U.S. Virgin Islands, American Samoa, or Guam), you may bring back $800 worth of items duty-free, as long as you bring them with you (this is called accompanied baggage).

If you return directly or indirectly from a U.S. insular possession (U.S. Virgin Islands, American Samoa, or Guam), you are allowed a $1,200 duty-free exemption. You may include 1,000 cigarettes as part of this exemption, but at least 800 of them must have been acquired in an insular possession. Only 200 cigarettes may have been acquired elsewhere. For example, if you were touring the South Pacific and you stopped in Tahiti, American Samoa, and other ports of call, you could bring back five cartons of cigarettes, but four of them would have to have been bought in American Samoa.

Firearms and ammunition. Non-residents arriving in U.S. waters with a firearm must apply for permission to enter with the weapon. Contact the Bureau of Alcohol, Tobacco, and Firearms for ATF Form 6 in advance of arrival. It can take up to 6 weeks for approval by ATF so submit the application well in advance. Failure to have an approved ATF Form 6 will result in firearms being seized. CBP will hold the firearms to allow an opportunity to apply for an ATF Form 6, but you will be liable for storage charges and you will have to make arrangements to personally retrieve the weapon from CBP custody. Alternately, you may make arrangements to export the firearm. Failure to either obtain the AFT temporary import approval or export the firearm will result in its seizure and destruction. Firearms can also be seized and destroyed if a CBP officer determines that failure to declare it on arrival was deliberate – so be sure to declare your weapon and ammunition – even if you do not have an approved ATF Form 6.

U.S. Residents traveling with firearms are reminded to register it with CBP on a CF 4457 prior to taking it out of the U.S. You will need to present the firearm in person to a CBP officer in order to register it. When you re-enter the U.S., a signed CF 4457 is proof that you did not acquire the firearm abroad. If you have the original receipt for a firearm purchased in the U.S., this can be used in lieu of a CF 4457 to demonstrate that it is American goods returned.

If you intend to bring back more than just a few items purchased abroad you should be familiar with all the rules and regulations, not just a summary. Contact a local office of the U.S. Customs and Border Protection or visit the CPB web site.

www.customs.ustreas.gov/xp/cgov/home.xml
www.customs.ustreas.gov/xp/cgov/travel/
      leavingarrivinginUS/
www.customs.ustreas.gov/xp/cgov/travel

Ports of Entry

There are many port of entry for use by recreational boaters. Contact your local Customs and Border Protection office for the entry ports in your area. A list is available on the Internet at www.boating.ncf.ca/usports.html.

Customs Decal for boats over 30 feet

You can apply online for a Customs Decal at www.customs.gov/travel/travel.htm.

Know before you go

The brochure can be downloaded for free from the CPB online at www.customs.ustreas.gov/xp/cgov/travel/leavingarrivinginUS/vacation/know_beforeu_go.xml.

Sample Form

The following U.S. Re-entry Information form can be used to write down some the information you will need for re-entry into the United States.

U.S. Re-entry Information

Your full name, birthdate, address and phone number.

_____

_____

Your boat name, type of boat, and length. _____

Boat Registration number or Coast Guard documention number. _____

Customs user fee Decal Number (if over 30') _____

Crew List

Full Name: _____
Nationality: _____
Residence Address: _____
Place & Date of Birth: _____

Full Name: _____
Nationality: _____
Residence Address: _____
Place & Date of Birth: _____

Full Name: _____
Nationality: _____
Residence Address: _____
Place & Date of Birth: _____

Full Name: _____
Nationality: _____
Residence Address: _____
Place & Date of Birth: _____

List or any items in your possession that you purchased while abroad and the value in U.S. dollars. _____

_____

_____

_____

Time and place that you left prior to re-entering the United States. _____

_____

Foreign Clearance Number: (assigned to you when you entered the foreign country from which you are returning:

_____

CanPass

For more information about CanPass visit the Canada Border Services Agency home page at www.cbsa-asfc. gc.ca/menu-e.html. The CanPass brochure is available at most customs offices and online. For more information call the Automated Customs Information Service (ACIS) toll free at 800-461-9999 from within Canada. If you are outside Canada, call 204-983-3500 or 506-636-5064.

Canadian Provincial Requirements

A list of provinces and territories and their official web sites is available on the Internet at www.gc.ca/othergov/ prov_e.html. From there, you can research boating regulations and restrictions for each province and territory. Alternatively, the relevant information is available in many popular cruising guides and boating publications.

Visiting Mexico by boat

The consulate list is obtainable on the Internet at www. mexonline.com/consulate.htm. Information is provided by the Mexican Secretariat of Tourism (SECTUR), which has offices all over the United States. A list of offices is available at www.mexonline.com/mxtur.htm. The SECTUR web site is at www.sectur.gob.mx/wb2/secturing/sect_2_home.

Visiting the Bahamas

Official information for entering the country can be obtained on the Internet by visiting www.bahamas.gov. bs/bahamasweb/home.nsf. A list of authorized ports of entry is also available at that web site. The following information is re-printed from that web site.

Bahamian Authorized Ports of Entry

Customs Procedures

Upon entering The Bahamas the master of a vessel must place the vessel ata n authorized port. The vessel must first clear customs prior to any crew coming ashore or the unloading or loading of any cargo.

Immigration Procedures

No person is to land in The Bahamas from a foreign territory without leave of an Immigration officer. All vessels must be landed at an authorized port of entry. Failure to comply with these regulations may result in imprisonment/forfeiture. Note the vessels restriction within the Immigration Act.

Note: No specified vessel (a vessel 100 net tons or below, inclusive of yachts) is to enter The Bahamas from any port in Haiti, except at the port of Matthew Town, Inagua. This provision is applicable to Bahamian owned vessels, as well. Vessels must obtain a transire (clearance) as under the Customs Management Act. There are other provisions relating to vessels sailing from Haiti to The Bahamas. It is essential that all parties are aware of the provisions.

Authorized Ports of Entry

The following is a list of authorized ports of entry within The Bahamas:

Abaco: Green Turtle Cay, Walker's Cay, Marsh Harbour, Spanish Cay, Treasure Cay
Andros: Fresh Creek, Congo Town, San Andros
Bimini: Alice Town, South Bimini

Berry Islands: Chubb Cay, Great Harbour Cay
Cat Cay
Cat Island: Bennett's Harbour, New Bight
Eleuthera: Rock Sound, Governor's Harbour, Cape Eleuthera, North Eleuthera, Harbour Island
Exuma: George Town, Moss Town
San Salvador: Cockburn Town
Grand Bahama: Freeport, West End, Lucaya Beach Marina, King's Inn Marina
Inagua: Matthew Town
Mayaguana
New Providence: Prince George Wharf

Sufferance Ports

Sufferance ports are referring to ports that are not authorized ports of entry; however provisions have be made where goods may be loaded/discharged (Vessels may clear customs, immigration etc. at sufferance ports. The following is a list of sufferance ports within The Commonwealth of The Bahamas.

Grand Bahama: South Riding Point (Burma), Freeport Container Facility, Bell Channel (Freeport), Jack Tar Marina (West End)

New Providence: Union Wharf, Kelly's Dock, John Alfred Dock, Nassau Yacht Haven, Nassau Harbour Club, East Bay Yacht Basin, Coral Harbour, Lyford Cay Marina, Clifton Pier, Brown Boat Basin, Hurricane Hole, Paradise Island, Ocean Cay, Bahmar/Cavalier Terminal, Arawak Cay, Seaboard Terminal

Section 9: United States Pollution Regulations

Sample Form

WASTE MANAGEMENT PLAN

Vessel Name _____

1. This plan describes policy and procedures for handling this vessel's garbage according to MARPOL Annex V and 33 CFR Subparts 151.51 through 151.77. As Captain, I am responsible for carrying out this plan. All crewmembers and embarked persons shall follow the instructions in this plan. **It is the general policy of this vessel that all food waste and garbage will be retained aboard for proper disposal ashore.**

2. Waste for this vessel is collected _____ (where) and stored _____ (location). When moored, all waste will be carried from the vessel and disposed of _____ (location of dumpster, etc.). **Plastics and waste containing plastic materials will never be discharged into the water from this vessel regardless of location.**

3. When sailing on inland waters or at sea within 12 nautical miles of land, no food, garbage or waste of any type will be discharged. When on an extended voyage, beyond 12 nautical miles from land, certain non-plastic and non-floating waste may be discharged if storage space is not available. In this case, all plastics (including foamed plastic) are to be segregated from other wastes and stored aboard for proper disposal ashore. Only those materials permitted for discharge according to the MARPOL Annex V placard may be discharged in the water. **In no case will waste of any kind be discharged into the water without my prior inspection and explicit permission.**

4. If you have any questions about this plan, waste handling procedures or materials that may be discharged, please consult me.

_____   _____
Captain   Date

Sample Form

A Sample Oil Discharge Placard

DISCHARGE OF OIL PROHIBITED

The Federal Water Pollution Control Act

Prohibits the discharge of oil or oily waste into on upon the navigable waters of the United States, or the water of the contiguous zone, or which may affect natural resources belonging to, appertaining to, or under the exclusive management and authority of the United States if such discharge causes a film or discoloration of the surface of the water or causes a sludge or emulsion beneath the surface of the water. Violators are subject to substantial civil penalties and/or criminal sanctions, including fines and imprisonment.

Report all discharges to the National Response Center at 1-800-424-8802 or to your local U.S. Coast Guard office by phone or VHF radio, Channel 16.

SAMPLE GARBAGE PLACARD (SAVE OUR SEAS)

It is illegal to dump:
Inside 3 miles and in U.S. Lakes, Rivers, Bays and Sounds and anywhere on the Great Lakes no matter how far from shore:
Plastic, dunnage, lining, and packing materials that float and any garbage except dishwater/graywater/fresh fish parts.
3 to 12 miles
Plastic, dunnage, lining, and packing materials that float and any garbage not ground to less than one square inch.
12 to 25 miles
Plastic, dunnage, lining, and packing materials that float.
Outside 25 miles
Plastic

Section 10: Marine Mammal Protection and Other Wildlife

A. Marine Mammals

The National Marine Fisheries Service has published the guidelines for observing Marine Mammals. The guidelines are divided into various regions and reflect the considerations for each region and considerations for the species of mammals in each region. You should be aware of the rules that apply in your area. Additional information can be obtained on the Internet at www.nmfs.noaa.gov/prot_res/index.html.

A good summary of the Marine Mammal Protection Act and the index with links to its provisions can be found at www.nmfs.noaa.gov/prot_res/laws/MMPA/MMPA.html.

Endangered Plants and Animals

Additional information about marine plants and animals that are listed as endangered can be obtained on the Internet at www.nmfs.noaa.gov/prot_res/overview/es.html. The following is a list of marine mammals currently listed as endangered.

- Blue Whale
- Bowhead Whale
- Fin Whale
- Gray Whale (Western North Pacific stock)
- Humpback Whale
- Northern Right Whale
- Southern Right Whale
- Sei Whale
- Sperm Whale
- Chinese River Dolphin (China)
- Indus River Dolphin (Pakistan)
- Dugong
- West Indian Manatee
- Gulf of California Harbor Porpoise
- Steller Sea Lion (Western stock)
- Caribbean Monk Seal
- Hawaiian Monk Seal
- Mediterranean Monk Seal
- Ringed Seal (Finland)

Penalties for Violations of the MMPA and the ESA

Marine Mammal Protection Act (16 U.S.C. 1375 Sec. 105)

(a) (1) Any person who violates any provision of this title or of any permit or regulation issued thereunder, except as provided in section 118, may be assessed a civil penalty by the Secretary of not more than $10,000 for each such violation. No penalty shall be assessed unless such person is given notice and opportunity for a hearing with respect to such violation. Each unlawful taking or importation shall be a separate offense. Any such civil penalty may be remitted or mitigated by the Secretary for good cause shown. Upon any failure to pay a penalty assessed under this subsection, the Secretary may request the Attorney General to institute a civil action in a district court of the United States for any district in which such person is found, resides, or transacts business to collect the penalty and such court shall have jurisdiction to hear and decide any such action.

(2) In any case involving an alleged unlawful importation of a marine mammal or marine mammal product, if such importation is made by an individual for his own personal or family use (which does not include importation as an accommodation to others or for sale or other commercial use), the Secretary may, in lieu of instituting a proceeding under paragraph (1), allow the individual to abandon the mammal or product, under procedures to be prescribed by the Secretary, to the enforcement officer at the port of entry.

(b) Any person who knowingly violates any provision of this title or of any permit or regulation issued thereunder (except as provided in section 118) shall, upon conviction, be fined not more than $20,000 for each such violation, or imprisoned for not more than one year, or both.

B. Other U.S. Environmental Regulations

Endangered Species Act
PENALTIES AND ENFORCEMENT
SEC. 11. (a) CIVIL PENALTIES.—

(1) Any person who knowingly violates, and any person engaged in business as an importer or exporter of fish, wildlife, or plants who violates, any provision of this Act, or any provision of any permit or certificate issued hereunder, or of any regulation issued in order to implement subsection (a)(1)(A), (B), (C), (D), (E), or (F), (a)(2(A), (B), (C), or (D), (c), (d), (other than regulation relating to recordkeeping or filing or reports), (f), or (g) of section 9 of this Act, may be assessed a civil penalty by the Secretary of not more than $25,000 for each violation. Any person who knowingly violates, and any person engaged in business as an importer or exporter of fish, wildlife, or plants who violates, any provision of any other regulation issued under this Act may be assessed a civil penalty by the Secretary of not more than $12,000 for each such violation. Any person who otherwise violates any provision of this Act, or any regulation, permit, or certificate issued hereunder, may be assessed a civil penalty by the Secretary of not more than $500 for each such violation. No penalty may be assessed under this subsection unless such person is given notice and opportunity for a hearing with respect to such violation. Each violation shall be a separate offense. Any such civil penalty may be remitted or mitigated by the Secretary. Upon any failure to pay a penalty assessed under this subsection, the Secretary may request the Attorney General to institute a civil action in a district court of the United States for any district in which such person is found, resides, or transacts business to collect the penalty and such court shall have jurisdiction to hear and decide any such action. The court shall hear such action on the record made before the Secretary and shall sustain his action if it is supported by substantial evidence on the record considered as a whole.

(2) Hearings held during proceedings for the assessment of civil penalties by paragraph (1) of this subsection shall be conducted in accordance with section 554 of title 5, United States Code. The Secretary may issue subpoenas for the attendance and testimony of witnesses and the production of relevant papers, books, and documents, and administer oaths. Witnesses summoned shall be paid the same fees and mileage that are paid to witnesses in the courts of the United States. In case of contumacy or refusal to obey a subpoena served upon any person pursuant to this paragraph, the district court of the United States for any district in which such person is found or resides or transacts business, upon application by the United States and after notice to such person, shall have jurisdiction to issue an order requiring such person to appear and give testimony before the Secretary or to appear and produce documents before the Secretary, or both, and any failure to obey such order of the court may be punished by such court as a contempt thereof.

(3) Notwithstanding any other provision of this Act, no civil penalty shall be imposed if it can be shown by a preponderance of the evidence that the defendant committed an act based on a good faith belief that he was acting to protect himself or herself, a member of his or her family, or any other individual from bodily harm, from any endangered or threatened species.

(b) CRIMINAL VIOLATIONS.—(1) Any person who knowingly violates any provision of this Act, of any permit or certificate issued hereunder, or of any regulation issued in order to implement subsection (a)(1)(A), (B), (C), (D), (E), or (F); (a)(2)(A), (B), (C), or (D), (c), (d) (other than a regulation relating to recordkeeping, or filing of reports), (f), or (g) of section 9 of this Act shall, upon conviction, be fined not more than $50,000 or imprisoned for not more than one year, or both. Any person who knowingly violates any provision of any other regulation issued under this Act shall, upon conviction, be fined not more than $25,000 or imprisoned for not more than six months, or both.

(2) The head of any Federal agency which has issued a lease, license, permit, or other agreement authorizing a person to import or export fish, wildlife, or plants, or to operate a quarantine station for imported wildlife, or authorizing the use of Federal lands, including grazing of domestic

livestock, to any person who is convicted of a criminal violation of this Act or any regulation, permit, or certificate issued hereunder may immediately modify, suspend, or revoke each lease, license, permit, or other agreement. The Secretary shall also suspend for a period of up to one year, or cancel, any Federal hunting or fishing permits or stamps issued to any person who is convicted of a criminal violation of any provision of this Act or any regulation, permit, or certificate issued hereunder. The United States shall not be liable for the payments of any compensation, reimbursement, or damages in connection with the modification, suspension, or revocation of any leases, licenses permits stamps, or other agreements pursuant to this section.

(3) Notwithstanding any other provision of this Act, it shall be a defense to prosecution under this subsection if the defendant committed the offense based on a good faith belief that he was acting to protect himself or herself, a member of his or her family, or any other individual, from bodily harm from any endangered or threatened species.

Section 11: Marine Law Enforcement

The following is a summary of some of the Regulations enforced by the Coast Guard, reprinted from www.navcen.uscg.gov/mwv/regulations/regs_home.htm. More information is available from the enforcement home page at www.uscg.mil/hq/g-o/g-opl/mle/welcome.htm.

Anchorages
- 33 CFR 110 - Anchorage Regulations

Bridges
- 33 CFR 117 - Drawbridge operations regulations

Coast Guard Jurisdiction
- 33 CFR 2 - Defines terms the Coast Guard uses in regulations, policies, and procedures, to determine whether it has jurisdiction on certain waters in cases where specific jurisdictional definitions are not otherwise provided.

Coast Guard Organization
- 33 CFR 3 - *Coast Guard Areas, Districts, Marine Inspection Zones, and Captain of the Port Zones.* This Rule describes the jurisdiction boundaries of each Coast Guard Area, District, Marine Inspection Zone (MIZ), and Captain of the Port (COTP) Zone.

COLREGS (International Navigation Rules)
- 33 CFR 80 - COLREGS Demarcation Lines • 33 CFR 81 - 72 COLREGS: Implementing Rules • 33 CFR 82 - 72 COLREGS: Interpretive Rules

Inland Navigation Rules
- 33 CFR 84 - Annex I: Positioning and technical details of lights and shapes • 33 CFR 85 - Annex II: Additional signals for fishing vessels fishing in close proximity • 33 CFR 86 - Annex III: Technical details of sound signal appliances • 33 CFR 87 - Annex IV: Distress signals • 33 CFR 88 - Annex V: Pilot Rules • 33 CFR 90 - Inland Navigation Rules: Interpretive Rules.

Regattas and Marine Parades
- 33 CFR 100 - The purpose of the regulations in this part is to provide effective control over regattas and marine parades conducted on the navigable waters of the United States so as to insure safety of life in the regatta or marine parade area.

Safety Zones
- 33 CFR 147 - Regulations adopted for safety zones may extend to the prevention or control of specific activities and access by vessels or persons, and include measures to protect the living resources of the sea from harmful agents.

St. Lawrence Seaway Regulations And Rules
- 33 CFR 401 - These regulations control the equipment and operation of vessels using the St. Lawrence Seaway (map), a set of channels and locks that connects the Great Lakes to the Atlantic Ocean.

US Army Corps of Engineers - Navigation Regulations
- 33 CFR 207 - Regulations regarding locks on US Navigable Waterways.

Section 12: The Basics of Chartering

The following information is the type collected by Charter Companies from prospective Charterers. Of course, the information varies from company to company as does the level of scrutiny of Charterers and the degree of training prior to departure. In addition to requested information some companies may include a short quiz.

- Full name, address, phone number, and e-mail address. Occupation and employer.

- Boat ownership: Type and size of boat owned, and number of years.

- Boating Experience: Lessons, training, education and certifications. Previous bareboat charter experience: When, where, type of boat, name of company.

- Cruising experience: Overnight trips, extended cruises, inshore, coastal, offshore, etc.

- Navigational experience: Piloting, use of charts, compass and electronics. Anchoring and mooring experience.

- Memberships in boating organizations: Yacht club, Coast Guard Auxiliary, etc.

Section 13: Boating Etiquette, Towing, and Salvage

Sample Form

Salvage Contract.

Boat Owners Association of The United States
STANDARD FORM YACHT SALVAGE CONTRACT

It is hereby agreed this _____ day of _____, 20_____, at _____ hours at _____ (location) by and between: _____ (Owner or Captain) for the Yacht named "_____," which is described as a _____ ("Vessel")(yr-manufacturer-length) and insured by: _____ ("Underwriter") and _____ (Salvage Company/Salvor) , to salvage the yacht under these terms and conditions:

1. Salvor agrees to render assistance to and endeavor to save said yacht and its property and deliver her afloat or ashore at _____ marina or port as mutually agreed, or to nearest safe port if unspecified herein, as soon as practicable.

2. Salvor shall have the requisite possession and control of the subject yacht and be entitled without expense to the reasonable use of the yacht and its gear in the performance of recovery or salvage operations.

3. Said salvage and any towage services by the Salvor shall terminate upon delivery of said yacht as designated herein. Owner and Underwriter shall be responsible for any storage, towing or other port or marina charges following delivery and for risk of loss thereafter.

    (a) NO CURE/NO PAY (Compensation, including special compensation, to be determined under ARTICLES 13 and 14, SALCON 89, and U.S. Admiralty Law.) INITIALS _____/_____ salvor / owner

    (b) NO CURE/NO PAY, AT A FIXED PRICE of $_____ INITIALS _____/_____ salvor / owner

    (c) NO CURE/NO PAY at $_____/per hour/per day/per vessel (or in accordance with SALVOR's published rates, initialed and attached hereto). INITIALS _____/_____ salvor / owner

    (d) OTHER:

4. Compensation to Salvor for the services performed hereunder shall be in accordance with a billing and any supportive analysis of the salvage operation to be presented to Owner and Underwriter's agents upon completion of salvage. Billing to be calculated on the basis specified in No. 3. No agreement on price or its reasonableness has been made at the scene unless agreed to in writing.

5. Services hereunder are rendered on a "No Cure, No Pay" basis; however, salvor shall be entitled to a reasonable allowance for prevention or minimization of environmental damage in accordance with Articles 13 & 14 of the 1989 International Convention on Salvage, as well as for clean up or wreck removal in the event the vessel is deemed a constructive total loss. Payment is due promptly upon presentation of Salvor's bill. Interest at the rate of one and one-half (1.5 percent) percent per month (or the maximum legal rate allowed) shall accrue on any unpaid balance from 30 days after completion of salvage and presentation of a salvage bill, or as determined in accordance with the findings of any Arbitration Award.

6. In the event of any dispute regarding this salvage or concerning the reasonableness of any fees or charges due hereunder, all parties agree to binding local arbitration utilizing individual(s) experienced in maritime and salvage law. The Boat Owners Association of The United States Salvage Arbitration Plan, though not required, is available as a public service through Boat Owners Association of The United States wherever the parties agree to its use. In the event Owner is uninsured for payment of these services, Salvor may, at its election, agree with Owner to use any agreeable arbitration system or to proceed with all available legal remedies to recover sums believed due and owing.

7. It is understood that services performed hereunder are governed by the Admiralty and Maritime Jurisdiction of the Federal Courts and create a maritime lien against the yacht or its posted security. Salvor's lien shall be preserved until payment. Salvor agrees in lieu of arrest or attachment to accept from the yacht's Underwriter, a Letter of Undertaking for an amount equal to one and one-half (1.5) times the presented billing with a copy of the insurance policy and coverage information. If the yacht is uninsured or its Underwriter cannot provide a Letter of Undertaking, Salvor may demand the posting of a Surety Bond with its designated Escrow Agent in an amount equal to 1.5 times the Salvor's bill. Salvor may satisfy collection of fees or charges hereunder by recourse to any security posted and shall be entitled to any costs incurred in collection of payments due hereunder including reasonable attorneys fees subject to the findings of any arbitration.

8. Salvor hereby warrants that it is acting on its own behalf and on behalf of any subcontractors retained by Salvor to perform services in the recovery or delivery of the yacht. Salvor shall be responsible for any such subcontractors' compensation.

9. In the event the Salvor has already rendered salvage services to the described yacht prior to execution of this contract, the provisions of this contract shall apply to such salvage services.

SIGNED: _____   _____

Owner/Captain or Owner's Agent   Salvage Company
Print Name & Address: Print Name & Address:

_____   _____

_____   _____

Phone: (_____) _____   Phone: (_____) _____

Fax: (_____) _____   Fax: (_____) _____

Section 14: State Laws and Regulations

State Boating Law and Enforcement Agencies

The NASBLA Reference Guide to State Boating Laws can be downloaded free from the NASBLA web site at www. nasbla.org. You can find the web site for your state's boating law and enforcement agency by visiting www.nasbla.org/ blas.htm. Below is a list of state offices and agencies. This information is taken from the NASBLA Reference Guide.

ALABAMA	ALASKA	ARIZONA
Marine Police Division	Alaska Public Lands Information Center	Game and Fish Department
Folsom Administrative Building	605 W 4th Avenue	2222 W Greenway Road
64 N Union Street, Room 438	Anchorage, AK 99501	Phoenix, AZ 85023
Montgomery, AL 36104	907-271-2737	602-942-3000
334-242-3673		
ARKANSAS	**CALIFORNIA**	**COLORADO**
Game and Fish Commission	Department of Boating and Waterways	Division of Parks and Outdoor
Boating Safety Section	1629 S Street	Recreation
2 Natural Resources Drive	Sacramento, CA 95814	13787 S Highway 85
Little Rock, AR 72205	916-445-6281	Littleton, CO 80125
501-223-6351	916-657-8013 (Boat registration)	303-791-1954
501-223-6378 (Boat registration)		
CONNECTICUT	**DELAWARE**	**DISTRICT OF COLUMBIA**
Department of Environmental	Department of Natural Resources and	Police Department Harbor Patrol
Protection Boating Division	Environmental Control	550 SW Water Street
P.O. Box 280	P.O. Box 1401	Washington, DC 20024
Old Lyme, CT 06371	Dover, DE 19903	202-727-4582
860-434-8638	302-739-3440	
860-566-1556 (Boat registration)	302-739-3498 (Boat registration)	
FLORIDA (Freshwater)	**FLORIDA (Saltwater)**	**GEORGIA**
Game & Freshwater Fish Commission	Marine Patrol, MS 630	Department of Natural Resources
620 S Meridian Street	3900 Commonwealth Boulevard	Wildlife Resources Division
Tallahassee, FL 32399-1600	Tallahassee, FL 32399	2070 SE Highway 278
904-488-6257	904-488-5600 Ext. 28	Social Circle, GA 30279
		770-918-6408
		770-414-3337 (Boat registration)
HAWAII	**IDAHO**	**LLINOIS**
Department of Land and Natural	Department of Parks and Recreation	Department of Natural Resources
Resources	P.O. Box 83720	Office of Law Enforcement
Division of Boating and Ocean	Boise, ID 83720-0065	524 S Second Street, 3rd Floor
Research	208-334-3180 Ext. 224	Springfield, IL 62701-1787
333 Queen Street, Suite 300		217-782-6431
Honolulu, HI 96813		217-782-2138 (Boat registration)
808-587-1970		

INDIANA Department of Natural Resources Law Enforcement Division IGCS 255D- 402 W Washington Street Indianapolis, IN 46204 317-232-4010 317-232-2821(Boat registration)	**IOWA** Department of Natural Resources Recreational Safety Division Wallace State Office Building Des Moines, IA 50319 515-281-8652 515-281-5267 (Boat registration)	**KANSAS** Department of Wildlife and Parks 512 SE 25th Avenue Pratt, KS 67124 316-672-5911 Ext. 156 316-672-5911 Ext.127 (Boat registration)
KENTUCKY Department of Fish and Wildlife Water Patrol 1 Game Farm Road Frankfort, KY 40601 502-564-3074	**LOUISIANA** Department of Wildlife and Fisheries P.O. Box 98000 Baton Rouge, LA 70898-9000 504-765-2988 504-765-2898 (Boat registration)	**MAINE** (Freshwater) Inland Fisheries and Wildlife Department Maine Warden Service 284 State Street, Station 41 Augusta, ME 04330 207-287-2766 207-287-5209 (Boat registration)
MAINE (Saltwater) Maine Marine Patrol Special Services State House Station #21 Augusta, ME 04330 207-624-6550	**MARYLAND** Department of Natural Resources 580 Taylor Avenue Annapolis, MD 21401 410-974-3211	**MASSACHUSETTS** Department of Fisheries, Wildlife and Environmental Law 175 Portland Street Boston, MA 02114 617-727-3905 617-727-3900 (Boat registration)
MICHIGAN Department of Natural Resources Steven T. Mason Building P.O. Box 30031 Lansing, MI 48909 517-335-3414 517-322-1460 (Boat registration)	**MINNESOTA** Department of Natural Resources Boat and Water Safety 500 Lafayette Road St. Paul, MN 55155-4046 612-296-3310 612-296-2316 (Boat registration)	**MISSISSIPPI** Department of Wildlife, Fisheries and Parks P.O. Box 451 Jackson, MS 39205 601-364-2240 601-364-2032 (Boat registration)
MISSOURI Department of Public Safety State Water Patrol P.O. Box 1368 Jefferson City, MO 65102 314-751-3333 314-751-4509 (Boat registration)	**MONTANA** Fish, Wildlife and Parks Boating Safety Division 1420 E 6th Street Helena, MT 59620 406-444-2452 406-846-1423 (Boat registration)	**NEBRASKA** Game and Parks Commission 2200 N 33rd Street Lincoln, NE 68503-0370 402-471-0641
NEVADA Division of Wildlife Law Enforcement Bureau P.O. Box 10678 Reno, NV 89520-0022 702-688-1500	**NEW HAMPSHIRE** Department of Safety Marine Patrol 31 Dock Road Gilford, NH 03246 603-293-2037	**NEW JERSEY** State Police Marine Law Enforcement Bureau P.O. Box 7068 West Trenton, NJ 08628-0068 609-292-4630 or 800-DMV-2222 (In-State Boat Registration)

NEW MEXICO New Mexico State Parks Boating Safety Section P.O. Box 1147 Santa Fe, NM 87504-1147 505-827-7465 505-827-0612 (Boat registration)	**NEW YORK** Office of Parks, Recreation & Historic Preservation Marine & Recreational Vehicles Empire State Plaza Agency Bldg. 1 Albany, NY 12238 518-474-0445	**NORTH CAROLINA** Wildlife Resources Commission Archdale Building Raleigh, NC 27604-1188 919-733-3391 919-662-4373 (Boat registration)
NORTH DAKOTA Game & Fish Department 100 N. Bismarck Expressway Bismarck, ND 59501-5095 701-328-6300	**OHIO** Department of Natural Resources Division of Watercraft 4435 Fountain Square Drive Fountain Square, Building. A Columbus, OH 43224-1300 or 614-265-6480	**OKLAHOMA** Department of Public Safety 3600 N. Martin Luther King Oklahoma City, OK 73136-0415 405-521-3221 405-521-2439 (Boat registration)
OREGON State Marine Board 435 Commercial Street N.E. #800 Salem, OR 97310 503-378-8587 Ext. 241	**PENNSYLVANIA** Fish & Boat Comm. Bureau of Boating P.O. Box 67000 Harrisburg, PA 17106-7000 717-657-4540 717-657-4551 (Boat registration)	**PUERTO RICO** Departmet of Natural Revenue Commissioner of Navigation P.O. Box 588, Pta. de Tierra San Juan, PR 00906 809-724-2340
RHODE ISLAND Dept. of Environmental Management 83 Park Street Providence, RI 02903 401-277-2284 401-277-6647 (Boat registration)	**SOUTH CAROLINA** Department of Natural Resources Division of Boating P.O. Box 12559 Charleston, SC 29412 803-762-5034	**SOUTH DAKOTA** Department of Game Fish & Parks 523 E Capitol Avenue Pierre, SD 57501-3182 605-773-3630
TENNESSEE Wildlife Resources Agency P.O. Box 40747 Nashville, TN 37204 615-781-6682	**TEXAS** Parks & Wildlife Department 4200 Smith School Road Austin, TX 78744 512-389-4800 512-389-4828 (Boat registration)	**U.S. VIRGIN ISLANDS** Department of Planning & Natural Resources 396-1 Annas Retreat, Foster Plaza St. Thomas, VI 00802 809-771-7397
UTAH Division of Parks & Recreation 1636 W. North Temple St. Salt Lake City, UT 84116 801-538-7220 801-972-5320 (Boat registration)	**VERMONT** State Police-Marine Division 565 St. George Road Williston, VT 05495 802-244-8778 802-828-2000 (Boat registration)	**VIRGINIA** Department of Game & Inland Fisheries Boat Section 4010 W. Broad Street Richmond, VA 23230-1104 804-367-1000
WASHINGTON State Parks & Recreation Commission P.O. Box 42654 Olympia, WA 98504-2654 360-902-8551 360-902-3770 (Boat registration)	**WEST VIRGINIA** Div. of Natural Resources Law Enforcement Section Capitol Complex, Bldg. 3 Charleston, WV 25305 304-558-2784	**WISCONSIN** Dept. of Natural Resources Law Enforcement P.O. Box 7921 Madison, WI 53707 608-266-2141 608-267-7799 (Boat registration)
WYOMING Department of Game & Fish 5400 Bishop Blvd. Cheyenne, WY 82006 307-777-4579	**MEXICO** Secretaria Turismo Presidente Masaryk 172 Bosque Chapultepec 11587 Mexico City, Mexico 525-250-2501, 525-250-1954 and 525-250-8617	**CANADA** Canadian Coast Guard AMEC-9th floor, 344 Slater Street Ottawa, ONT K1A 0N7 613-990-7011 or 800-267-6687 (in Canada) 613-991-3150 (Boat registration)

The following table summarizes some State law requirements.

SUMMARY OF STATE LAWS

State Name:	State Agency	Internet Address	Legal Requirements						
			min. age boat or PWC	Educ. req'd?	Lic. reg'd?	MSD req'd	Y-valve lock?	Boat title?	Alcohol (BUI) law?
Alabama	Conservation & Natural Resources	www.dcnr.state.al.us/boating	12	no	yes	no	no	no	yes
Alaska	Department of Natural Resources	www.alaskaboatingsafety.org	none	no	yes	no	no	no	yes
Arizona	Game & Fish Department	www.azgfd.com	12	no	no	no	no	no	yes
Arkansas	Arkansas Game and Fish Commission	www.agfc.state.ar.us	12	yes	no	no	yes	no	yes
California	California Resources Agency	www.dbw.ca.gov	16	no	no	no	yes	yes	yes
Colorado	Department of Natural Resources	www.parks.state.co.us	16	yes	no	no	yes	no	yes
Connecticut	Department of Environ. Protection	www.dep.state.ct.us/rec/boating/index.htm	12	yes	yes	yes	no	no	yes
Delaware	Division of Fish & Wildlife Enforcement	www.dnrec.state.de.us/dnrec2000/	none	yes	no	no	yes	no	yes
Dist. Columbia	Harbor Patrol	www.mpdc.org	13	yes	no	yes	yes	yes	yes
Florida	Fish & Wildlife Conservation Commission	www.myfwc.com/boating/	14	yes	no	yes	yes	yes	yes
Georgia	Department of Natural Resources	www.georgiawildlife.dnr.state.ga.us/	12	yes	no	yes	yes	no	yes
Hawaii	Div. of Boating and Ocean Recreation	www.hawaii.gov/dlnr/dbor/dbor.htm	none	no	no	yes	yes	no	yes
Idaho	Department of Parks & Recreation	www.idahoparks.org/rec/boating.html	none	yes	no	no	yes	yes	yes
Illinois	Department of Natural Resources	www.dnr.state.il.us/admin/systems/boats.htm	10	yes	no	no	yes	yes	yes
Indiana	Department of Natural Resources	www.in.gov/dnr/boating/	15	yes	yes	yes	yes	yes	yes
Iowa	Department of Natural Resources	www.iowadnr.com/	12	yes	yes	no	no	yes	yes
Kansas	Department of Wildlife & Parks	www.kdwp.state.ks.us/boating/boating.html	12	yes	no	yes	yes	no	yes
Kentucky	Department of Fish & Wildlife	www.fw.ky.gov/	12	yes	no	yes	yes	yes	yes
Louisiana	Department of Wildlife & Fisheries	www.wlf.state.la.us	13	yes	yes	yes	yes	no	yes
Maine	Dep't of Inland Fisheries & Wildlife	www.state.me.us/ifw/	12	no	no	yes	no	no	yes
Maryland	Department of Natural Resources	www.dnr.state.md.us/boating/	none	yes	no	yes	yes	yes	yes
Massachusetts	Massachusetts Environmental Police	www.mass.gov/dfwele/dle/dle_toc.htm	12	yes	no	no	no	yes	yes
Michigan	Department of Natural Resources	www.dnr.state.mi.us	12	yes	no	no	yes	yes	yes

State	Agency	Website	Age						
Minnesota	Department of Natural Resources	www.dnr.state.mn.us/boating/index.html	12	yes	no	no	yes	yes	yes
Mississippi	Dept. of Wildlife, Fisheries & Parks	www.mdwfp.com	12	yes	no	yes	no	no	yes
Missouri	Department of Public Safety	www.mswp.state.mo.us	14	yes	no	yes	n/a	no	yes
Montana	Dept. of Fish, Wildlife & Parks	www.fwp.state.mt.us	13	no	no	yes	no	yes	yes
Nebraska	Game & Parks Commission	www.ngpc.state.ne.us/boating	14	yes	no	yes	yes	yes	yes
Nevada	Dept. of Cons. & Natural Resources	www.boatnevada.org/	none	yes	no	yes	yes	yes	yes
New Hampshire	Department of Safety	www.nh.gov/safety/	16	yes	no	yes	n/a	n/a	yes
New Jersey	Department of Law & Public Safety	www.nj.gov/lps/	16	yes	yes	no	yes	yes	yes
New Mexico	New Mexico State Parks	www.emnrd.state.nm.us/nmparks/	13	no	no	yes	yes	yes	yes
New York	NY State Parks & Recreation	www.nysparks.com/boats	10	yes	no	yes	yes	yes	yes
North Car.	Environmental & Natural Resources	www.state.nc.us/wildlife	12	no	no	no	no	yes	yes
North Dakota	Game and Fish Department	www.state.nd.us/gnf/boating/	12	no	no	yes	yes	yes	yes
Ohio	Department of Natural Resources	www.dnr.state.oh.us/watercraft/	12	yes	no	no	no	yes	yes
Oklahoma	Highway Patrol, Lake Patrol Section	www.dps.state.ok.us	none	no	no	yes	yes	yes	yes
Oregon	State Marine Board	www.boatoregon.com	12	yes	no	no	no	yes	yes
Pennsylvania	Fish & Boat Commission	www.fish.state.pa.us	12	yes	no	yes	yes	yes	yes
Rhode Island	Dept. Environmental Management	www.state.ri.us/dem	none	no	no	yes	yes	yes	yes
South Carolina	Department of Natural Resources	www.dnr.state.sc.us/etc/boating.html	none	yes	no	no	no	yes	yes
South Dakota	Dept. of Game, Fish & Parks	www.sdgfp.info/Wildlife/Boating/	12	no	no	no	no	yes	yes
Tennessee	Parks & Wildlife Department	www.state.tn.us/twra/boatmain.html	12	no	no	yes	yes	yes	yes
Texas	Parks & Wildlife Department	www.tpwd.state.tx.us/boat/	13	yes	no	yes	yes	yes	yes
Utah	Division of Parks & Recreation	www.parks.state.ut.us/boating/default.htm	16	no	no	no	no	yes	yes
Vermont	Vermont State Police, Marine Division	www.dps.state.vt.us/vtsp/	12	yes	no	no	no	yes	yes
Virginia	Dept. of Game & Inland Fisheries	www.dgif.state.va.us/boating/	14	no	no	no	no	yes	yes
West Virginia	Division of Natural Resources, L.E. Section	www.wvdnr.gov/lenforce/boating.shtm	15	yes	no	no	no	yes	yes
Washington	Parks & Recreation Commission	www.parks.wa.gov/boating.asp	14	no	no	yes	yes	yes	yes
Wisconsin	Department of Natural Resources	www.dnr.state.wi.us/OutdoorActivities.html	10	yes	no	yes	yes	yes	yes
Wyoming	Game & Fish Department	www.gf.state.wy.us/fish/boating/index.asp	16	no	no	no	no	no	yes

Section 15: Equipment Information and Specifications to Keep Aboard

Sample Form

The following Equipment Information form can be used to keep track of the equipment on your boat.
Equipment Information

A. Radios (VHF, Single Side Band, CB, etc.)

Description:	Make & Model	Serial #	Price	Date & Place Purchased

B. Radar

Description:	Make & Model	Serial #	Price	Date & Place Purchased

C. GPS

Description:	Make & Model	Serial #	Price	Date & Place Purchased

D. Battery Charger-Inverter

Description:	Make & Model	Serial #	Price	Date & Place Purchased

E. Other instruments (depth sounder, wind speed, knot meter, fish finder, etc)

Description:	Make & Model	Serial #	Price	Date & Place Purchased

F. Genset

Description:	Make & Model	Serial #	Price	Date & Place Purchased

G. Windlass

Description:	Make & Model	Serial #	Price	Date & Place Purchased

H. Other Equipment

Description:	Make & Model	Serial #	Price	Date & Place Purchased

Glossary of Nautical Terms

ABAFT - Toward the rear (stern) of the boat. Behind.

ABEAM - At right angles to the keel of the boat, but not on the boat.

ABOARD - On or within the boat.

ABOVE DECK - On the deck.

AFT - Toward the stern of the boat.

AGROUND - Touching or fast to the bottom.

AHEAD - In a forward direction.

AIDS TO NAVIGATION - Artificial objects to supplement natural landmarks to indicate safe and unsafe waters.

ALOFT - Above the deck of the boat.

AMIDSHIPS - In or toward the center of the boat.

ANCHOR - A heavy metal device, fastened to a chain or line, to hold a vessel in position, partly because of its weight, but chiefly because the designed shape digs into the bottom.

ANCHORAGE - A place suitable for anchoring in relation to the wind, seas and bottom.

ASTERN - In back of the boat, opposite of ahead.

ATHWARTSHIPS - At right angles to the centerline of the boat.

BATTEN DOWN - Secure hatches and loose objects both within the hull and on deck.

BEACON - A lighted or unlighted fixed aid to navigation attached directly to the earth's surface.

BEAM - The greatest width of the boat.

BEARING - The direction of an object expressed either as a true bearing as shown on the chart, or as a bearing relative to the heading of the boat.

BELOW - Beneath the deck.

BIGHT - The part of the rope or line, between the end and the standing part, on which a knot is formed. Also, a shallow bay.

BILGE - The interior of the hull below the floor boards.

BITTER END - The last part of a rope or chain. The inboard end of the anchor rode.

BLOCK- A wooden or metal case enclosing one or more pulleys and having a hook, eye, or strap by which it may be attached.

BOAT - A fairly indefinite term. A waterborne vehicle smaller than a ship. One definition is a small craft carried aboard a ship.

BOAT HOOK - A short shaft with a fitting at one end shaped to facilitate use in putting a line over a piling, recovering an object dropped overboard, or in pushing or fending off.

BOW - The forward part of a boat.

BOW LINE - A docking line leading from the bow.

BOW SPRING LINE - A bow pivot line used in docking and undocking, or to prevent the boat from moving forward or astern while made fast to a pier.

BOWLINE KNOT - A knot used to form a temporary loop in the end of a line.

BOWSPRIT - A spar extending forward from the bow.

BRIDGE - The location from which a vessel is steered and its speed controlled. "Control Station" is really a more appropriate term for small craft.

BULKHEAD - A vertical partition separating compartments.

BUOY - An anchored float used for marking a position on the water or a hazard or for mooring.

CABIN - A compartment for passengers or crew.

CAPSIZE - To turn over.

CAST OFF - To let go.

CATAMARAN - A twin-hulled boat, with hulls side-by-side.

CHAFING GEAR - Tubing or cloth wrapping used to protect a line from chafing on a rough surface.

CHANNEL - 1. That part of a body of water deep enough for navigation through an area otherwise not suitable. It is usually marked by a single or double line of buoys and sometimes by range markers. 2. The deepest part of a stream, bay, or strait, through which the main current flows. 3. A name given to a large strait, for example, the English Channel.

CHART - A map for use by navigators.

CHINE - The intersection of the bottom and sides of a flat or v-bottomed boat.

CHOCK - A fitting through which anchor or mooring lines are led. Usually U-shaped to reduce chafe.

CLEAT - A fitting to which lines are made fast. The classic cleat to which lines are belayed is approximately anvil-shaped.

CLOVE HITCH - A knot for temporarily fastening a line to a spar or piling.

COAMING - A vertical piece around the edge of a cockpit, hatch, etc. to prevent water on deck from running below.

COCKPIT - An opening in the deck from which the boat is handled.

COIL - To lay a line down in circular turns.

COMPASS - Navigation instrument. Magnetic (showing magnetic north) or gyro (showing true north).

COMPASS CARD - Part of a compass, the card is graduated in degrees, to conform with the magnetic meridian-referenced direction system inscribed with direction which remains constant; the vessel turns, not the card.

COMPASS ROSE - The resulting figure when the complete 360° directional system is developed as a circle with each degree graduated upon it, and with the 000° indicated as True North. True North is also known as true rose. This is printed on nautical charts for determining direction.

CURRENT - The horizontal movement of water.

DAYBEACON - A fixed navigation aid structure used in shallow waters upon which is placed one or more daymarks.

DAYMARK - A signboard attached to a daybeacon to convey navigational information presenting one of several standard shapes (square, triangle, rectangle) and colors (red, green, orange, yellow, or black). Daymarks usually have reflective material indicating the shape, but may also be lighted.

DEAD AHEAD - Directly ahead.

DEAD ASTERN - Directly aft or behind.

DEAD RECKONING - A plot of courses steered and distances traveled through the water.

DECK - A permanent covering over a compartment, hull or any part of a ship serving as a floor.

DISPLACEMENT - The weight of water displaced by a floating vessel.

DISPLACEMENT HULL - A type of hull that plows through the water, displacing a weight of water equal to its own weight, even when more power is added.

DOCK - A protected water area in which vessels are moored. The term is often used to denote a pier or a wharf.

DRAFT - The depth of water a boat draws.

EASE - To slacken or relieve tension on a line.

EBB TIDE - A receding tide.

EVEN KEEL - When a boat is floating on its designed waterline it is said to be on an even keel.

EYE OF THE WIND - The direction from which the wind is blowing.

EYE SPLICE - A permanent loop spliced in the end of a line.

FAST - Said of an object that is secured to another.

FATHOM – Six feet. Usually a measurement of depth.

FENDER - A cushion, placed between boats, or between a boat and a pier, to prevent damage.

FIGURE EIGHT KNOT - A knot in the form of a figure eight, placed in the end of a line to prevent the line from passing through a grommet or a block.

FLAME ARRESTER - A safety device, such as a metal mesh protector, to prevent an exhaust backfire from causing an explosion; operates by absorbing heat.

FLARE - The outward curve of a vessel's sides near the bow. A distress signal.

FLYING BRIDGE - An added set of controls above the level of the normal control station for better visibility. Usually open, but may have a collapsible top for shade.

FOLLOWING SEA - An overtaking sea that comes from astern.

FORE AND AFT - In a line parallel to the keel.

FORWARD - Toward the bow of the boat.

FOULED - Any piece of equipment that is jammed or entangled, or dirtied.

FOUNDER - when a vessel fills with water and sinks.

FREEBOARD - The minimum vertical distance from the surface of the water to the gunwale

GAFF - A spar to support the head of a gaff sail.

GALLEY - The kitchen area of a boat.

GANGWAY - The area of a ship's side where people board and disembark.

GEAR - A general term for ropes, blocks, tackle and other equipment.

GIVE-WAY VESSEL - A term, from the Navigational Rules, used to describe the vessel that must yield in meeting, crossing, or overtaking situations.

GRAB RAILS - Hand-hold fittings mounted on cabin tops and sides for personal safety when moving around the boat.

GROUND TACKLE - Anchor, anchor rode (line or chain), and all the shackles and other gear used for attachment.

GUNWALE - The upper edge of a boat's sides.

HARBOR - A safe anchorage, protected from most storms; may be natural or man-made, with break-waters and jetties; a place for docking and loading.

HATCH - An opening in a boat's deck fitted with a watertight cover.

HEAD - A marine toilet. Also the upper corner of a triangular sail.

HEADING - The direction in which a vessel's bow points at any given time.

HEADWAY - The forward motion of a boat. Opposite of sternway.

HEAVE TO - To bring a vessel up in a position where it will maintain little or no headway, usually with the bow into the wind or nearly so.

HEEL - To tip to one side.

HELM - The wheel or tiller controlling the rudder.

HITCH - A knot used to secure a rope to another object or to another rope, or to form a loop or a noose in a rope.

HOLD - A compartment below deck in a large vessel, used solely for carrying cargo.

HULL - The main body of a vessel.

HYPOTHERMIA - A life-threatening condition in which the body's warming mechanisms fail to maintain normal body temperature and the entire body cools.

INBOARD - More toward the center of a vessel; inside; a motor fitted inside the boat.

KEDGE - To use an anchor to move a boat by hauling on the anchor rode; a basic anchor type.

KEEL - The centerline of a boat running fore and aft; the backbone of a vessel.

KETCH - A two-masted sailboat with the smaller after mast stepped ahead of the rudderpost.

KNOT - A measure of speed equal to one nautical mile (6076 feet) per hour. A fastening made by interweaving rope to form a stopper, to enclose or bind an object, to form a loop or a noose, to tie a small rope to an object, or to tie the ends of two small ropes together. .

LEEWARD - The direction away from the wind. Opposite of windward.

LEEWAY - The sideways movement of the boat caused by either wind or current.

LINE - Rope and cordage used aboard a vessel.

LOG - A record of courses or operation. Also, a device to measure speed.

LUBBER'S LINE - A mark or permanent line on a compass indicating the direction forward; parallel to the keel when properly installed.

MAST - A spar set upright to support rigging and sails.

MONOHULL - A boat with one hull.

MOORING - An arrangement for securing a boat to a mooring buoy or a pier.

MOORING BUOY - A buoy secured to a permanent anchor sunk deeply into the bottom.

NAUTICAL MILE - One minute of latitude; approximately 6076 feet - about 1/8 longer than the statute mile of 5280 feet.

NAVIGATION - The art and science of conducting a boat safely from one point to another.

OUTBOARD - Toward or beyond the boat's sides. A detachable engine mounted on a boat's stern.

OUTDRIVE - A propulsion system for boats with an inboard engine operating an exterior drive, with drive shaft, gears, and propeller; also called stern-drive and inboard/outboard.

OVERBOARD - Over the side or out of the boat.

PAINTER- A line attached to the bow of a boat for use in towing or making fast.

PAY OUT - To ease out a line, or let it run in a controlled manner.

PENNANT (sometimes PENDANT) - The line by which a boat is made fast to a mooring buoy.

PERSONAL FLOTATION DEVICE (PFD) - PDF is official terminology for life jacket. When properly used, the PDF will support a person in the water. Available in several sizes and types.

PIER - A loading/landing platform extending at an angle from the shore.

PILOTING - Navigation by use of visible references, the depth of the water, etc.

PITCH - 1. The alternate rise and fall of the bow of a vessel proceeding through waves; 2. The theoretical distance advanced by a propeller in one revolution; 3. Tar and resin used for caulking between the planks of a wooden vessel.

PITCHPOLING - A small boat being thrown end-over-end in very rough seas.

PLANING HULL - A type of hull shaped to glide easily across the water at high speed.

PORT - The left side of a boat looking forward. A harbor.

PROPELLER - A rotating device, with two or more blades, that acts as a screw in propelling a vessel

QUARTER - The sides of a boat aft of amidships.

QUARTERING SEA - Sea coming on a boat's quarter.

REEF - To reduce the sail area.

RIGGING - The general term for all the lines of a vessel.

RODE - The anchor line and/or chain.

ROLL - The alternating motion of a boat, leaning alternately to port and starboard; the motion of a boat about its fore-and-aft axis.

ROPE - In general, cordage as it is purchased at the store. When it comes aboard a vessel and is put to use, it becomes a line.

RUDDER - A vertical plate or board for steering a boat.

RUNNING LIGHTS - Lights required to be shown on boats underway between sundown and sunup.

SCOPE - The ratio of the length of an anchor line, from a vessel's bow to the anchor, to the depth of the water.

SCREW - A boat's propeller.

SEA ANCHOR - Any device used to reduce a boat's drift before the wind.

SECURE - To make fast.

SHACKLE - A "U" shaped connector with a pin or bolt across the open end.

SHEAR PIN - A safety device, used to fasten a propeller to its shaft; it breaks when the propeller hits a solid object, thus preventing further damage.

SHEET BEND - A knot used to join two ropes. Functionally different from a square knot in that it can be used between lines of different diameters.

SHIP - A larger vessel usually used for ocean travel. A vessel able to carry a boat aboard.

SHOAL - An offshore hazard to navigation at a depth of 16 fathoms (30 meters or 96 feet) or less, composed of unconsolidated material.

SLACK - Not fastened; loose. Also, to loosen.

SLOOP - A single masted vessel with working sails (main and jib) set fore and aft.

SPLICE - To permanently join two ropes by tucking their strands alternately over and under each other.

SPRING LINE - A pivot line used in docking, undocking, or to prevent the boat from moving forward or astern while made fast to a dock.

SQUALL - A sudden, violent wind often accompanied by rain.

SQUARE KNOT - A knot used to join two lines of similar size. Also called a reef knot.

STANDING PART - That part of a line which is made fast. The main part of a line as distinguished from the bight and the end.

STAND-ON VESSEL - That vessel which continues its course in the same direction at the same speed during a crossing or overtaking situation, unless a collision appears imminent. (Was formerly called *the privileged vessel*.)

STARBOARD - The right side of a boat when looking forward.

STERN - The after part (back) of the boat.

STERN LINE - A docking line leading away from the stern.

STOW - To pack or store away; especially, to pack in an orderly, compact manner.

SWAMP - To fill with water, but not settle to the bottom.

TACKLE - A combination of blocks and line to increase mechanical advantage.

THWART - A seat or brace running laterally across a boat.

TIDE - The periodic rise and fall of water level in the oceans.

TILLER - A bar or handle for turning a boat's rudder or an outboard motor.

TOPSIDES - The sides of a vessel between the waterline and the deck; sometimes referring to onto or above the deck.

TRANSOM - The stern cross-section of a square-sterned boat.

TRIM - Fore and aft balance of a boat.

TRIMARAN - A boat with three hulls.

TRIPLINE - A line fast to the crown of an anchor by means of which it can be hauled out when dug too deeply or fouled; a similar line used on a sea anchor to bring it aboard.

TRUE NORTH POLE - The north end of the earth's axis. Also called North Geographic Pole. The direction indicated by 000° (or 360°) on the true compass rose.

TRUE WIND - The actual direction from which the wind is blowing.

TURNBUCKLE - A threaded, adjustable rigging fitting, used for stays, lifelines and sometimes other rigging.

UNDERWAY - Vessel in motion, i.e., when not moored, at anchor, or aground

V BOTTOM - A hull with the bottom section in the shape of a "V."

VARIATION - The angular difference between the magnetic meridian and the geographic meridian at a particular location.

VHF RADIO - A very high frequency electronic communications and direction finding system.

WAKE - Moving waves, track or path that a boat leaves behind when moving across the waters.

WATERLINE - A line painted on a hull which shows the point to which a boat sinks when it is properly trimmed.

WAY - Movement of a vessel through the water, such as headway, sternway, or leeway.

WHARF - A man-made structure bonding the edge of a dock and built along or at an angle to the shoreline, used for loading, unloading, or tying up vessels.

WINCH - A device used to increase hauling power when raising or trimming sails.

WINDWARD - Toward the direction from which the wind is coming. Opposite of leeward.

YAW - To swing off course, as when due to the impact of a following or quartering sea.

YAWL - A two-masted sailboat with the small mizzenmast stepped abaft the rudderpost.

Boating Organizations and Agencies

American Boat and Yacht Council, Inc.
3069 Solomon's Island Road
Edgewater, MD 21037
410-956-1050
www.abycinc.org

American Power Boat Association
P.O. Box 377
EastPointe, MI 48021-0377
810-773-9700
www.apba-boatracing.com

American Red Cross
8111 Gatehouse Road
Falls Church, VA 22042
703-206-7180
www.redcross.org

American Sail Training Association
P.O. Box 1459
Newport, RI 02840
401-846-1775
www.tallships.sailtraining.org

American Sailing Association
5301 Beethoven Street, Suite 265
Los Angeles, CA 90066
310-822-7171
www.american-sailing.com

Boat Owners Association of The United States
880 S. Pickett Street
Alexandria, VA 22304
703-823-9550
www.boatus.com

Canadian Power and Sail Squadron
26 Golden Gate Court
Scarborough, ON M1P 3A5
416-293-2438
www.cps-ecp.ca

Federal Communications Commission
Wireless Telecommunications Bureau
2025 M Street NW, Room 8308
Washington, DC 20554
202-418-0569
www.fcc.gov

Insurance Information Institute
110 William Street
New York, NY 10038
212-669-9200
www.iii.org

National Association of State Boating Law Administrators
1500 Leestown Road, Suite 33o
Lexington, KY 40511
859-225-9487
www.nasbla.org

National Boating Federation, Inc.
P.O. Box 4111
Annapolis, MD 21403
410-626-8566

National Marine Manufacturers Association
200 E Randolph Drive, Suite 5100
Chicago, IL 60601
312-946-6200
www.nmma.org

National Oceanographic and Atmospheric Administration (NOAA)
National Ocean Service, Public Affairs Office,
14th Street and Constitution Avenue NW
Room 6013
Washington, DC 20230
202-482-6090
www.noaa.org

National Safe Boating Council, Inc.
P.O. Box 1058
Delaware, OH 43015
740-666-3009
www.safeboatingcouncil.org

National Sailing Industry Association
200 E Randolph Drive, Suite 5100
Chicago, IL 60601-6528
312-946-6200

National Vessel Documentation Center
2039 Stonewall Jackson Drive
Falling Waters, WV 25419
800-799-8362

Personal Watercraft Industry Association
1819 L Street NW, Suite 700
Washington, DC 20036
202-721-1620
www.pwia.org

U.S. Army Corps of Engineers
20 Massachusetts Avenue NW
Washington, DC 20314-1000
202-761-0660
www.usace.army.mil

U.S. Coast Guard Office of Boating Safety
Headquarters Commandant (G-OPB)
2100 Second Street SW
Washington, DC 20593
202- 267-1077 or 800-368-5647
www.uscgboating.org

U.S. Coast Guard Auxiliary
Headquarters Commandant (GOCX)
2100 Second Street SW
Washington, DC 20593
202-267-1001
www.cgaux.org

U.S. Power Squadrons National Headquarters
1504 Blue Ridge Road
P.O. Box 30423
Raleigh, NC 27622
888-367-8777
www.usps.org

United States Sailing Association
P.O. Box 1260
15 Maritime Drive
Portsmouth, RI 02871-6015
401-683-0800
www.ussailing.org

References

There are numerous resources available for vessel owners and operators, often with free publications and references. The following list contains some useful internet websites, and other references used in writing this book. All the internet links were operational at the time this list was prepared. However, it is possible that some will have disappeared or changed by the time you read this.

Books & Publications:

Boater's Source Directory. (2004). BoatU.S. Foundation for Boating Safety and Clean Water. 880 South Pickett Street, Alexandria VA 22304

Bond, Bob. (1992) Handbook of Sailing. Revised edition. Knopf

Calder, Nigel. (2004). How to Read a Nautical Chart. McGraw Hill.

Council on Environmental Quality. (1977) The Evolution of National Wildlife Law.

Fletcher, Sue. (2002). Boater's Guide to VHF and GMDSS, International Marine/Ragged Mountain Press.

Maritime Law and Practice. (1980) Florida Bar Association Continuing Legal Education.

Maloney, Elbert. (2003) Chapman: Piloting and Seamanship. 64th edition. Hearst Books

Maritime Strategy for Homeland Security. 2002. Department of Homeland Security, United States Coast Guard.

Purcell, Charles. (1996). Washington, Oregon, and Alaska Limited Liability Company. Data Trace Publishing Co.

Reference Guide to State Boating Laws, 2000. National Association of State Boating Law Administrators.

Rousmaniere, John. (1999) Annapolis Book of Seamanship. 3rd Rev&up edition. Simon & Schuster.

Rules of the Road: United States Coast Guard. www.boatingsafety.com

United States Department of the Treasury, Internal Revenue Service: IRS Publications, 463, 527, 535.

Articles:

Boat insurance basics: Need boat insurance? Compiled by FirstBoat.com Staff writers. 2002

Boating In Canada (Pat's Boating In Canada): www.boating.ncf.ca/index.html#reg (Marine Radio in Canada: Required Boat Equipment in Canada: Canada Pleasure Craft Operator Card.)

Chartering from 2nd Tier Fleets, The Yacht Charter Information Source, www.sailonline.com

Childress, Lynda Morris, Bareboat Chartering 101, August 1, 2001, Cruising World,

Federal Requirements and Safety Tips for Recreational Boats, Quick Reference Chart. U.S. Coast Guard, Office of Boating Safety: www.uscgboating.org

Forms and Fess. Federal Communications Commission, Wireless Telecommunications Bureau. www.wireless.fcc.gov/feesforms/index.html

Frequently Asked Questions: National Vessel Documentation Center. United States Coast Guard. www.uscg.mil/hq/g-m/vdoc/nvdc.htm

Frequently Asked Questions: No Discharge Zones. BoatU.S. Government Affairs. www.boatus.com

Giaschi, Christopher. Chris Giashi's Maritime Law Page. www.admiraltylaw.com. Giaschi & Margolis, 401-815 Hornby St. Vancouver, BC, V6Z 2E6, Canada

Guide to Mexico. Reproduced in Mexico Connect, by permission of Latitude 38 Publishing Co., Inc., 1998-2001

Kenyon, Todd. (2002) Admiralty and Maritime Law Guide, Marine Insurance. www.admiraltylawguide.com/insurance

Mex-online, Taking your Boat to Mexico: www.mexonline.com/boatmex.htm. Mexico Online 5638 Lake Murray Bl. #218, La Mesa, CA 91942

Nalder, Eric. (2004). "Buyers defend deductions, saying they help create jobs": "Declaring your boat a second home can bring big tax relief": "Finding boat scofflaws a daunting task for agency": "Yacht owners enjoying a huge perk—tax breaks": "Yacht owners will cruise international waters to save a bundle": "Ruling could end sweet 'bare-boat' deals": "Small and large companies use boat write-offs": *Seattle Post-Intelligencer*.

Pleasure Boat Fact Sheet, Laws and Regulations Governing Pleasure Boats, Title 8, United States Code, Section 1225 (a)(3). 2004. Department of Homeland Security, Customs and Boarder Protection.

Port Safety and Security. (2003). U.S. Coast Guard Marine Safety Office. MSO Puget Sound 1519 Alaskan Way S., Bldg. 1, Seattle, WA

Ullrich, Amy. (2004). Bareboat Basics: Want to get off the beach and charter a bareboat? Sail Magazine 2004 Buyers Guide Bareboat Basics

Internet Websites:

Bahamas Government: www.bahamas.gov.bs/bahamasweb/home.nsf. The Official Website of the Government of the Bahamas.

Bahamas Tourism Web page: www.bahamas.com/bahamas/index.aspx. Commonwealth of the Bahamas Official Tourism Website of The Islands Of The Bahamas.

Blue Water Cruising Association: www.bluewatercruising.org/ Bluewater Cruising Association, 8886 Hudson Street, Vancouver, BC V6P 4N2

Boat Owners Association of the United States: www.boatus.com. Boat U.S. 880 S. Pickett St, Alexandria VA, 22304

Boat Owners World: www.boatowners.com Boat Owner's World, Inc. 104 Rouville Drive Dollard Des Ormeaux, Quebec H9B 2B1

Canadian Yachting Association: www.sailing.ca/ Canadian Yachting Association, Portsmouth Olympic Harbour, 53 Yonge Street, Kingston, Ontario, K7M 6G4

Canadian Coast Guard: www.ccg-gcc.gc.ca/main_e.htm. Fisheries and Oceans Canada, Canadian Coast Guard.

Canada Immigration: www.cic.gc.ca/, Citizenship and Immigration Canada.

Canada Transport: www.tc.gc.ca/en/menu.htm. Transport Canada, Tower C, Place de Ville, 330 Sparks Street, Ottawa, Ontario, K1A 0N5

Cruiser Log: The One Stop Cruising Resource. www.cruiser.co.za/

Internal Revenue Service: www.irs.ustreas.gov. United States Department of the Treasury.

Marine Telecommunications. United States Coast Guard Communications Template, U.S.C.G. Navigation Center. www.uscg.mil/USCG.

Mariners Guide: www.marinersguide.com PO Box 5647, Annapolis, MD 21403

Maritime Law Association of the United States: www.mlaus.org/ Philip A. Berns, Membership Secretary, 2607 Savannah Springs Avenue, Henderson, NV 89052

Mexican Consulate: www.mexonline.com/consulate.htm

Mexican Liability Insurance: www.mexonline.com/legal. htm

Mexico Ministry of Tourism: www.sectur.gob.mx/wb2. Government of Mexico, Ministry of Tourism Information.

National Association of Marine Surveyors: www.nams-cms.org/ The National Association of Marine Surveyors, Inc. P.O. Box 9306. Chesapeake, Virginia 23321-9306

National Association of State Boating Law Administrators: www.nasbla.org/.National Association of State, Boating Law Administrators, 1500 Leestown Road, Suite 330, Lexington KY 40511

National Boat Owners Association: www.nboat.com. National Boat Owners Association, 800-248-3512

National Ocean Service: www.oceanservice.noaa. gov/welcome.html. United States Department of Commerce, National Oceanographic and Atmospheric Administration.

National Vessel Documentation Center. www.uscg.mil/ hq/g-m/vdoc/nvdc.htm. United States Department of Homeland Security, United State Coast Guard.

NFBC: www.safeboatingcouncil.org. National Safe Boating Council, P.O. Box 509, Bristow, Virginia, 20136

National Oceanographic and Atmospheric Administration: www.noaa.gov NOAA Public, Constituent & Intergovernmental Affairs, Room 6217, 14th Street & Constitution Avenue, NW, Washington, DC 20230

National Recreational Boating Survey Report, Nov. 2003, Strategic Research Group. (www.strateginresearchgoup.com)

NOAA Protected Resources: www.nmfs.noaa.gov/pr/. Office of Protected Resources, National Marine Fisheries Service, 1315 East-West Highway, 13th Floor, Silver Spring, MD 20910

NOAA National Marine Fisheries Service: www.nmfs. noaa.gov/. NOAA Fisheries Service, Office of Constituent Services, 1315 East West Highway, 9th Floor, Silver Spring, MD 20910

Office of Coast Survey Nautical Charts: www. nauticalcharts.noaa.gov/staff/charts.htm. NOAA, National Ocean Service, Office of Coast Survey, 1315 East West Highway, Silver Spring, MD 20910-3282

Sea Sources.Net Training for Mariners: www.seasources.net SeaSources, 812 Main Rd., Islesboro, Maine, 04848

Society of Accredited Marine Surveyors: www. marinesurvey.org/ Society of Accredited Marine Surveyors, National Office, 4605 Cardinal Boulevard, Jacksonville, Florida 32210

Tetley, William. Professor, Faculty of Law, McGill University. Tetley's Maritime and Admiralty Law. www.mcgill.ca/maritimelaw/

Tides Online: www.tidesonline.noaa.gov/ National Oceanographic and Atmospheric Administration, National Ocean Service, Center for Operational Oceanographic Products and Services.

Vessel Traffic Services. 2003. U.S.C.G. Navigation Center. www.uscg.mil

U.S. and International Law, Homepage of George d'Angelo, Esq. 1717 K Street, N.W., Washington, D.C., 20036. www.members.aol.com/DangeLaw/ homepage.html

U.S. Coast Guard Auxiliary: www.cgaux.org Coast Guard Auxiliary Association, Inc.

U.S. Coast Guard: www.uscg.mil United States Department of Homeland Security, United State Coast Guard.
U.S. Coast Guard, Office of Boating Safety: www.uscgboating.org United States Department of Homeland Security, United State Coast Guard.

U.S. Dep't of Homeland Security: www.dhs.gov/ dhspublic United States governement, Department of Homeland Security, Washington, D.C. 20528

U.S. Sailing: www.ussailing.org/ United States Sailing Assoc., P.O. Box 1260, 15 Marine Drive, Portsmouth, R.I. 02871-0907

United States Power Squadron: www.usps.org 1504 Blue Ridge Road, P.O. Box 30423, Raleigh, NC 27622

World Cruising Club: www.worldcruising.com/ World Cruising Club, 120 High Street, Cowes PO31 7AX UK

Miscellaneous:

B & S Associates V Indemnity Casualty and Property, 641 So. 2d 436, 19 Fla. Law W.D 1706 (1994)

CANADA SHIPPING ACT, Pleasure Craft Sewage Pollution Prevention Regulations. Source: www.laws. justice.gc.ca/en/S-9/SOR-91-661/52923.html

CANADA SHIPPING ACT, Small Vessel Regulations. Source: www.laws.justice.gc.ca/en/S-9/C.R.C.-c.1487/54533.html

Title 46, part 67, Vessel Documentations Regulations, Code of Federal Regulations.

U. S. Coast Guard Documentation Regulations, Superintendent of Documents, United States Government.

VHF Frequencies for Pleasure Vessels in the Pacific Northwest. 14th Edition, Recreational Boating Association of Washington, North Pacific Marine Radio Council.

Whale Watching Guidelines. (2004) National Oceanographic Atmospheric Administration: National Marine Fisheries Service.

Other titles in the Fine Edge Nautical Knowledge Series

The Radar Book
Kevin Monahan

The complete picture on how to maximize the use of your marine radar system. By using practical examples, illustrated with screen displays and the corresponding charts, the newcomer to radar as well as the experienced mariner will learn how to tune a radar system, interpret the display in a variety of conditions, take advantage of all of the built-in features and use radar effectively as a real-time navigational tool. Today's next generation radar systems, which combine the chart plotter display and their usage, are described in this comprehensive explanation of marine radar systems.

Local Knowledge: A Skipper's Reference
Tacoma to Ketchikan
Kevin Monahan

A must-have reference for the skipper of any boat traveling the Inside Passage! Includes over 50 pages of handy distance tables and strategies for managing tides and currents in Johnstone Strait and Cordero Channel, time, distance and speed tables, weather data and much, much more!

GPS Instant Navigation, 2nd Edition
A Practical Guide from Basics to Advanced Techniques
Kevin Monahan and Don Douglass

In this clear, well-illustrated manual, mariners will find simple solutions to navigational challenges. Includes 150 detailed diagrams, which illustrate the many ways you can use GPS to solve classic piloting and navigation problems.

Enjoy these other publications from Fine Edge

Exploring the Pacific Coast—San Diego to Seattle
Don Douglass and Réanne Hemingway-Douglass
All the places to tie up or anchor your boat from the Mexican border to Victoria/ Seattle. Over 500 of the best marinas and anchor sites, starting from San Diego to Santa Barbara—every anchor site in the beautiful Channel Islands, the greater SF Bay Area, the lower Columbia River, and the greater Puget Sound.

Exploring the San Juan and Gulf Islands—2nd Edition
Cruising Paradise of the Pacific Northwest
Don Douglass and Réanne Hemingway-Douglass
Describes the most scenic and accessible marine area in the world—a cruising paradise of 300 tree-covered islets and islands surrounded by well-sheltered waters, comfortable resorts, quaint villages, secure moorings and anchorages.

Exploring Southeast Alaska
Dixon Entrance to Glacier Bay and Icy Point
Don Douglass and Réanne Hemingway-Douglass
Almost completely protected, these waters give access to a pristine wilderness of breathtaking beauty—thousands of islands, deeply-cut fiords, tidewater glaciers and icebergs.

Exploring Vancouver Island's West Coast—2nd Ed.
Don Douglass and Réanne Hemingway-Douglass
With five great sounds, sixteen major inlets, and an abundance of spectacular wildlife, the largest island on the west coast of North America is a cruising paradise.

Exploring the North Coast of British Columbia—2nd Ed.
Blunden Harbour to Dixon Entrance—Including the Queen Charlotte Islands
Don Douglass and Réanne Hemingway-Douglass
Describes previously uncharted Spiller Channel and Griffin Passage, the stunning scenery of Nakwakto Rapids and Seymour Inlet, Fish Egg Inlet, Queens Sound, and Hakai Recreation Area. Includes the beautiful South Moresby Island of the Queen Charlottes, with its rare flora and fauna and historical sites of native Haida culture.

Exploring the South Coast of British Columbia—2nd Ed.
Gulf Islands and Desolation Sound to Port Hardy and Blunden Harbour
Don Douglass and Réanne Hemingway-Douglass
"Clearly the most thorough, best produced and most useful [guides] available . . . particularly well thought out and painstakingly researched." — NW Yachting

Exploring the Marquesas Islands
Joe Russell
Russell, who has lived and sailed in the Marquesas, documents the first cruising guide to this beautiful, little-known place. Includes history, language guide, chart diagrams, mileages and heading tables and archaeology. "A must reference for those wanting to thoroughly enjoy their first landfall on the famous Coconut Milk Run."—Earl Hinz, author, *Landfalls of Paradise—Cruising Guide to the Pacific Islands*

Exploring the Virgin Islands
By Joe Russell and Mark Bunzel
The warm tropical waters and easy sailing make the US and British Virgin Islands one of the most popular cruising destinations in the world. "Exploring the Virgin Islands" provides up to date information on all of the coves and anchorages in both Island chains including many never published before. Many anchorages are illustrated with color aerial photos and diagrams showing the best means for entry and where to anchor. GPS waypoints for each harbor are provide along with the best routing to get there. Local sites, restaurants, beach bars and hiking trails are included along with suggested itineraries and tips on how to prepare for your trip to this Caribbean paradise.

Dreamspeaker Vol. 1 - Gulf Islands and Vancouver Island
By Anne & Laurence Yeadon-Jones

Anne and Lauren Yeadon-Jones have spent thousands of hours cruising British Columbia's coast in their yacht *Dreamspeaker*. Their cruising guides feature informative, hand-drawn shoreline plans of marinas and small boat anchorages. Numerous color photographs show each area in all its splendor. With this book explore the inside coast of Vancouver Island from Victoria to Nanaimo with extensive coverage of charming Gulf Islands.

Dreamspeaker Vol. 2 - Desolation Sound and the Discovery Islands
By Anne & Laurence Yeadon-Jones

The pristine vistas and coves and anchorages with soaring rock walls make the Desolation Sound area dn the Discovery Islands a favorite for cruisers in British Columbia. This cruising guide, Volume 2 in the Dreamspeaker series, features informative, hand-drawn shoreline plans of more than 100 selected marinas and small boat anchorages. Numerous color photographs show the area in all its splendor.

Dreamspeaker Vol. 3 - Vancouver, Howe Sound and the Sunshine Coast
By Anne & Laurence Yeadon-Jones

This colorful, illustrated guide—the third in the popular Dreamspeaker series—offers charts, tips and data that will enhance any boater's enjoyment of one of North America's most popular cruising areas: the Strait of Georgia's captivating eastern shoreline, including metropolitan Vancouver and nearby Indian Arm and Howe Sound. Northwest from Gibsons lie the delights of the Sunshine Coast, an area blessed with many clear-blue-sky days. Volume 3 contains several hundred color photos and hand-drawn maps, plus detailed information on dozens of popular (and secret!) anchorages up and down the coast.

Dreamspeaker Vol. 4 - The San Juan Islands
By Anne & Laurence Yeadon-Jones

Volume 4 of the Dreamspeaker series captures the San Juan Islands like they have never been captured before. Watercolor harbor diagrams and illustrations of popular boating locations such as Roche Harbor, Rosario Resort as well as the quiet anchorages such as Garrison, Wescott and Blind Bay or Sucia are all shown along with many of the interesting shoreside parks and attractions. Anne & Laurence Yeadon-Jones present their colorful tour of this Pacific Northwest Paradise.

Proven Cruising Routes, Vol. 1—Seattle to Ketchikan
Kevin Monahan and Don Douglass

With our 34 routes you have the best 100 ways to Alaska! We've done the charting! This route guide contains precise courses to steer, diagrams and GPS waypoints from Seattle to Ketchikan.

Also available: Companion 3.5" IBM diskette to directly download routes into electronic charts.

Pacific Coast Route Planning Maps

The perfect complement for the *Exploring the Pacific Coast—San Diego to Seattle* book. In beautiful color and full topographic detail, each 24' x 60" map includes the GPS waypoints for the three popular routes for cruising the coast, the Bluewater Route, the Express Route and the Inshore Route.

Inside Passage Maps—North and South

The Inside Passage to British Columbia and Alaska is one of the most sheltered and scenic waterways in the world. Now, for the first time, our maps include an index to all harbors and coves in this superb wilderness allowing you to customize your own routes.

San Juan and Gulf Islands Nautical and Recreational Planning Map
By Don Douglass and Réanne Hemingway-Douglass

Boating and exploring one of the most popular cruising areas in the world is now easy with this colorful planning map of the San Juan and Gulf Islands. The map covers the area from Deception Pass west to Victoria, and north from Bellingham to Nanaimo. All harbors, coves, anchorages, and Cascade Marine Trail sites for kayaks or canoes are noted as well as and public and provincial parks are shown along with Fine Edge's Proven Cruising Routes© to help you get there.

Index